St Antony's/Macmillan Series

General Editors: Archie Brown (1978–1985) and Rosemary Thorp (1985–), both Fellows of St Antony's College, Oxford

Recent titles include:

Amazia Baram
CULTURE, HISTORY AND IDEOLOGY IN THE FORMATION OF BA'THIST IRAQ, 1968–89

Gail Lee Bernstein and Haruhiro Fukui (editors)
JAPAN AND THE WORLD

Archie Brown (*editor*)
POLITICAL LEADERSHIP IN THE SOVIET UNION

Deborah Fahy Bryceson
FOOD INSECURITY AND THE SOCIAL DIVISION OF LABOUR IN TANZANIA, 1919–85

Victor Bulmer-Thomas
STUDIES IN THE ECONOMICS OF CENTRAL AMERICA

Sir Alec Cairncross
PLANNING IN WARTIME

Helen Callaway
GENDER, CULTURE AND EMPIRE

Colin Clarke (*editor*)
SOCIETY AND POLITICS IN THE CARIBBEAN

David Cleary
ANATOMY OF THE AMAZON GOLD RUSH

Roger Cooter (*editor*)
STUDIES IN THE HISTORY OF ALTERNATIVE MEDICINE

Robert Desjardins
THE SOVIET UNION THROUGH FRENCH EYES

Guido di Tella and Carlos Rodríguez Braun (*editors*)
ARGENTINA, 1946–83: THE ECONOMIC MINISTERS SPEAK

Guido di Tella and D. Cameron Watt (*editors*)
ARGENTINA BETWEEN THE GREAT POWERS, 1939–46

Guido di Tella and Rudiger Dornbusch (*editors*)
THE POLITICAL ECONOMY OF ARGENTINA, 1946–83

Saul Dubow
RACIAL SEGREGATION AND THE ORIGINS OF APARTHEID IN SOUTH AFRICA, 1919–36

Ann Lincoln Fitzpatrick
THE GREAT RUSSIAN FAIR

Heather D. Gibson
THE EUROCURRENCY MARKETS, DOMESTIC FINANCIAL POLICY AND INTERNATIONAL INSTABILITY

David Hall–Cathala
THE PEACE MOVEMENT IN ISRAEL, 1967–87

John B. Hattendorf and Robert S. Jordan (*editors*)
MARITIME STRATEGY AND THE BALANCE OF POWER

Linda Hitchcox
VIETNAMESE REFUGEES IN SOUTHEAST ASIAN CAMPS

Derek Hopwood (*editor*)
STUDIES IN ARAB HISTORY

Amitzur Ilan
BERNADOTTE IN PALESTINE, 1948

Hiroshi Ishida
SOCIAL MOBILITY IN CONTEMPORARY JAPAN

J.R. Jennings
SYNDICALISM IN FRANCE

Maria d'Alva G. Kinzo
LEGAL OPPOSITION POLITICS UNDER AUTHORITARIAN RULE IN BRAZIL

Bohdan Krawchenko
SOCIAL CHANGE AND NATIONAL CONSCIOUSNESS IN TWENTIETH–
CENTURY UKRAINE

Robert H. McNeal
STALIN: MAN AND RULER

Iftikhar H. Malik
US-SOUTH ASIAN RELATIONS, 1940–47

Amii Omara-Otunnu
POLITICS AND THE MILITARY IN UGANDA, 1890–1985

Ilan Pappé
BRITAIN AND THE ARAB-ISRAELI CONFLICT, 1948–51

J.L. Porket
WORK, EMPLOYMENT AND UNEMPLOYMENT IN THE SOVIET UNION

Brian Powell
KABUKI IN MODERN JAPAN

Alex Pravda
HOW RULING COMMUNIST PARTIES ARE GOVERNED

Laurie P. Salitan
POLITICS AND NATIONALITY IN CONTEMPORARY SOVIET JEWISH
EMIGRATION, 1968–89

H. Gordon Skilling
CZECHOSLOVAKIA, 1918–88
SAMIZDAT AND AN INDEPENDENT SOCIETY IN CENTRAL AND EASTERN
EUROPE

J.A.A. Stockwin, A. Rix, A. George, J. Horne, Daichi Itô, M. Collick
DYNAMIC AND IMMOBILIST POLITICS IN JAPAN

Verena Stolcke
COFFEE PLANTERS, WORKERS AND WIVES

Jane E. Stromseth
THE ORIGINS OF FLEXIBLE RESPONSE

Joseph S. Szyliowicz
POLITICS, TECHNOLOGY AND DEVELOPMENT

Jane Watts
BLACK WRITERS FROM SOUTH AFRICA

Philip J. Williams
THE CATHOLIC CHURCH AND POLITICS IN NICARAGUA AND
COSTA RICA

Culture, History and Ideology in the Formation of Ba'thist Iraq, 1968–89

Amatzia Baram
Lecturer in the Department of the History of the Middle East
Haifa University, Israel

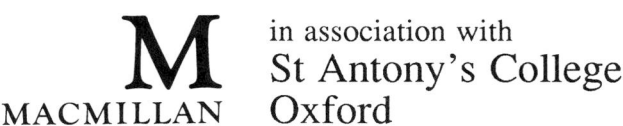

MACMILLAN

in association with
St Antony's College
Oxford

First published 1991

Published by
MACMILLAN ACADEMIC AND PROFESSIONAL LTD
Houndmills, Basingstoke, Hampshire RG21 2XS
and London
Companies and representatives
throughout the world

Printed in the United States of America

British Library Cataloguing in Publication Data
Baram, Amatzia
Culture, history and ideology in the formation of Ba'thist
Iraq, 1968–89.
1. Iraq, political events, 1960–
I. Title. II. St Antony's College
956.704
ISBN 0–333–54845–0

In memory of my young brother, Gabriel,
who died aged only 18 in his burning Patton tank on the eastern
bank of the Suez Canal on Yom Kippur, 6 October 1973.

May this book contribute to a better understanding
between Arabs and Jews.

Contents

List of Plates

Preface

This book is about the metamorphosis of national ideology in Ba'thist Iraq. By 'ideology' the reference is to a very broad sense of the term, closer to a 'collection of political proposals, . . . somewhat intellectualistic',[1] than to a comprehensive world view or an interpretation of history fully, systematically and rigorously thoughtout, presented and elaborated. Speeches by leading politicians, historiography and the writings of intellectuals in general, to the extent that they contain coherent and consistent ideas in regard to Iraq's political community, are considered here as ideology, even if these ideas do not constitute a complete 'politico-social program'.[2] Furthermore, for our purposes, even non-verbal statements such as a work of art, let alone a music festival or a massive monument in a central city square, are an integral, sometimes an essential part of a regime's ideology, so long as their relevance to the regime's thought (or to that of any other group under study) can be ascertained. Thus, for example, Jawad Salim's colossal Monument of the Fourteenth of July, erected in 1961 at Baghdad's Tahrir Square by the republican regime of General 'Abd al-Karim Qasim (1958–63), was as much a political and ideological declaration of Iraqi independence of Western domination and separateness from the Arab world as it was a work of art. And while to Qasim culture was an auxiliary technique, under the Ba'th it became a major tool. Indeed, when in the late 1960s they decided to launch their new national ideology, they chose to do this almost exclusively under a cultural guise (see Chapter 2).

This book is an attempt to follow and analyze the change in the Ba'th party's perception and representation of Iraq as a political community. By resurrecting and imbuing with great national significance elements previously rejected, ignored or downplayed in Ba'th ideology such as territory, race and local pre-Islamic and pre-Arab historical epochs, the Ba'th regime of Iraq has sought to reshape the collective identification of its countrymen. In several cases, this reshaping took the form of re-enforcing and fully legitimizing an already existing identification that hitherto the party had looked upon unfavorably.

Iraqi localism – the identification of nationhood with the ancient territory between the Tigris and the Euphrates – was given equal status to and, occasionally, even priority over pan-Arabism, in direct contravention of former Ba'th orthodoxies. In essence, the Ba'th regime had relinquished the party's traditional approach to the existing political entities of the Arab world wherein they were all equal, and equally illegitimate entities, arbitrarily created by Western imperialism and destined to disappear within an integrative pan-Arab union. Indeed, corollaries to the new idea were the notions that the Iraqi entity is eternal and that by virtue of its illustrious particular history and centrality to the Arab cause, Iraq deserves to lead the Arab world. Thus, traditional Ba'th egalitarian and integrationist pan-Arabism was gradually replaced by a clear-cut Iraqi-centered pan-Arab credo, that exposed occasional imperial tendencies.

To better understand the ideological trend under study it is necessary to understand the historical context within which it developed. Chapter 1 is therefore dedicated to the historical circumstances that gave birth to the pan-Arab ideology of the ruling Sunni-Arab elite in Baghdad under the monarchy and of the infant Ba'th party in Syria in the 1940s, but also to strong reservations vis-à-vis this ideology in large segments of Iraqi society. On the governmental level these reservations found expression for the first time under the military government of General Bakr Sidqi and his Prime Minister, Hikmat Sulayman, in 1936–37, and more forcefully, both in Baghdad's streets and on the highest political and military level under the rule of General 'Abd al-Karim Qasim. Qasim and his regime were toppled by the Ba'th in February 1963, but the social forces that drove him and his predecessors to distance themselves from integrative pan-Arabism did not disappear. Partly due to these forces the Ba'th regime of 1963 failed in its attempts (and, apparently, never tried in earnest) to unite with Egypt and Syria. Within a few months they lost power in Baghdad, to be replaced by another pan-Arab regime. The latter, too, was unable to bring about unification with any Arab country. The Ba'th spent the next four and a half years in jail, exile and underground activity. During these years the party's activists had time to reflect on the dismal results of the interplay between their egalitarian and integrationist pan-Arab ideology and the Iraqi (and all-Arab) political environment. Chapter 1 also deals with a few other developments that occurred in the mid-and-late 1960s which added weight to the party's need to reassess its national ideology, if it wanted it to have any relevance to political reality. This reassessment did not bear fruits, however, before the party, having come to power for the second time in 1968, tried again to carry out radical pan-Arab policies. These policies, the dangers to which they exposed the second Ba'th regime and, as a result, the party's decision to change course and adopt Iraqi-centered policy and ideology, are the subject of the Chapter 2.

The new Iraqi-centered credo was seen by the regime as instrumental, in the first place, in dealing with the Kurdish and Shi'i populations. To enforce its rule over Kurdish nationalists and Shi'i traditionalists the central government, almost entirely Sunni-Arab, resorted, in the first place, to repression that was unprecedented in the history of modern Iraq. Yet to complement these measures it also tried positive social and economic incentives. Chapter 2 also briefly discusses both coercion and enticement.

The regime, however, felt that one more dimension was indispensable in order to secure mass support or, at least, to prevent the Shi'i and Kurdish masses from rendering their support to the opposition. In order to send a clear message to all citizens of Iraq, that Iraq comes first, before any pan-Arab cause, the Ba'th decided, not surprisingly for an ideology-oriented party, that it was necessary to adopt a new cultural-ideological policy that would fortify the Iraqi identity and give Shi'is and Kurds a sense of true belonging to and equality within an integrated Iraqi political community. These policies, the central theme of the present book, are examined in the following chapters.

Almost immediately following its rise to power in 1968 the second Ba'th regime embarked on a campaign contrived to create a secular culture that would be both uniquely Iraqi and desegregative, i.e., common to Kurds, Shi'i and Sunni Arabs. As will be shown in Chapters 7 and 8, while in the 1970s and 1980s this campaign was fully orchestrated and sponsored by the Ba'th regime, an extremely rich and uniquely single-minded totalitarian regime that left little room for spontaneity, in fact it rested on earlier beginnings, initiated voluntarily by groups of young Iraqi artists and a few poets in the late 1940s and early 1950s.

Not all aspects of Iraqi culture under the Ba'th are discussed here. This book focuses on the regime's effort in one area: the creation of the cultural-historical foundations upon which a new secular national doctrine that would replace the traditional doctrine of the Ba'th party could be established.

The cultural campaign started initially in a three-pronged thrust. One direction was a major boost to Iraqi folklore; music, folk-tales and poetry in local dialects, folk dances, arts and crafts, were recovered, recreated and occasionally invented by a plethora of government-sponsored institutions. In doing so the regime was confronted with two problems: one was the great diversity of Iraq's society. Developing the folklore of the various communities could accentuate this diversity instead of playing it down. The other difficulty was that the promotion of uniquely-Iraqi folklore could be construed as isolationism. The way in which the Ba'th cultural commissars treated these and other issues is discussed in Chapter 3.

The second direction, examined in Chapter 4, was an extensive and expensive campaign of archeological excavations and reconstructions and the establishment of archeological museums in all parts of the country. This campaign received extensive coverage in the media which explicitly or by insinuation created the connection between the ancient civilizations of Mesopotamia and the modern Iraqi people.

Chapter 5 is dedicated to the third direction of the new cultural policy – the introduction of a modern version of the ancient Mesopotamian spring rite. To create a vertical fusion between the Iraqi Man and his soil, but also to reinforce the horizontal bonds between Arabs and Kurds, Muslims and Christians, the regime initiated a colorful Spring Festival in Mosul, followed by similar state-sponsored events in other parts of Iraq.

Other facets of the cultural-ideological campaign took a few years to manifest themselves. One was the gradual introduction of ancient Mesopotamian and Medieval-Islamic names to the administrative map of Iraq and the various institutions of the state, with the result that by the end of the 1970s long-vanished names like Babylon, Nineveh, Tammuz, Ishtar, Gilgamesh, Qadisiyya and al-Anbar, became by necessity household names in Ba'thi Iraq. This subject is treated in Chapter 6.

Since 1968–69 Iraqi artists, poets, novelists and playwrites have been encouraged to derive their inspiration from the civilizations and cultures that flourished in Mesopotamia-Iraq from remote antiquity to the modern age. The results are delineated and analyzed, with the help of illustrations, in Chapters 7 and 8.

From its first days the new policy ran into a major difficulty; even though during the first few years it had been carefully limited to the cultural sphere (as different from that of political ideology *per se*), a stress on the Iraqi identity was an unmistakable departure from party orthodoxy. To retain a sense, or at least a semblance of ideological continuity, party ideology shifted the emphasis to a deeper plain, that of pan-Arabism in general. As long as the regime remained broadly within pan-Arab parameters, a different approach from that of party orthodoxy to the question of how this ideal should be realized could have been and, indeed, was presented as a continuation of, rather than a departure from the party's intellectual tradition (see Chapter 11). A continued stress on Arabism and pan-Arabism, however, was incompatible with the new emphasis on Iraq's pre-Islamic and, more importantly, pre-Arab history. The way in which the regime's politicians, ideologues and historians attempted to resolve this contradiction is analyzed in Chapters 9 and 10.

A return to pagan pre-Islamic cultures also threatened to exacerbate the already tense relations between the regime and the more traditional circles in Iraq, in particular the Shi'i clergy. This issue is discussed briefly in

Chapter 10 and in the Conclusion. The broader issue of Islam and the state in Ba'thist Iraq, however, deserves a far more thorough study which is outside the scope of the present book.

Finally, to place the new Ba'thi approach to Iraq's national identity within a wider, all-Iraqi context, Chapter 12 compares it with the approach of the most important opposition groupings in Iraq and suggests that in the 1980s the Ba'th is no exception.

In preparing this volume, being an Israeli citizen I have been unable to visit Iraq. To compensate for this deficiency I have relied on Iraqi sources which, except for school text books that could not be found anywhere outside Iraq, are amply available in libraries; the Ba'th regime that sought to make use of artists, poets and historians in order to spread its political message to the masses spared no effort in giving them wide publicity, making sure that their production would reach the widest audience possible, far byond the confines of art exhibitions and limited intellectual circles. It has to be made very clear, however, that due to the nature of the Ba'th regime even people who visited Iraq under its rule found it extremely difficult to discuss with people their attitude towards the Ba'th ideology, let alone conduct a field study. This book, therefore, limits itself to the study of the regime's practice in introducing its new secular national ideology, and does not attempt to investigate the degree of its popularity. In the Conclusion, however, an attempt is made to evaluate its long-term chances of success.

AMATZIA BARAM

Acknowledgements

I would like to express my thanks to the institutions and people without whose material assistance and moral support this book could not have been written: to The Harry S. Truman Institute on Mount Scopus; to the Jewish-Arab Center at Haifa University; to Mr Stanley M. Bogen of New York and Mr Irving Young of London who helped me with grants; to the following institutions that provided me with fellowships between 1987 and 1990: to The Institute of Advanced Studies at the Hebrew University in Jerusalem and to Professor Emanuel Sivan who was kind enough to invite me to participate in the Seminar on Political Radicalism there; to the Woodrow Wilson Center at the Smithsonian Institution in Washington, D.C.; and to St Antony's College at Oxford University.

Many colleagues have helped me with valuable advice, encouragement and intellectual stimulation. Professor Robert McCormick Adams, the Secretary of the Smithsonian Institution, Washington, D.C.; the late Professor Gabriel Baer of the Hebrew University, Jerusalem; Professor Shaul Bakhash of George Mason University; Dr Charles Blitzer, of the Woodrow Wilson Center, Washington D.C.; Professor Israel Gershoni of the Hebrew University; Dr Sylvia Haim-Kedourie of London; Dr Derek Hopwood and Mr Albert Hourani of Oxford University; Professor James Jankowski of the University of Colorado; Professor Elie Kedourie of the London School of Economics; Professor Bernard Lewis, Director of the Annenberg Research Institute, Philadelphia; Dr Robert Litwak of the Woodrow Wilson Center, the Smithsonian Institution, Washington, D.C.; Professor Moshe Ma'oz of the Hebrew University; Dr Phebe Marr of the National Defense University, Washington, D.C.; Professor Emanuel Marx of Tel-Aviv University; Dr Barry Rubin, of the Washington Institute for Near Eastern Studies; Dr Julie Meisami-Scott of Oxford University; Professor Shmuel Moreh of the Hebrew University; Dr Roger Owen and Dr Julian Raby of Oxford University; Professor Aaron Shaffer and Professor Emanuel Sivan of the Hebrew University; Professor Sasson Somekh of Tel-Aviv University; Mrs Rosemary Thorp of Oxford University; Mr Samuel F. Wells Jr., Deputy Director of the Woodrow Wilson Center, the Smithsonian Institution, Washington, D.C. I am deeply grateful to all of them for their counsel and support. The views presented in this volume and any factual mistakes, however, are exclusively my own responsibility.

My thanks go also to Mr Peretz Kidron of Jerusalem, and to Mrs Sylvia Platt of Oxford for going over the manuscript and greatly improving its style. May I also thank the managements and staffs of the Israel National Library in Givat Ram; The Harry S. Truman library on Mount Scopus, Jerusalem; the Dayan Center at Tel-Aviv University and the library at Haifa University; the SOAS library and the British Library in London; the Bibliothèque Nationale de France and the library of the Institute des Langues Orientales Vivents in Paris; the central libraries at Princeton and Harvard Universities, at the Woodrow Wilson Center in Washington, D.C., and The Library of Congress; to the libraries at the Middle East Centre, St Antony's College and the Oriental Institute and the Bodleian Library, Oxford, and the library of the Middle East Centre at Durham University.

This study would not have seen the light of day without the love, patience, and sound judgement of my fiancee, Bonnie Belkin, who typed and commented on it. My greatest debt is to her.

AMATZIA BARAM
Haifa, Israel, April 1990.

1 The Historical Setting

The Monarchy, 1921–58

Since its inception as a nation-state in the wake of World War I, Iraq has been burdened with a number of acute problems, the most important of which, though interrelated, may be divided into two main categories: issues concerning Iraq's borders, and those associated with its political community.

After a lengthy period of deliberation and indecision the occupying British authorities decided to unite the three disparate Ottoman provinces (*wilayas*) of Basra, Baghdad and Mosul into one nation-state that would be called 'Iraq', a name borrowed from the medieval past of the region. In 1921 it was decided that the new state would be ruled, under a British mandate, by Prince Faysal ibn Husayn (since August 1921 King Faysal I) of the Hashimite house of the Hijaz. With no army to speak of the new monarchy had to settle a controversy over its long, ill-defined and histori-cally problematic border with a formidable neighbor, Iran. The settlement that was reached in 1937 lasted for more than three decades. Iraq was also threatened by another superior neighbor, Turkey, which claimed the large and oil-rich province of Mosul. This dispute was settled, with massive British support, in the Treaty of Lausanne, signed by Turkey and the Allies in July 1925. Yet, the Turkish claim over Mosul did not subside overnight, thus causing occasional acute concern in Baghdad. Iraq found itself also sharing a long and contentious border with the hostile Saudi monarchy, with whom both the Shi'a of the Iraqi south and the Hashimites had a long feud.

More difficult to manage, however, were the internal divisions running through Iraqi society, particularly religious sectarianism and differences in language and culture. As will be shown, these divisions were not unbridgeable, and indeed, during the seventy years of the existence of the Iraqi nation-state Iraqi society, and especially its Arabic speaking majority, became much more integrated. Yet, these divisions were, and still are, a serious impediment to the formation of a nation.

In their effort to overcome these divisions and bring the various com-munities under effective central control (or, as they saw it, to cement the internal unity of the Iraqi people), the various regimes that ruled over Iraq applied a range of measures, from all out military campaigns against Shi'i and Kurdish uprisings, through social and economic incentives and the development of the country's infrastructure, to the creation of a unifying national ideology. This book concerns itself with the creation of such an ideology, and the cultural tools through which it was introduced under the Ba'th regime (1968–). This ideology is meant to serve as the intellectual and emotional force binding together the diverse components of Iraq's society and molding them into an integrated and well-defined people.

When Iraq became a state in 1920–21 some 55 percent of its population consisted (and, apparently, still consists today) of Shi'i Arabs, concentrated in the basin of the Tigris and the Euphrates rivers south of Baghdad. The Shi'a started off as a political movement soon after the death of the Prophet, when they challenged the order of succession and claimed that 'Ali, the Prophet's cousin and son-in-law, and his descendants, alone are the legitimate successors (*khulafa*, or caliphs) of the Prophet and the leaders, or *Imams* of the Muslim community. To them, the three caliphs who preceded 'Ali, and who are greatly admired by the Sunnis (as well as the Umayyads and the 'Abbasids who followed them, and who were and are regarded by the Sunna as legitimate rulers), were immoral, ignorant, and despotic usurpers. Often these caliphs are perceived as sinners, even as infidels, who adopted Islam only outwardly, in order to further their personal ambitions.[2] After the disappearance of the Twelfth Shi'i Imam in the ninth century, authority to interpret Quranic sources and spiritual (and, to various degrees, political) leadership of the Shi'i community passed to the senior religious scholars, the *mujtahids*, and especially to the more senior among them, the *maraji'* (singular *marji'*, collective *marji'iyya*, 'sources of authority').

What started as a political movement became a religious sect following the violent death of Imam Husayn, 'Ali's son and the Prophet's grandson, at the hands of Umayyad troops on the tenth day of the month of Muharram in 60 after the Hijra (AD 680) at Karbala. While in terms of substantive law the Shi'a never strayed too far from Sunni orthodoxy, they nevertheless do differ from the latter over a few points of law, and in the course of time they developed several distinctive rituals, the most important of which is the *'ashura*, commemorating al-Husayn's death. Among others are the fortieth day after his death, and his and his father's birthdays. Being a minority in most of the Muslim lands, and having suffered persecution (sometimes as a result of attempts to overthrow the Sunni government), over the years the Shi'a acquired the characteristics of a persecuted minority: alienation from the Sunni society and government, a strong sense of communal cohesion,[3] and a rich and very popular literature of martyrdom. As observed in the early 1930s by a British scholar well acquainted with the Iraqi scene: 'the Sunni-Shi'a differences have come to mean more than a doctrinal schism. The two communities are now deeply colored by the results of the split – educationally, emotionally and politically.'[4]

In Iraq, the Shi'i religious leadership and institutions were almost entirely concentrated in the holy cities of Karbala and Najaf (some 50 and 100 miles respectively by road south of Baghdad), and Kazimiyya (or Kazimayn, a few miles up the Tigris, north-west from Baghdad). All three cities, being the burial places of, among others, the Imams 'Ali (in Najaf), al-Husayn (in Karbala) and Musa al-Kazim (in Kazimayn), became important centers of learning and pilgrimage for the whole Shi'i world. (A small center of learning was also in Samarra, north of Baghdad, where the 12th Imam is believed to have disappeared.)

Between 17 and 20 percent of Iraq's population were (and probably still are) Kurds, the vast majority of whom are Sunni Muslims. The Kurds, whose Indo-European language is akin to Persian (and very different from Arabic), occupied the mountainous parts of Northeast Iraq, as well as a large part of the Kirkuk area, and great numbers of Kurds also used to live around Mosul. With the advent of language-and-culture-based nationalism in the Middle East after World War I (i.e., in Turkey, Iran and the Arab world), the Kurds, too, gradually adopted this European concept, which, together with their traditional aversion to central government control, set them apart from Iraq's Arabic-speaking majority. Indeed, in the abortive Treaty of Sevres, signed in August 1920 between the victorious European powers and the Ottoman sultan, the Kurds of Turkey and Iraq were promised an autonomous state, and it was stipulated that within a year they could apply for membership in the League of Nations. Even after the Treaty was made obsolete by Mustafa Kamal Ataturk, the British still briefly contemplated a Kurdish autonomy in the Mosul *wilaya*.[5] These promises and plans further encouraged separatist Kurdish national aspirations, as they gave the Kurds hope of international recognition. During the time of the monarchy there were a number of Kurdish armed revolts against the state. In some cases these revolts could not have been put down without massive support from the British Royal Air Force.

Sunni-Arabs, comprising some 20 percent or slightly more of the population, were the majority in Baghdad, and in the central and central- northern parts of Iraq that roughly correlate with the triangle extending between Baghdad, Mosul and the Syrian border.[6] There were also other much smaller groups: along the Ottoman trade route leading from Anatolia to Baghdad, mainly in Kirkuk, there lived (and still live today): Turkomans

(2–3 percent); Persian-speaking Shi'is, mainly living in the Holy Cities, comprised some 1–2 percent; and there were Christians (some 3 percent), Jews (some 2.5 percent), Yazidis and Shabaks (under one percent) and others, in very small numbers.[7]

The difficulties stemming from the Sunni-Shi'i divide within Iraq's Arabic-speaking community were compounded by three facts. One was the presence of a large number of Persians in the holy cities of Iraq, and the traditionally close religious, political and family ties between the Arab and Persian Shi'i clergy. Even though this affinity was not free from friction and conflicts, it led Faysal's Sunni-Arab political elite to suspect the loyalty of Shi'is of Iranian stock or with strong Iranian connections to Iraq, sometimes with good reason.[8] Two other complicating factors were the fact that the Sunni-Shi'i divide was not only religious but also geographical (which made integration more difficult), and the fact that it overlapped, to a large extent, with social and economic differentiation. Thus, for example, many land owners and merchants in the south were Sunni Arabs, while the poor peasants were, as a rule, Shi'is. Despite King Faysal's attempts to accelerate the absorption of Shi'i and Kurdish youngsters into the government machinery,[9] the Ottoman tradition of excluding the Shi'i community from government service proved extremely resilient, and throughout the monarchy the civil service remained, essentially, the domain of Sunnis, mainly Arabs. In the army, too, while the majority of foot soldiers were Shi'i Arabs, the vast majority of the officers were Sunnis. This included a number of Kurds who, unlike the Shi'ites, served as officers in the Ottoman army, and were subsequently absorbed into the nascent Iraqi army. Kurdish penetration into the civil service was proportionately more substantial than that of Shi'ites, but they, too, were clearly outnumbered by Sunni Arabs. This situation was perpetuated under the monarchy by the fact that, as under the Ottomans, the Sunni-Arab areas continued to enjoy better secular education and by the tendency for the bureaucracy and the military command to recruit officials and cadets from among their own community, even their own town, tribe or village. This is not to say that the Shi'a and the Kurds did not make any inroads into the propertied classes and 'official' Iraq . Thus, for example, by 1958 six out of Iraq's seven biggest landlords were Shi'ites, and among the 49 largest land-owning families 23 were Shi'i and 11 were Kurdish. These, and other landed families, mostly tribal shaykhs, wielded influence in Baghdad through Parliament, where they were heavily represented, and through personal contacts. Yet this influence was used in most part to serve their class interests rather than to further the interests of their communities as such.

Massive Shi'i immigration to Baghdad and improved education contributed to growing Sunni-Shi'i integration on the popular level during
and after the 1930s; Shi'ites also became very prominent in trade and
finance, and there was a growing Shi'i middle class of professionals and
entrepreneurs in the cities. Also, in the last decade of the monarchy, while
44 percent of the more important political leaders were still Sunni Arabs, all
the same 33 percent were already Shi'i Arabs and 19 percent were Kurds.[10]
Yet, the overall picture under the monarchy was still that of unchallenged
Sunni-Arab supremacy.[11] Shi'i penetration into the higher-middle and
middle echelons of the civil service was slow, and in the senior command
of the army it was almost non-existent.[12] In the same way, while some of
the richest people in Iraq were Shi'i tribal shaykhs, the vast majority of
the very poor – landless peasants and dwellers of the vast shanty towns
on Baghdad's outskirts – were also Shi'is. Kurds, for their part, did not
move *en masse* to Baghdad. Thus, on the eve of the 1958 revolution both
the huge mass of economically deprived Shi'is in the rural south, and the
Kurds of the rural north (though better off economically) were still cut off
from the main processes of modernization and, like the Shi'i dwellers of
Baghdad's shanty-towns, from the process of national integration.

On the level of national ideology, the monarchy offered its citizens
a blend of Iraqi patriotism[13] and militant pan-Arabism, with the main
stress on the latter. The ruling Sunni Arab elite sought an Arab union[14]
for a variety of reasons, one of which being the wish to change Iraq's
demographic balance.[15] On the political level this concept of pan-Arabism
was furthered energetically by King Faysal I in his last years, and with
much more zest by his successors (King Ghazi and the Regent 'Abd
al-Ilah), and by politicians like Yasin al-Hashimi and Nuri al-Sa'id.
On the ideological-educational level it was furthered with great zeal by
devout pan-Arabs who served as directors general and inspectors general
of education, and by Palestinian and Syrian teachers who taught in Iraq's
secondary schools and teacher training colleges.[16]

Lack of information makes it difficult to gauge the Shi'i attitude towards
the regime's pan-Arabism. Criticism of such a strongly-held tenet of
official faith as pan-Arabism was considered unwise, and thus was hard
to come by; vociferous (and wholehearted) support for pan-Arabism
was easier to trace. This came from a number of Shi'is intellectuals
such as Fadil al-Jamali, who served as both prime minister and minister of education, Muhammad Mahdi Kubba, one of the leaders of the
opposition pan-Arab Istiqlal party of the 1940s and 1950s, and Sadiq
al-Bassim, who served as minister several times (all of them were also
members of the radical pan-Arab al-Muthanna Club in the 1930s). To

these Western-educated politicians and intellectuals this ideology was an important vehicle for Shi'i-Sunni equality. Yet, as observed by Elie Kedourie, these pan-Arab politicians were seen as camp-followers of the Sunni regime and were not representative of their Shi'i community. 'Iraqi pan-Arab policy would be regarded with hostility by the bulk of the population,' concludes Kedourie, 'for neither the Shi'ites nor the Kurds relish the prospect of being swamped by Arab-Sunnis in the Arab state to which Faysal and his followers aspired.'[17] According to Marion and Peter Sluglett, immediately following the downfall of the monarchy, the Shi'a (as well as Christians, Jews and members of other minority communities) 'could feel at ease' with General 'Abd al-Karim Qasim's rule, in part due to 'the Iraqi patriotic component' of his nationalism[18] (namely, his objection to unity with 'Abd al-Nasir's United Arab Republic – Qasim himself was born of a Sunni-Arab father and a Shi'i-Kurdish mother). Hanna Batatu, too, points out that although pan-Arabism in Iraq 'counted not a few Shi'i devotees, for its mass support it could draw only upon Sunni Arabs'.[19] Samir al-Khalil (pseudonym) in his *Republic of Fear*, is even more outspoken: 'to an Iraqi Shi'ite, pan-Arabism and Sunnism go hand in hand. Just as for the Arabic-speaking Christian, pan-Arabism and Islam are inseparable . . . Arabism was in the end bound to be perceived as the hegemony of a minority of Sunnis over Kurds, Shi'ites and non-Muslims, on terms set by this minority, and designed to secure for it a new eventual majority.'[20]

The strong support for the Communist party (which usually preferred local Iraqi patriotism to pan-Arabism) among secular Shi'is in the holy cities of Najaf and Karbala in the 1950s indicates the same tendency, and it is significant that it was Shi'i quarters in Baghdad which became the strongholds of the Communists and the pro-Qasim forces during the Ba'th-Nasirite coup d'état of February 1963 which toppled him.[21] At the same time, however, as will be shown below, the 1950s also witnessed the emergence of a young generation of pan-Arab Shi'is, people who rose to prominence in the infant Ba'th party. Indeed, the issue of the attitude of the various strata and interest groups of Shi'i society to the official pan-Arab ideology of the monarchy (and the regimes that followed it, at that) is far from settled. The overall impression from the existing evidence, however, is that, to the extent that any generalization at all can be made, the Shi'i community, while being and feeling Arab, were still suspicious of, or at least unenthusiastic about, the virulent pan-Arab ideology of the Sunni-Arab regime. This is because they were alienated from and mistrustful of the regime itself, and suspicious of its ulterior motives. Furthermore, it seems that the overwhelmingly Sunni-Arab Ba'th elite which came to power in 1968 suspected that the attitude of the Shi'i masses towards the equally virulent pan-Arab ideology of the Sunni-Arab elite under their own short-lived rule in 1963, as well as that of the 'Arif brothers that followed it had changed very little. This may provide a partial explanation for the fact that they focused much of their new ideology and culture, which emphasized the local Iraqi identity, on the Shi'i south.[22]

As for the Kurds, to them Faysal's pan-Arabism was anathema. A series of Kurdish revolts against the monarchy (the last was crushed in 1945)[23] showed, among other things, that the Kurds felt deeply alienated in a state that on the ideological and political levels ignored their national aspirations.

The Republic 1958–68

The first decade of republican rule brought with it mixed results for the Shi'a. As for the Kurds, a conciliatory beginning was eventually followed by further Arab-Kurdish estrangement. Excluding the Qasim era (July 1958–February 1963), the republican regimes were radically pan-Arab, and Kurds were both alienated and out of favor. Worse still, Qasim's preference for Iraqi patriotism over pan-Arab unity, important as it was politically and ideologically, did not satisfy the Kurds, and they demanded meaningful autonomy. After two years of negotiations the two sides resorted to arms. This pattern of negotiations, then warfare, also repeated itself under the first Ba'th regime (February–November 1963), and the 'Arif brothers' regime ('Abd al-Salam ousted the Ba'th from power in November 1963 and died in a helicopter crash in April 1966. He was replaced by his brother, 'Abd al-Rahman, April 1966–July 1968) with the result that throughout the decade the Kurds paid heavily for their *de facto* autonomous rule in terms of the devastation of large parts of their countryside, and a standstill in urbanization, economic development, health and education. Kurdish integration at the center, too, suffered a clear setback.[24] Under such circumstances, the sense of alienation between Kurdish and Arab nationalists could only increase.

The Shi'a fared better, but their advance was not easy nor was it uniform; indeed, in certain areas they even suffered some setbacks. The land reform, initiated by Qasim's regime, his important housing projects designed to eliminate Baghdad's Shi'i slums, and his stress on expanding education and health services, clearly benefitted many Shi'i peasants and urban poor.

According to a sympathetic Shi'i secular source, Qasim also removed the invisible obstacles barring Shi'is from joining the Military Academy and attending the Staff Academy, and thus made the promotion of Shi'i officers to senior positions possible.[25] Yet although Qasim improved the lot of the peasants, by breaking the power of the Shi' landed class, he also removed an important center of Shi'i influence in Baghdad, however faulty, without replacing it with another. In addition, if the report of Qasim's policy of recruiting and promoting Shi'i officers is accurate, it did not have time to bear fruit before he was overthrown. The regimes that succeeded him between 1963 and 1968, all led by army officers, made no similar effort so that the top echelon of all the republican regimes between 1958 and 1968 had very few Shi'i members (16 percent), and the Shi'a also suffered from clear under-representation (only 35 percent) at the second level.[26] In addition, the fact that under the monarchy those Shi'a who opted for secular education were channelled into private enterprise, rather than into government and military service, meant that their middle and upper middle classes suffered particularly heavily from the nationalization policies of the 'Arif regime in the mid-1960s.[27]

As for the Shi'i clergy, under the monarchy they were far from satisfied with the status of their community, with British tutelage[28] and, in the 1950s, with the state of religious affairs in Iraq.[29] Yet, at least after the May 1941 Rashid 'Ali anti-British revolt their opposition was essentially passive, having reached a de facto *modus vivendi* with the regime. This situation changed very soon after the July 1958 revolution. At first, a number of Shi'i clergy gave their support to Qasim's regime (again, only after it became a *fait accompli*). Yet, within a few months, in response to a new, secular Law of Personal Status and to the ascendancy of the communists under his rule (and, as they saw it, the danger of atheism), the Shi'i clergy changed their attitude. Led by the Chief *Mujtahid* Muhsin al-Hakim, they criticized Qasim openly, and called for a change of policy.

Under the 'Arif brothers relations between the regime and the *mujtahid*s remained tense, with the main criticism directed against his nationalization policies and his adherence to 'Abd al-Nasir's pan-Arabism, but 'Abd al-Salam 'Arif was also accused of anti-Shi'i sentiments and designs. Under Qasim and the 'Arifs a number of groups of activist Shi'i *'ulama* (religious scholars) came into being, with the intention of fighting atheism.[30]

The tension between the Shi'i religious establishment and its followers and the secular ruling Sunni elite came to a head, however, only in 1968–69, upon the ascent to power of the second Ba'th regime.

THE GENESIS OF THE BA'TH PARTY[31]

The Arab Ba'th (Resurrection) party came into being in Damascus in 1940. However, it was only on 7 April 1947 that the party's First Pan-Arab Congress approved its constitution, and this date is the party's official anniversary as observed in Iraq and Syria, the two countries where it holds power.

The main intellectual driving force behind the new party was a Damascus-born and Sorbonne-educated Greek Orthodox school teacher named Michel 'Aflaq. His co-founder was another Sorbonne-educated Damascene, Salah al-Din al-Baytar, a Sunni Muslim. A significant intellectual contribution to the party's thinking was provided by another Sorbonne graduate, Zaki Arsuzi, an 'Alawite from Alexandretta; although he himself never joined the Ba'th of 'Aflaq and Baytar (in 1940 he established his own minuscule Arab Ba'th party) many of his disciples eventually did. In 1953, the Arab Ba'th party in Syria merged with the anti-feudalist Arab Socialist party of Akram Hawrani, a Hama-based Sunni Muslim, son of a family of impoverished landowners and a seasoned politician. The union was named the Arab Ba'th Socialist Party. The party adopted a number of principles which, though later significantly modified, remained staples of its doctrine well into the 1980s; in varying degrees, these principles were subsequently incorporated into the theories of other pan-Arab movements, notably that of 'Abd al-Nasir.

The party's most important principle was that of Arab unity (*al-wahda al-'arabiyya*), which envisioned the political unification of all the Arab lands – from the Atlantic Ocean to the Persian Gulf, (or, in Ba'th vernacular: The Gulf of Basra) and from the Taurus mountains in the north to the Indian Ocean to the south – whereby the Arabs would rise from the ashes and fulfil a worldwide 'eternal mission' (*risala khalida*) of civilization and enlightenment. Though he never discussed it in a methodical way, preferring vague formulas like 'love before anything else', Arab nationalism was perceived by 'Aflaq in terms of language, culture and history. Very little thought was dedicated to the issue of other national (or ethnic-lingual) groups living in Arab countries as minorities (such as the Kurds or Berbers). When referring to this problem in his early (and formative) writings, 'Aflaq settled for the claim that these minorities were very close to the Arabs, that they share a common history and that they have a common destiny. As will be shown, in later years, when the party was in power in Iraq, the unresolved issue of the Kurdish minority and its political rights came to haunt its leaders. As for the Shi'a, in their vast majority Arabic speaking, there was no reason, at least in theory, why they should not fit well into the Ba'th national mould. Indeed, as will be shown below, during its early years in Iraq Shi'i youngsters occupied the most important leadership positions in the Ba'th party. Another principle of the young party was 'liberty' (*huriyya*) meaning, in the first place, relentless struggle against Western imperialism and its influence upon the Arab world. This entailed opposition to Western strategic pacts, and a struggle against the local 'compradore' classes: namely, feudalists (*al-iqta'*) and capitalists. A further principle was a mild form of socialism (*ishtirakiyya*), combining both Fabian and etatist influences. Up to the early 1960s, however, socialism was perceived merely as an expedient for drawing the deprived classes into the camp of unity. In its Sixth Pan-Arab Congress in October 1963, the party placed socialism on a level equal to unity. It also adopted a quasi-Marxist terminology, using expressions like 'class struggle' and 'popular democracy'. Indeed, the Soviet political system, a dictatorship of one party, claiming to represent the interests of the 'toiling masses', appealed to the young, radical party as early as 1960 and possibly earlier, when it was in opposition.[32] This became a part of its official doctrine in 1963, the year in which it came to power in Iraq and Syria. From that moment the principle of liberal democracy, however vague in the party's 1947 constitution, became identified with social exploitation and Western imperialism.

Yet another party principle was the separation of religion from politics. In a Muslim country, this notion came naturally to a Christian intellectual such as 'Aflaq (and his Druze and 'Alawite disciples). Confining Islam to the mosque also appealed to secularly-minded Muslim high-school and university students and young Damascene intellectuals who, under the influence of Western thinkers like Ernest M. Renan, regarded Islam as an impediment to progress. However, unlike the Communists, who turned to atheism, they avoided a rift with the more traditional masses by paying lip-service to religion, while striving simultaneously to defuse Islam as a political and social force. The principle of a separation between mosque and state had promising potential in the Iraqi context, as it could ease the integration of secularly-minded Shi'i (as well as Christian) Arabs into the political system.

Secular nationalism, anti-imperialism and socialism were fused into an amalgam whose potency was illustrated shortly after the establishment of the party, when new branches were founded in Jordan, Iraq and Lebanon.

EARLY YEARS IN IRAQ

Principally as a result of the 1948 debacle in Palestine, the Ba'th party was founded in Iraq in the first half of 1949, by a number of Syrian students from Alexandretta and Aleppo who were studying in Baghdad. At the same time, Iraqi students returned home from Syria and Lebanon where they had come under the influence of Ba'th ideas. From Baghdad, the organization spread in the early and mid-1950s to Shi'i Basra and Nasiriyya, to Sunni-Arab Ramadi and to other places, and included a mixed membership of Sunni and Shi'i Arabs (few Kurds ever joined the party because of its radical pan-Arab credo). The members were mostly college and secondary school students later to be joined by a few army officers and a few workers and peasants. Party membership at first was minute and its leadership fluctuated up to 1951, when the Shi'i engineering student from Nasiriyya, Fuad al-Rikabi, emerged as its predominant figure. Under him membership rose from about fifty in 1950 to around one hundred by mid-1952, when it was formally recognized by the center in Syria. Throughout the 1950s the party was deeply involved in anti-government demonstrations and other opposition activities. Despite police crackdowns, the party held its First Regional Congress in December 1955. (In 1954 the Ba'th had restructured itself at the all-Arab level, initiating the hitherto non-existent level of 'country' or 'region' (*al-qutr*). From this point, Iraq – like Lebanon and Jordan, and, of course, Syria – was regarded as one of the party's 'regional' branches.)

On the eve of the officers' revolt of July 1958 the party membership reached no more than a few hundred.[33] Though making an undisputable contribution to the pre-revolutionary atmosphere, the party's influence within the army was negligible, as it had only very few officer-members, the most prominent being Col. Ahmad Hasan al-Bakr, who joined the party formally only after the downfall of the monarch.[34] This fact was reflected in the party's modest role in the government in the early days of the Free Officers' rule.[35] Immediately after the officers' coup, the Ba'th joined other pan-Arab groups and individuals headed by Col. 'Abd al-Salam 'Arif in calling for an immediate unification with 'Abd al-Nasir's United Arab Republic (UAR, the Egyptian-Syrian union formed in February 1958). Qasim and his regime correctly construed this call as a direct challenge to their Arab policy, which sought to avoid political union with the UAR. Within a year after the Qasim revolution, following a number of confrontations with the ruling officers, the party fell from favor, and after trying to assassinate Qasim in October 1959 they had to go underground.

Notwithstanding these setbacks, the party expanded significantly between mid-1958 and the end of 1962, numbering by then hundreds of 'active' (i.e., full) members, and thousands of supporters in their various ranks in the party hierarchy. All the same it was not before February 1963 that the party felt strong enough to challenge the regime again, and even then they needed to recruit non-Ba'thi support. The party's rapid expansion had its own drawbacks, as it brought in large numbers of members inadequately screened and disciplined.

On 8 February 1963, the party overthrew Qasim in a bloody coup d'état with the help of Nasirite and other pan-Arab army officers headed by Col. 'Abd al-salam 'Arif. 'Arif was made a figurehead president, but real control was in the hands of the Ba'th: its unruly militia, controlled by the civilian leadership, and its army officers, led by Col. (later General) Ahmad Hasan al-Bakr, who secured the army's support.

Within a few weeks the party was divided into three rival groups, split along personal and factional and, to some extent, sectarian lines, and using social ideology as an effective weapon in their bickering. A self-proclaimed 'leftist' group consisted mostly of civilians, many of them Shi'is, was led by the new party's 'strong man', the Shi'i 'Ali Salih al-Sa'di, who had control of the party militia. Another group, dubbed by the 'left' 'rightists', was headed by the Shi'is Hazim Jawad and Talib Shabib. The leadership of a third group, headed by the Sunni-Arab army Generals Ahmad Hasan al-Bakr and Salih Mahdi 'Ammash (with Saddam Husayn as a middle-ranking operator), consisted mainly but not exclusively of Sunni Arabs. This group was usually referred to as 'centrist'. Eventually, it was this group which seized power in Baghdad again in July 1968, after the party lost it in November 1963 to 'Arif.

In addition to warring with each other and creating havoc in Iraq's economy, all factions bore varying degrees of responsibility for a massive campaign of arrests, executions and murder of real and perceived communists carried out mainly, but not exclusively, by the party militia. This campaign damaged the party's prestige among left-wing circles in Iraq and the Arab world. Even more importantly, it severely damaged Iraqi-Soviet relations, thus jeopardizing Iraq's only reliable source of economic aid and arms, at a time when relations with Iran were unstable and there was active fighting in Kurdistan.[36] Finally, the party also failed in its attempt to realize what was traditionally its highest ideal, when talks about unity with 'Abd al-Nasir's Egypt and twin-Ba'thi Syria failed to produce any tangible results.

On 18 November 1963, after Ba'thi in-fighting came to a head, President 'Arif and the military, with the support of some 'centrist' Ba'th officers (including General Ahmad Hasan al-Bakr) and politicians, put an end to the Ba'th agony, and ousted it from power. Bakr and his 'centrist' colleagues were rewarded with government portfolios, but within a few months they found themselves out of office. In September 1964, to abort a new Ba'thi coup d'état, they and many of their colleagues, were rounded up and tossed unceremoniously into jail. This was the beginning of four years of imprisonment, exile and underground activity aimed at purging and re-building the shattered party organization, this time as a unified body under the leadership of General Bakr and his civilian youthful and energetic aid, Saddam Husayn.[37] It looks as if it was during these years that party members revised their national ideology so that soon after they came to power in 1968 they hesitantly revealed a new credo.

PREPARING FOR A NEW START: WHY A NEW IDEOLOGY?

Five developments that occurred during the party's period of underground activity, between November 1963 and July 1968, and very soon after it came to power again in 1968, greatly influenced its course when in power. When seen as a whole, these developments explain the party's recourse to a new national ideology and a new cultural policy. One development, the June 1967 Six Day War, occurred in the all-Arab arena. Another, which occurred on the regional level, was the eruption of an acute conflict with the Shah's Iran. Another was on the internal Iraqi level, namely the failure of the central government to defeat the Kurdish revolt or reach an agreement with the Kurds. Two other developments occurred within the party itself. One was the disappearance of the Shi'is from its leadership, to be replaced by Sunni-Arabs, many of whom were from the city of Tikrit. The other was an internal rift within the party between 'pro' and 'anti' Syrians. When the 'anti-Syrian' faction came to power in Baghdad, this internal rift became an inter-Arab enmity between Damascus and Baghdad. This necessitated major ideological changes.

The most important development on the all-Arab arena that occurred before July 1968, but which strongly influenced the Ba'th party, its doctrine and its political behavior after they came to power in 1968, was the 1967 Six Day War. The downfall of 'Abd al-Rahman 'Arif and the rise to power of the Ba'th party in July 1968 were in no small measure the outcome of the failure of the Iraqi army to support Jordan and Syria effectively in their war against Israel. This failure, and the failure of Iraq and the other combatant states to resume the war with Israel, served as the rallying cause of massive anti-government demonstrations in late 1967, in which the Ba'th party was a major instigator.[38] Indeed, following the Six

Day War the prestige of all the Arab regimes that lost suffered a heavy blow. Concomitantly, the prestige of the Palestinian armed organizations, the only Arab fighting force that still continued the armed struggle against Israel, soared to unprecedented heights. Having come to power, by its own admission, largely on the wave of public resentment against 'Arif's insufficient contribution to the war, the Ba'th party was expected by its pan-Arab supporters both within Iraq and outside to prove that it was better than all the regimes that had lost the war, and thus to adopt very radical pan-Arab policies and ideology.[39]

At the same time, however, there were other developments that worked in the opposite direction. One was the eruption of a border conflict with Iran in the spring of 1969. This conflict, and the need to secure Iraqi strategic interests on the Gulf became a powerful incentive to turn inward, at least for a while. As pointed out by the Eighth Regional Congress:

> The eruption of the threats to the Arab Gulf came at a time [1969] when the [Ba'th] Revolution was totally preoccupied, on the military and political levels alike, with the issue of Palestine. This fact greatly affected the degree and quality of [Iraq's] action and efforts in the Gulf area.[40]

The 'Arif brothers' failure to reach a political or a military solution to the Kurdish problem was another fact that influenced Ba'th practice and ideology in an inward-looking direction. On the eve of the second Ba'th takeover, the Kurds already enjoyed a state of de facto autonomy in Iraqi Kurdistan. A large section of this area (some 35,000 sq. kilometers with almost half of the population of Iraqi Kurdistan) was actually ruled by the Mulla Mustafa al-Barazani and the Kurdish Democratic Party with its armed force, the Peshmerga, which numbered some 21,000 in 1970.[41] If the Ba'th regime intended to solve this problem through peaceful means, it needed to provide the Kurds with ideological, as well as with other demonstrations of its commitment to Kurdish-Arab equality. But, in view of their military weakness, even if the Ba'th were to embark on a military campaign they would have to look for means to attract as much Kurdish support as possible away from Barazani and the KDP. Ideological concessions could well be (and indeed were) a part of the price to be paid. In either case, then, a new trend in national ideology and culture that would foster an Iraqi identity, at the expense of radical integrative pan-Arabism, was called for.

Two other developments that influenced the Ba'th to counter-balance its pan-Arab zeal with local Iraqi patriotism occurred within the party.

One was the near-disappearance of the Shi'i element from the first rank of its leadership, and apparently from the lower echelons as well. While between 1952 and November 1963 some 54 percent of the various regional leaderships were Shi'is, as a result of a series of historical coincidences (as different from a premeditated policy), between November 1963 and 1970 they were replaced by Sunni-Arabs, and their representation dropped to some 14 per cent.[42] Furthermore, when the party came to power again in 1968 there were no Shi'is in the Revolutionary Command Council (RCC), the highest decision-making institution in Ba'thi Iraq, or in the Regional Leadership of the party (RL), the second most important institution, and there were only 12.5 percent of them in the government, the third institution in the hierarchy.[43] Never before since World War II had the Sunni-Arab minority monopolized political (and, with the advent of nationalization also economic) power so totally and blatantly. As for the activist circles within the Shi'i religious establishment, the mutual alienation between them and the Ba'th was such that the party decided on a policy of confrontation, making no effort to win them over.[44]

Yet, to the secular Shi'is who wanted to integrate into the political system, or those whose position was somewhere in the middle between the two poles (and as the Gulf War has later shown, these groups consisted of the majority of the Shi'a), the near-total Sunni Arab monopoly of political power appeared as hypocrisy; after all, the Ba'th party supposedly spoke in the name of Sunni-Shi'i (and Christian) equality within the Arab nation. Such a monopoly was a sufficient cause for alienation, and the Ba'th could ill afford to lose the support (or the acquiescence) of the 'quiet majority' of the Shi'a, let alone to see them lured into the *mujtahids*' camp. Soon after the party came to power this problem had to be and, indeed, was addressed both on the level of political practice and on that of culture and ideology. On the latter, while pan-Arabism was not abandoned it was restrained by a new stress on the local Iraqi identity, a stress which the party seems to have felt could improve its relations with the Shi'a.

The second important development that occurred within the party in the mid-1960s, and which encouraged it to adopt a new ideology, was the rift between pro-and-anti-Syrians. Since 1963–64 the larger faction within the Iraqi party, headed by General Bakr, had made common cause with Michel 'Aflaq and other Ba'th civilian old-timers in Syria against a 'leftist' group of young Ba'thi army officers, headed by Colonels Salah Jadid and Hafiz al-Asad. When in February 1966 the 'leftist' officers ousted 'Aflaq and his supporters from power in Damascus, General Bakr's pro-'Aflaq party faction in Iraq found itself in bitter conflict with the new rulers of Damascus. Within months, Damascus had announced their expulsion from the party and channelled all aid to the other pro-Syrian faction in Iraq.[45] These policies marked the beginning of a long feud. When, in 1968, General Bakr's faction succeeded in toppling the 'Arif regime in Iraq and achieving power, this became an inter-state rivalry. Strengthening the Iraqi identity was necessary in order to limit public expectation of immediate Iraqi-Syrian unification. Such unification was perceived as a threat to the new and yet insecure regime in Baghdad, because within a collective leadership they stood a good chance of being eclipsed by their better-entrenched and more popular Syrian counterparts. Iraqi patriotism was also needed to provide the Iraqi people with a political entity with which they could identify at least until the moment when unity with Syria would be possible. And, as was evident from their political practice upon assuming power, the Ba'th regime in Baghdad were in no hurry to unite with Ba'thi Damascus.[46] Similarly, enhancing local Iraqi patriotism at the expense of radical integrative pan-Arabism was also necessary in order to combat the influence of Egypt's Gamal 'Abd al-Nasir. This influence has been greatly augmented under the 'Arifs, particularly within the Iraqi armed forces. The Ba'th tackled this problem in the first place on the administrative level, when they dismissed more than 2,000 officers from the army, including the chief of staff and four divisional commanders, who were ousted as early as December 1968.[47] Yet the stress on Iraqi patriotism was seen as an essential long-term means to achieve the same goal. The development of local-territorial nationalism – the subject of this book – came to serve this purpose, too. That it conflicted with the most sacred party ideal of total Arab unity did not deter the Ba'th politicians when the survival of their rule was at stake: having lost power once through factionalism and mismanagement they were determined not to allow it to happen again.[48]

It may be suggested that there were two other, though far less tangible developments that encouraged the Ba'th to introduce the new ideology. Both developments, however, were exposed only after the party took over. One was the decline, at least temporarily, of radical pan-Arabism as a result of the repeated failures to achieve Arab unity in the 1960s, and in the wake of the devastating Arab defeat by Israel in 1967. Indeed, while this defeat brought with it great admiration for the Palestinians it also seriously tarnished the image of the two most radical and revolutionary pan-Arab regimes, namely, that of 'Abd al-Nasir in Egypt and the 'leftist' officers in Damascus. And while in the short term Arab wrath and national sentiments reached unprecedented heights following the defeat, the long-term influence of the failure of the Messianic pan-Arab trend embodied by 'Abd al-Nasir was, dialectically, to lower public expectations, at least for a while. Even if only for the time being, radical integrative pan-Arabism was increasingly out of fashion.[49] A second development of which the Ba'th regime apparently became aware only a few years after it came to power was that of growing 'consumerism' among the Iraqi masses. Alternatively, it may be that the Iraqi masses had not changed in any way, but that until the late 1960s and early 1970s they had not been asked to lower their standard of living (which was never very high to start with) in order to support the pan-Arab battle for Palestine (between the Arab-Israeli war of 1948–49 and June 1967 there was no meaningful Iraqi military presence on Israel's borders). The stark contrast between Ba'thi calls upon the Iraqi masses to sacrifice their economic well-being for the cause of the battle for Palestine in 1968–70, and their explicit admission in the mid-1970s that Iraq should come first, and that economic well-being and highly developed social services were indispensible to win the party public legitimacy, implies Ba'th realization that they had misunderstood the public's attitude.[50]

The Ba'th regime's treatment of the Shi'a and the Kurds and its attempt to resolve the tension between the pan-Arab and local Iraqi policies are the subject of Chapter 2. The attempts to resolve the tension between pan-Arabism and local patriotism on the cultural-ideological level are the subject of the other chapters of this book.

2 The Ba'th in Power: The Political and Ideological Setting

In the political, social and economic spheres the infant regime embarked on a policy of 'stick and carrot' or, as it came to be known among the populace of Iraq, *al-tarhib wal-targhib* ('intimidation and attraction'). Ba'th coercion on both the Shi'a and the Kurds was unprecedented in the history of modern Iraq; and for the Shi'a, after the rise in oil revenues following the Arab-Israeli war in 1973, the inducements of the carrot policy were likewise unprecedented.

After early 1969, the regime made efforts to bring the Shi'i religious establishment and its educational system under its full control. This signalled the beginning of a long and violent clash between the regime and the activist *mujtahids* and their followers. The former accused the latter of serving the Shah of Iran and the CIA, and the latter accused the former of trying to legalize the sale of alcoholic drinks and spread moral corruption in the holy cities. As a result of the clash in the summer and fall of 1969 the regime closed down religious institutions and imprisoned or deported many hundreds of students of religion and their teachers. In 1974, apparently in response to Shi'i protests over heavy Shi'i casualties in the regime's campaign against the Kurds in the north, the first five activists of the underground movement *al-Da'wa al-Islamiyya* (The Islamic Call) were executed. (*Al-Da'wa* was established in 1957–58 as a cultural-educational circle to combat the decline of religious consciousness and the Communist-Atheist ascendancy under Qasim. Under the Ba'th it became a political and military organization.) After more clashes the confrontation between the two sides reached massive proportions in February 1977, when the regime tried to prevent a mass religious procession from Najaf to Karbala to mark the fortieth day of al-Husayn's martyrdom. Two thousand were arrested, and a few were again executed. The number of teachers and students in Najaf and Karbala declined steeply to no more than 600.

After *Ayat Allah* Khomeini's rise to power in Tehran two years later, the conflict between the Ba'th regime and the Shi'a, led by the activist *mujtahids*, came to a head. In response to violent demonstrations in the Shi'i south, but also in the huge Shi'i al-Thawra slum of Baghdad, and to calls to overthrow the 'infidel Ba'th regime', the latter executed a few hundred religious activists (including their spiritual leader, *Ayat Allah* Muhammad Baqir al-Sadr), arrested around 10,000 and, during the first half of 1980, deported close to 40,000 Shi'is to Iran. Many of these were Iraqi citizens whom the regime defined as Iranians, 'whose unfaithfulness to the [Ba'th] revolution and the homeland was proven'. Deportations, arrests and executions (including those of non-political *'ulama* to deter their activist relatives) continued during the Gulf War. Ba'th tactics vis-à-vis the Shi'a were to remove known or suspected activists, the radical religious leadership and potential supporters from the scene, and to replace the radical *'ulama* with others who would be ready to tow the regime's line or at least to stay out of politics. In addition, the regime set out to intimidate the traditional Shi'a masses, discouraging them from taking part in political demonstrations.[1]

While engaging in such massive coercion the regime also used positive incentives to encourage the Shi'i masses to join the party or at least to lend it passive support. Between 1968 and 1980 the party made sure that a number of Shi'i-Ba'thi activists rose to the highest echelons of its leadership (the RCC and RL), and other Shi'is were able to rise to the middle and higher-middle echelons of party and state. Thus, for example, by 1974, 23 percent of the RL (which is the second stratum in the political hierarchy) were Shi'is. In late 1977 at least 28 percent of the RCC, 26 percent of the RL and 25 percent of the government were Shi'is. However, the most important positions in the government, army and internal security remained safely in Sunni-Arab hands (and, to a large extent, in the hands of people hailing from Tikrit, General Bakr's and Saddam Husayn's home town). Yet, the new prominence of Shi'is in party and government (as well as in the army during the Gulf War) was designed to signal to Shi'i youngsters that if they towed the line laid down by party and president and acquiesced in *de facto* Sunni-Arab supremacy, they could realistically expect upward social mobility.[2]

In May 1969 the regime embarked simultaneously on a new and far-reaching policy of land reform, accompanied by compulsory membership in cooperatives, a mechanism that increased the central government control over the peasantry; it introduced further nationalization and enacted a new and more progressive labor code, and when its oil revenues mushroomed after the 1973 Arab-Israeli war, the Ba'th regime invested huge resources in advancing education and medical services in the countryside, in developing country roads and providing local electricity and fresh water supply systems throughout the country.[3] These measures were designed to win over the peasants and the urban poor, the majority of whom were Shi'is, and attract them away from other political or religious bodies. In the case of the Shi'a, these were represented mainly by the *mujtahid*s who, for religious as well as economic reasons, objected to any socializing measures. However, it was also hoped that such measures would help to deter the secular Shi'is from supporting the Communist party which, as pointed out above, enjoyed a fairly wide following among the Shi'i poor.

In addition to greater Shi'i representation and social and economic improvements, the party had also to come up with an ideology that would give Shi'i Arabs a sense of equality with their Sunni counterparts and of true belonging to the Iraqi political community. Being essentially a secular party, and being ideologically committed to minimizing the religious antagonism between Sunnis and Shi'is,[4] it was only natural for the Ba'th to produce a secular credo. On the face of it, the party's traditional secular pan-Arabism should have been an adequate solution to this problem. Judging by the party's practice, however, their conclusion was that secular pan-Arabism, while not to be relinquished, could no longer serve as its sole national credo. In addition to its realization (or suspicion) that integrationist pan-Arabism left the Shi'i masses 'cold' for historical reasons, the regime apparently also felt that the less sophisticated Iraqis needed a national ideology that would be more tangible than pan-Arabism. Thus, for example, in 1975, in a lecture to educational committees assembled to rewrite Iraq's school textbooks, the then Deputy Vice President, Saddam Husayn, warned the Iraqi educators that 'the Arab homeland . . . is still an unfulfilled goal', and as such it was highly abstract. At the same time, however, Iraqi patriotism was a far more tangible concept. 'This means,' he summed up, 'that we must not submerge ourselves in the theoretical pan-Arab and neglect the direct local patriotic (*al-watani*).'[5]

As for the Kurds, for some eighteen months, until December 1969, the new regime tried to impose its control over the Kurdish areas and defeat the Kurdish national movement. They tried to achieve this through a combination of a military campaign, an alignment with Kurdish anti-Barazani groups, and cultural-ideological and administrative concessions designed to win the support of those Kurds not strongly attached to Barazani and his rebels. Amongst the cultural-ideological concessions the regime established a Kurdish Academy of Science and a university in Sulaymaniyya; it announced the Newruz, the Kurdish New Year (March 21), as an all-Iraqi National Holiday; it allowed Kurdish writers to establish their own association and made a few other minor concessions.[6] This was also the time when the First Mosul Spring Festival was inaugurated. In this Festival it was Iraqi rather than Arab history which became the central theme for the first time, though intertwined with a concept of an Iraqi pan-Arab mission. The festival signaled the genesis of Iraqi territorialism under the Ba'th. Indeed, if the Ba'th wanted to have a chance of attracting any real support from the Kurdish population, they had to find a new national formula for Iraq. The Kurds were traditionally strongly opposed to any attempt to involve Iraq in schemes for Arab unity. (In April 1963, for example, when the Ba'th regimes of Iraq and Syria were conducting unity talks with Egypt, the Kurds threatened to secede if such unity materialized.) Thus, as long as the Kurdish nationalists could wield the threat of secession or even of continued revolt, the regime had good reason to play down its pan-Arab commitment in order to prevent further Kurdish defection to the nationalist camp. However, since there were other forces at work that pushed the Ba'th regime to display a very high pan-Arab profile, the least that it could do, on the ideological and cultural levels, was to add a strong local dimension to its pan-Arab credo. Through the full legitimization of local Iraqi patriotism and the implied message that the Iraqi nation would not melt away even if Arab unity were achieved, they hoped to dampen Kurdish nationalist fervour. No less importantly, the Mesopotamian component, which was introduced in 1969, was designed to satisfy, on the ideological level, Kurdish demands to be treated as equals to Arabs in their common homeland, because it presented Iraqi history from remote antiquity as a common history of Arabs and Kurds alike.

In 1970 the regime reached an agreement with the Kurdish nationalists in which it recognized the Kurdish right to autonomous rule, but the new national myth was still needed: whether or not the regime intended to carry out the agreement, Kurdish power meant that the central government could not ignore Kurdish aspirations. Within a year relations again started to deteriorate, and in the spring of 1974 the regime launched a new offensive against the Kurds in the north. After the Kurdish revolt was crushed as a result of the Iraqi-Iranian March 1975 agreement, there was less need to appease the Kurds. The intimate connection between the political and the ideological in Ba'thist Iraq was exposed when, at this moment, other considerations (which will be discussed below) were allowed to take precedence and the regime's historiography changed again; unlike their Arab compatriots, Iraqi Kurds were no longer regarded as descendants and heirs of the great civilizations of Mesopotamia. This new interpretation that banished the Kurds from the paradise of Mesopotamian history remained in force even after Khomeini's rise to power in Tehran in

February 1979 when the Kurdish revolt was revived as a result of renewed Iranian support.

As soon as the ceasefire with Iran came into effect Iran's support for the Kurds was stopped for the second time, as it had been in March 1975. The Iraqi army could now turn its full might against the Kurds. In a six-week offensive from August to October 1988 in which chemical weapons were used against Kurdish civilians for the second time (the first being in Halabja in March 1988, in which thousands died), some 120,000 Kurds in the areas bordering Turkey and Iran fled across the borders and the Iraqi army regained effective control of all the Kurdish areas of Iraq. The Kurdish leadership was scattered in Iran, Turkey, Syria and Europe and a massive operation of evacuating towns and villages from a security zone thirty kilometers wide along the Iranian-Iraqi and Turkish-Iraqi borders was initiated by Baghdad. By the end of 1989 no less than 250,000 Kurds had been evacuated to be resettled in other parts of Kurdistan.[7] Some semblance of recognition of Kurdish national rights remained in the sense that an autonomy was established in March 1974 and retained even after the end of the Kurdish revolts in 1975 and 1988. This formal autonomy, however, was a far cry from the minimum demands and expectations of the Kurdish national movement. Some Kurdish cultural rights, too, were retained and the ideological-political commitment to refrain from dissolving the Iraqi nation even in the event of unification with other Arab states was made even more explicit in the late 1970s and in the 1980s than ever before. And although this was not done for the benefit of the Kurds (at least not in the first place), it was potentially a useful approach that could have allayed some Kurdish fears. However, in view of the widening political gulf and the growing acrimony between the most important Kurdish political and military organizations and the Ba'th regime during and following the Gulf War, and of the devastation wrought upon large parts of Kurdistan, this issue paled into insignificance.

IRAQ'S ARAB POLICY AND ITS METAMORPHOSIS

When the Ba'th party came to power in Iraq in July 1968 it tried to put into political practice its revolutionary pan-Arab ideology. In view of the Arab mood following the 1967 war the regime hoped that in this way they could regain the popular support that the party had lost as a result of its dismal performance in 1963. Indeed, for more than two years their Arab policies were exceptionally extreme. They kept a large expeditionary force in Jordan and Syria, which they pledged to put 'at the disposal' of the Palestinian organizations against Israel or any Arab power that threatened them. Although this force avoided an all-out clash with Israel it was occupied far away from home at a time when the Kurdish revolt was simmering in northern Iraq and a serious conflict was brewing with Iran, after the latter abrogated the 1937 agreement over the Shatt al-Arab. The party accused all the Arab regimes of betraying the Palestinian cause, defining each as either 'reactionary' and serving American imperialism (meaning Saudi Arabia and the Gulf states), as treacherous, boastful, and deceitful (meaning the Ba'th regime in Syria) or as 'petty bourgeois' and detached from the masses (meaning 'Abd al-Nasir's Egypt). The alternative which they offered was the 'Arab revolution', sometimes called 'the permanent revolution'. In essence, it meant replacing all the existing Arab regimes with truly popular, socialist, and pan-Arab ones in the image of the Ba'th regime in Baghdad. These new regimes would achieve political unity and start a major transformation of Arab society from semi-feudalism to socialism. The popular (as different from the regular) military struggle for the liberation of Palestine, being the training ground for the new revolutionary cadres, was supposed to serve as an indispensable catalyst for this process.

At the same time, however, Iraq also demanded a new offensive by the Arab regular armies against Israel. The degree of ideological chaos in Baghdad was demonstrated very clearly when the same Iraqi politicians on one occasion called for the downfall of 'Abd al-Nasir and the Syrian Ba'th, and on another called for unification between Iraq and the same two 'corrupt' regimes.

As it happened, Iraq paid heavily for commitment to the Palestinian cause and its ultra-revolutionary theory of action, and it would have stood a good chance of paying a much heavier price had it decided to stick to its guns. On the economic level, the cost of keeping some 25 percent of its armed forces in Jordan was, as admitted by the regime, crippling. On the strategic level, these troops were needed on the Iranian and Kurdish fronts (the March 1970 agreement with the Kurds was seen by both sides as a means to gain time, rather than a lasting solution). Finally, Iraq also suffered a major setback to its political status in the Arab world; its offensive style, its subversive activities in Syria, Jordan, the Gulf states and even in Egypt and the Sudan, and its advocacy of an immediate new war against Israel, when Egypt, Jordan and Syria were still licking their wounds, made close relations with any Arab regime very difficult to cultivate. Thus, when it needed Arab support when its confrontation with Iran reached a head in November–December 1971, it was abandoned by most Arab states.

In the same way, by its own belated admission, Iraq became the subject of general Arab scorn when, for reasons of state, it reneged on its promise to help the PLO against the Jordanian regime when the two clashed in 'Black' September 1970. This brought about a long-overdue internal debate regarding Iraq's national priorities. An important circle within the party, the most conspicuous member of which was the Deputy Chairman of the all-powerful Revolutionary Command Council Saddam Husayn, demanded that Iraq depart from her policy of sacrificing her own interests on the altar of the Arab Revolution, which, they argued, could result in the destruction of both the party and the state. By this they did not, however, imply a break with the Arab world. In fact, this group envisaged an Iraqi return to the Arab arena and even a bid for Arab leadership from a position of great strength in the more distant future, in a decade or two. During the 1970s and possibly part of the 1980s, however, they demanded that Iraq would strike a very different balance between pan-Arab nationalism (*qawmiyya*) and local-Iraqi patriotism (*wataniyya*), with the emphasis shifting towards the latter. By the early 1970s Iraq started gradually to turn away from direct military involvement in the Arab-Israeli conflict and from its revolutionary policy. This process was slow, full of inconsistencies, and accompanied by constant assurances that Iraq would eventually turn out again to spread the revolution and to liberate Palestine. In addition, Iraq adopted a 'rejectionist' stance over the Arab-Israeli conflict (*al-rafd*), and viciously attacked any Arab regime that showed signs of readiness to enter into peace talks. The oscillations, the pervasive radical promises of an ultra-revolutionary future and the rejectionist stance reflected internal struggle and the party leadership's fear of criticism from within the party and from the radical left of the Arab world for its betrayal of its own ideals, as well as an attempt to resolve their own cognitive dissonance. Yet the shift in policy was unmistakable. In late 1970 and early 1971 Iraq recalled its troops from Jordan and Syria, though it promised to send them back when the confrontation states were ready for war. After mid-1972 it no longer promised an early unification with Syria (or with any other Arab country). In October 1978, following the Camp David Accords, this promise was renewed, but it died out again within a few months. In 1975–76 Iraq allowed its relations with Syria, the only radical state bordering Israel, to deteriorate, thus making a new confrontation with Israel less likely, but making it also more difficult for the Ba'th regime in Damascus to penetrate the party in Baghdad.

In 1975 Baghdad reached an agreement with the Shah in which, in return for territorial concessions, it received an Iranian commitment to stop all aid to the Kurds and the Shi'i underground. This agreement opened the way to reconciliation with the pro-American monarchies in the Gulf and with Jordan. Indeed, after 1974 Iraq also endeavored to improve its economic (and, by necessity, political) relations with the 'imperialist countries' of the West, in order to accelerate its economic development. These political changes that came to serve particular Iraqi interests at the expense of the party's pan-Arab ideals were heralded and then accompanied by a new cultural and ideological policy. By giving historical depth and cultural substance to what it saw as a still poorly formed and hitherto little recognized Iraqi national identity, the regime thus sought to forget a double-edged sword that could cut both ways. On the one hand, as pointed out above, it was designed to assure Shi'is, Kurds and others who feared unity that their future was secure, as under no circumstances would Iraq dissolve in a pan-Arab crucible. On the other hand, however, the regime endeavored to legitimize its Iraqi-oriented policies in the eyes of Iraqi pan-Arabs. As perceived by the Ba'th, regime pursuing local Iraqi interests was made much easier when there were no doubts as to the actual existence of an Iraqi nation.

Most of the above mentioned shifts of policy are not new to the student of Iraqi contemporary history.[8] However, the new cultural-ideological policy is little known outside Iraq[9] and is discussed below.

A CULTURAL CAMPAIGN TO OVERCOME IDEOLOGICAL CONSTRAINTS

Less than a year after it came to power, the Ba'th regime launched a policy which sought to create (or as the case may have been, to invigorate and reinforce) a national-territorial consciousness resting upon the particular history of Iraq and, equally significantly, of what the regime, or a powerful circle within it, presented as the history of the Iraqi people. One course adopted was an extraordinary official drive to foster local archeological research, and to make the Iraqi people aware of the importance and relevance of the country's ancient history – including that of the pre-Islamic era. Another path followed was the introduction of ceremonies, names and symbols, dating back to Islamic, but also pre-Islamic Mesopotamia, into the administrative, political and cultural life of modern Iraq. An additional avenue was the cultivation of local folklore, for the dual purpose of inspiring the various communities with a sense of internal Iraqi unity, and of emphasizing Iraq's uniqueness among the nations of the world at large – and the Arab world in particular. By claiming a connection between Iraq's contemporary folklore and the cultures of ancient Mesopotamia,

Iraqi intellectuals enhanced this effect of endowing Iraq with a unique character.

This multi-faceted drive began in the spring of 1969, but it was only in the late 1970s that it came to the notice of political observers and students of the political history of present-day Iraq. The reason for this was that throughout the first decade of Ba'th rule the campaign was promoted under an exclusively cultural guise.

While the cultural plane is a predictable setting for a campaign designed to endow a nation with a historical foundation such a campaign could nevertheless be expected to find expression at the doctrinaire level, as for example in the president's speeches on Revolution Day, or in resolutions by the party congresses (at the regional, if not the pan-Arab, level), or in statements by the Revolutionary Command Council (RCC) and the government – the two highest executive bodies in the land. But throughout that first decade, nothing of the sort occurred.

There are two possible explanations for this extraordinary omission. One is negative: prominent ideologues of the Arab national movement were firmly opposed to the cultivation of a myth resting upon any local pre-Islamic and pre-Arab history. The other is positive: the existence in Iraq since the early 1950s of a cultural trend drawing inspiration from ancient Mesopotamia made it possible to pursue the campaign as an extension of an existing (and well-established) practice. With regard to the negative reason, as I shall endeavor to show, the Ba'th – unlike the followers of Egyptian Pharaonism in the 1920s and early 1930s, or Antun Sa'ada in Lebanon in the 1930s and 1940s – had no intention of disowning its links with the Arab nation at large. However, any attempt to cultivate the Mesopotamian myth – that is to revive a local civilization which, in addition to being pre-Islamic, was widely regarded as pre-Arab – was liable to rouse opposition from the more radical pan Arab circle in Iraq, and severe criticism from similar circles in the Arab world. In the view of Sati' al-Husri, the most important ideologue of modern-day pan-Arabism (and the person who shaped public education in Iraq under King Faysal I), for example, the ancient civilizations of the Middle East had been 'buried under the sands of time for thousands of years', and any bid 'to revert to those lost epochs' was nothing more than 'an attempt to revive . . . that which is dead and mummified'. Al-Husri conceded a possible racial connection between modern Egyptians and the ancient inhabitants of their land, or between present-day Iraqis and the Babylonians of antiquity; but as far as he was concerned, such a connection was totally irrelevant. Islamic-Arab culture, he contended, had brought about a total transformation of those who adopted it; from that time and up to the present day, they had found 'spiritual forefathers' exclusively in Muslim-Arab heroes like Khalid n. al-Walid or philosophers like al-Ma'arri, not in the Pharaohs or the Sumerian kings. Arab history, according to Husri, commenced with the Arab kingdoms of the Yemen, and, subsequently, in the Ghasan and Nabatean states, and flowered in the Golden Age of Islamic-Arab civilization.[10]

Michel 'Aflaq, the intellectual moving force behind the Ba'th party, wrote in a similar vein. In one place, with his argument that the heritage of the civilizations predating that of the Muslim-Arabs had merged into it, and is now a hidden component thereof, he comes very close to claiming that most of the Middle Eastern peoples of antiquity were Arabs. Yet, he never went so far as to characterize them as 'Arab', and, in any case, he affirmed that modern-day Arab nationalism possesses its own unique 'personality', 'is careful to avoid regression into small loyalties [al-'asabiyyat al-saghira]', and is free of 'surrender to factors of the local environment . . . '.[11]

> If it were correct that there is a necessity to acknowledge every civilizational stage which passed over our country as a special nationality, and revive it, there would be numerous categories of this kind of 'nationalism' in every [Arab] country,[12]

he asserted. And whether or not he considered the ancient peoples of the Middle East Arab, clearly to 'Aflaq the period of Muhammad and his prophetic mission, not the remote pre-Islamic eras, was the high point in Arab history.[13] Another notable pan-Arab ideologue, the Iraqi 'Abd al-Rahman al-Bazzaz, was crystal clear in his position towards the pre-Islamic heritage; he regarded it quite unequivocally as part of the history of the Arab *land* or *territory*, rather than of the Arab *nation*:

> In Egypt Mesopotamia and Syria . . . there arose mighty civilizations, including the civilizations of the ancient Egyptians . . . the Akkadians and Babylonians . . . and the civilization of the Phoenicians . . . it would not harm our Arab nationalism to take pride in them . . . but when we do take pride in them . . . let us not for a single moment forget our Arabism, to which our first affiliation must [belong]. For an Iraqi must not forget, when taking pride in the grandeur of the Babylonians and Assyrians, that he is not of the seed of the Babylonians, nor of the Assyrians; he is an Arab, in every sense of Arabism: in his language, in his culture and his living, active history . . . the sons of the Arab nation are today required to emphasize the common, collective characteristics

of their history, and to proudly ignore the local aspects, particularly in public education and in popular culture.[14]

Although al-Husri, 'Aflaq and Bazzaz were referring to separatist movements par excellence, their warnings may certainly be assumed to have exerted a far broader influence; any attempt to resurrect those ancient pre-Islamic cultures, and endow them with political significance, was therefore liable to encounter suspicion and opposition. This was particularly the case in Iraq, which, before the Ba'th takeover, was the sole Arab state of modern times save Egypt where an effort to salvage the pre-Islamic heritage, and render it a legitimate and central component of national consciousness, was made, not by groups of intellectuals or opposition parties, but by the regime itself. Disconcertingly, this was the 'isolationist' regime of 'Abd al-Karim Qasim. Two salient examples will suffice to illustrate the course Qasim sought to follow. One relates to symbols. Under Qasim, Iraq made its national emblem the Akkadian sun (an eight-pointed star with coherent light waves between its points) while the hectagonal star of Ishtar became a prominent element in its national flag. Not surprisingly, both symbols vanished without trace under 'Arif and his pan-Arab regime.[15] The second example relates to the first Revolution Day celebrations on 14 July 1959. The principal feature of the anniversary procession was large floats depicting scenes from the life of ancient Mesopotamia: the first writing in human history; the great breakthrough in science; a large stele bearing Hammurabi's laws under the title: 'Justice is the foundation of government'; day-to-day life in Babylon; a large model of the Ziggurat of Ur; a full-scale replica of a Sumerian ship and its crew; and at the head, a large portrait of General Qasim, flanked by the symbols of 'Tammuz-Dumuzi, the spring god of the ancient Iraqis'. Beneath the name of the deity, the Iraqi archaeologists who organized the procession identified their own immediate god by the cuneiform inscription: 'Dumu-zi Ab-du-ul Ka-ri-im [Qasim]'.[16]

From the viewpoint of the Ba'th party in Iraq, this early quest for national roots in the archeological excavations of Mesopotamia was more of a burden than an asset. If anyone in Iraq recalled it at all, it was associated with memories of an 'isolationist' policy; from the viewpoint of a pan-Arab party which had engineered Qasim's downfall in 1963, the association was therefore unredeemably negative. Introducing the new line via the indirect cultural route was accordingly less liable to draw fire. Such a path was also easier to abandon, without doctrinaire implications, in the event of strong opposition within the party.

But as we have seen, there was also a positive reason why the campaign was a purely cultural, rather than a political one; Iraq had, since the 1950s, witnessed the budding of art forms which sought inspiration in Mesopotamian culture and history. Some of the artists who took this tack were Marxist-inclined and their artistic quest for local Iraqi roots may have been connected with the Iraqi Communist party's traditional inclination towards local Iraqi patriotism. But such a motive is difficult to detect among other members of this school, some of whom, moreover, displayed a profound commitment to the pan-Arab movement. In short, the trend embraced artistic circles from various extremes of the Iraqi secular political spectrum; it could therefore not be unequivocally associated with political separatism. Equally important, followers of this trend included some of modern Iraq's (and, indeed, the modern Arab world's) greatest poets, painters and sculptors. A similar picture emerges in regard to folklore, whose cultivation, however hesitant, began during the period of 'Arif's pan-Arab rule. And finally: the decade between the mid-1930s and mid-1940s saw archeological research fostered and recognized as an important national asset (see the Conclusion). The cultural sphere had thus witnessed important initial steps which the Iraqi public memory did not associate with political isolationism. Accordingly, a start made in this field could be expected to be less provocative, and encounter milder resistance, than one launched in the political arena. Thus, culture became the spearhead of the new ideology.

3 Folklore and Mesopotamian Culture

THE REVIVAL OF LOCAL FOLKLORE

Shortly after the Ba'th accession to power, activities to promote Iraqi folklore received an enormous official boost,[1] which found its initial expression in legislation. A law promulgated early in 1969 created the 'General Directorate for Cinema and Theatre', whose province was to include festivals and congresses devoted to folklore, and the fostering of that art and its preservation on film 'so as to protect our historical, artistic and literary heritage'.[2] The first practical undertakings of this nature to enjoy official support were folklore museums. In 1969–70, a museum of folklore handicrafts was founded in Kirkuk, and a small folklore museum in Mosul was greatly expanded.[3] Apparently in response to an open letter to the president calling for the establishment of a special museum to preserve and exhibit 'life in old Baghdad',[4] such a museum was, indeed, established, housing traditional crafts, apparel, models of living quarters and domestic utensils, and scenes from social life in Baghdad, commencing from the city's foundation in the days of al-Mansur in the 8th century AD and up to the twentieth century. The museum was honored with visits by Iraqi leaders and quite frequent mentions in the press.[5]

Construction work also commenced, at the same time, on an all-Iraqi center of folklore. The center comprised eight departments: literature (folk tales and parables), popular poetry, songs, musical instruments and instrumental music; folk dancing; preservation, manufacture and sale of handicrafts; popular apparel, a reconstruction department and a large library. *Inter alia*, the center was expected to sponsor exhibitions throughout the length and breadth of the country.[6]

The Education Ministry, anxious to preserve and revive local folk arts and crafts, decided to offer schools incentives to establish special sections to teach traditional handicrafts,[7] and another Center for Popular Handicrafts and Industries undertook the preservation and development of traditional crafts from the country's various regions. It conducted special courses to train teaching staff, and founded smaller provincial branches, each specializing in the crafts for which its region had always

30

been distinguished.[8] In the same vein, the 1936 Antiquities Law, which defined 'antiquities' as objects 200 years old or more, received its first-ever amendment empowering the minister responsible to include newer articles within the definition, thereby enabling the government to prevent exports of old products of traditional handicrafts.[9]

Similar efforts in popular song and dance closely followed the Ba'th takeover. March 1970 witnessed the formation of the 'National Folklore Troupe', which included 73 artistes. In 1976, similar though smaller troupes were founded in Basra, in the southern (Shi'i) city of Samawa, in Kurdistan's Irbil and in the Sunni-Arab region of Nineveh. The central troupe's repertoire included dances, songs and instrumental music from Baghdad, from the Shi'i south and from the Kurdish north; and a contemporary choreographer's impression of what an ancient Babylonian dance would have looked like ('the Hammurabi dance'). The songs were performed in the local dialects and languages (the various colloquial Arabic dialects of Iraq, Kurdish and Syriac Aramaic). Arab nationalism was represented by a Palestinian dance. The Basra troupe, which had grown to seventy by 1978, specialized in dancing and instrumental music from the south, supplementing its repertoire with dances from Iraq's Assyrian and Kurdish communities.[10] Indeed, the general principle of the regional troupes appears to have been specialization in local folklore, but supplementing it by folklore from other parts of the country.

In the field of research, a series of books on Iraqi folklore began to appear in 1969. That same year witnessed the appearance of the journal *al-Turath al-Sha'bi* [Folklore]. Commencing with 3000 copies, its circulation had risen to 15,000 by the end of the 1970s.[11]

With regard to the arts surveyed hereto, the political significance is implicit; but one art form which is politically explicit and immediate is popular poetry. The popular poets, declared a correspondent for an intellectual journal, adopt a style 'closest to the souls of the inhabitants' for they 'address people's day-to-day feelings, without the barrier of [literary] language'.[12] These poets came together for occasional congresses where they read their poems outloud in their local dialects; their works, in no small part, glorified the political leadership, urging the masses to support it and its policies.

Predominant in this sphere is the Shi'i south; so Nasiriyya, which is particularly renowned for its folklore poetry, was chosen as the setting for the first Festival of Popular Poets in 1969.[13] Another such festival likewise held in the south, at Babylon, took place at a time when the regime – after nationalizing the assets of the Western-owned Iraqi Petroleum Company (IPC), and at the height of its confrontation with Iran – was clinging on for dear life, making it particularly anxious to rally support among the Shi'i population, where Iranian influence was to be particularly feared. Indeed, the festival was officially designated as a means to 'indoctrinate the masses'.[14] In 1980, a popular poetry festival was held in Baghdad, and the press stressed the attendance of President Saddam Husayn throughout its four-day duration. Somewhat paradoxically it was reported that the poems expressed in local dialects the 'deep roots of the pan-Arab revolution' and party principles. As may be expected in wartime, they also denounced Khomeini's Iran. The president wound up the festival by addressing its participants in terms suited to those whose principal occupation was with the colloquial, rather than the literary language:

> If you find difficulty in reading Ba'th principles . . . sniff the soil of this land . . . your land in the Euphrates valley, and ask your Arab brethren when they come from Sinai and the West Bank . . . to bring you a handful of soil for you to sniff, and then you will become familiar with the principles of the Ba'th.[15]

Such festivals became annual events during the war.[16] Indeed the subject was of sufficient political importance for the resolutions of the party's Ninth Regional Congress to offer the 'popular poets' special praise over their contribution towards recruiting the masses for the party and its leader.[17]

All of the above was backed up by reports on the activities of folklore theatres. Folklore programs were common on television, and playwrights called upon their colleagues to write plays in their local dialects.[18]

The regime's enthusiasm for preserving Iraq's material and cultural heritage engulfed also architecture. Occasionally the Iraqi press published demands that resources be made available for preservation of Baghdad's unusual throughways and its traditional buildings, particularly those possessing the so-called *shanashil* (wooden verandas surrounded by a kind of trellis of carved wood). There were also calls for building new buildings in the old Baghdad style,[19] and Iraqi engineers and architects conducted symposiums to discuss the planning and implementation of a 'modern Iraqi building [style]'.[20] By 1969, the first such buildings were preserved,[21] and in subsequent years more houses were renovated. During the 1980s the old Turkish building of Khan Mirjan was renovated and turned into a restaurant; parts of Haifa Street were reconstructed and a house in Abu Nuwas St. and a group of some five houses in the old quarter of Kazimiyya was preserved as well, but the inclination was to concentrate mainly on the more monumental, old public buildings, rather than on small private houses. In 1982, even as the Gulf War was raging, the Baghdad municipality was willing to invest great sums in restoring the Suk al-Thulatha to its 'Arab-Baghdadian' style.[22] In the late 1980s the Department of Antiquities and Heritage embarked on two important reconstructions. One was that of the impressive medieval Mustansiriyya College (completed in 1989). The other was that of the largest building in old Baghdad, the L-shaped 180m long Ottoman Qushla. Established in 1861 on the Tigris, it served mostly as a barracks for the Ottoman army. In 1921 King Faysal I's coronation ceremony took place there and in the early 1920s it served the Iraqi National Museum. Its reconstruction was reported to cost some $1.5m and it was meant to become a cultural center.[23] During the 1987 battle for Basra, an astonished American journalist saw that restoration of *shanashil* in the ancient quarter was proceeding 'as if assigned a high priority'.[24]

An extravagant contribution towards fostering Iraqi folklore came from the Iraqi Fashion House (*Dar al-Azya*), founded under a law promulgated in 1970. Its goals were to preserve traditional attire from the various parts and communities of Iraq, and thus create a horizontal fusion, but also 'to protect and cultivate ancient Iraqi fashion', and 'to raise the standard of design' of Iraqi textiles with 'designs inspired by the ancient Iraqi paintings', thus establishing a vertical connection with Iraq's pre-Islamic past.[25] The Fashion House was to not only study the dress styles of times gone by in Iraq's provinces, but also to duplicate these sources in collections of clothing designed for display throughout Iraq and the world. These articles of clothing were

> to reflect the figures and living landscapes which flourished in Mesopotamia thousands of years ago. [The clothes] are a kind of summons to profound thought about our history and the channels of our civilization from the most ancient epochs up to the present.[26]

If a certain student of Iraqi folklore was indeed correct in claiming that 'Mesopotamian princes . . . wore clothes and headcoverings with an astonishing resemblance to certain traditional Iraqi clothes of the present day',[27] then bridging the ages by designing fashions on such motifs should not have been too difficult.

In the course of the 1970s, the Fashion House presented its collection numerous times in Iraq and abroad, and some were televised. Dozens of attractive models exhibited 130 costly and beautiful outfits, which drew upon patterns of folklore clothing from the medieval illustrations by the famous Iraq-based painter Yahya al-Wasiti to *Maqamat al-hariri*, and of

Sumerian and other Mesopotamian apparel found in wall paintings, seals and other historical relics.[28] The Iraqi press offered incessant acclaim to 'the historic exhibition which draws its inspiration from the cultures of Sumer, Akkad . . . Basra, Kufa, Baghdad, Samarra and Mosul'.[29]

In February 1979, while Iraq and Syria were conducting talks on unification, the entire Fashion House collection was exhibited in Damascus, as part of an Iraqi culture week aimed at rubbing in Iraq's cultural pre-eminence. According to an Iraqi report 'the show stunned Damascus'.[30] The Fashion House's unique status is also reflected in the scale of resources channelled into it: a 1982 report on a visit to the House by Deputy Prime Minister and RCC member Tariq 'Aziz mentioned that, at a time of war, the government was erecting a new 5 million dinar ($15 million) building for them. The two-and-a-half-acre site was to include various display and entertainment sections, and was designed to draw masses of visitors.[31]

The intensive cultivation of folklore embraced three mutually complementary ideological aims. The first was to bring home to the public the unity underlying the variegated assortment of ethnic communities which compose the Iraqi political entity. A second aim was to illustrate the existence of a popular Iraqi tradition both rich and unique, which deserved to be preserved and fostered for the sake of a heightened awareness of Iraq's uniqueness among the nations of the world and of the Arab world. A third aim was to point up the cultural and possibly the ethnic links connecting the Iraqi people of modern times with the peoples who dwelled in Iraq in antiquity.

All of the aforementioned aims implied a unity arising from separateness, although I have only found this point explicitly discussed in one instance, and here too, the discussion, in various of its aspects, does not gear with the realities imposed upon Iraq by the Ba'th regime. In his 1975 address to the commission for reform of the school curriculum, Saddam Husayn drew a connection between the problem of Iraq's political community and the cultivation of folklore. In view of the sensitivity of the denominational (Sunni-Shi'i) cleavage, Husayn referred to the divide solely in its ethnic and lingual aspects; however, his words are equally valid with regard to the religious denominational divisions between the Sunni center and north-west, and the Shi'i south:

> In patriotic education, there is no evading discussion of [Kurdish] autonomy; [however] when we discuss autonomy, we should not . . . transform the administrative structures of autonomy into a Chinese Wall dividing Iraq's Arabs and Kurds. For example, when we consider Iraqi

folklore, there is nothing that requires us to talk endlessly about Kurdish folklore, and then Arab [folklore], and thirdly Turkoman [folklore] etc.; rather, it should be depicted exclusively as Iraqi folklore. Therefore we should say: this is a [Shi'i] dance from southern Iraq, from Nasiriyya, and this is a [Kurdish] dance from Sulaymaniyya . . . Assuming that one of the ways to prove equality between the Arab[s] and others is, for example, by the Arab wearing an *'aqal* [Arab headgear] and the Kurd a *laft al-ra's* [Kurdish headgear] . . . is a great error, for this . . . will lead to harmful long-term results, ideological and political . . . We must speak of the Iraqi who comes from Sulaymaniyya, and he who comes from Basra, without pointing to his ethnic origins . . . let us delete the words Arabs and Kurds, and replace them with [the term] the Iraqi people.[32]

In addition to an amazing admission that over stressing the Arab connection of the Iraqi people threatens the national unity inside Iraq, this declaration contains also an inherent contradiction: if the aim is expression of Kurdish folklore, how is the onlooker to know that a certain dance is Kurdish, unless the dancers wear the Kurdish headgear? Furthermore, the vice-president's words failed, in part at least, to reflect reality. In most cases, dances or apparel are indeed characterized in the Iraqi press by region; but equally frequent is an express reference to a specific dance or item of clothing as Kurdish or Assyrian. Various official documents specify efforts to foster the 'national heritage' of Kurds, Arabs and other nationalities.[33] In addition, the vice-president appeared to endow the mere use of the term 'Kurdish' with nigh-magical properties, for there can be little doubt that expressions like 'our beloved north' or 'the autonomous region' or 'Najaf' or 'Nasiriyya' are translated by the listener or reader as 'Kurdish' or 'Shi'i' respectively. Realities cannot be changed by mere semantics. But precisely because of their irrationality, and, equally, their divergence from the aforementioned practical policies as pursued by the cultural commissars, these notions of Saddam Husayn highlight the tension between realities and official intentions. While it could be claimed to enfold an inherent contradiction, ethnic folklore was fostered for the dialectical purpose of bridging the gap between ethnicity and an all-embracing Iraqi nationalism. Expression and encouragement would be granted to the culture of every community, thereby heading off a sense of discrimination; but the final outcome would be a common Iraqi product, or something presented as such, thereby advancing towards an integrative nationalism.

This unity-in-diversity was to find its expression in the fact that Iraq's cultural variety was housed in full span under one roof in the principal folklore centers located around Baghdad, and to some extent even in provincial folklore museums, too.[34] A similar aim is evident in the festivals, which sought to bring together Kurds and Arabs, northerners and southerners, in an atmosphere that, while stressing the folklore of the various communities, symbolized national unity. One salient example, was the first 'Festival of Popular Arts and Dress', held in Mosul between June 28 and July 4, 1979, under the auspices of *al-Futuwua* (the General Association of Iraqi Youth). The festival was attended by youngsters from Sulaymaniyya in their Kurdish national dress, which they wore in the popular play they staged. Other youngsters from Basra, likewise in folklore dress, performed dances and songs from 'our Arab Gulf', and a group from the south presented 'the folklore of Najaf'. The youngsters from all the provinces, dressed in their respective local-folkloric costumes and singing in unison, marched in a joint procession to the *al-Hadba* woods near Mosul, thereby, as the party organ affirmed, 'implementing . . . our [unified] patriotic folklore'.[35]

This great investment in local folklore, much of which is uncharacteristic of the remainder of the Arab homeland (that of the Kurds, the Assyrians, the Chaldeans and the Turkomans), the extensive discussion thereof in the media, and its public depiction as representing Iraq alone – can all be construed as an effort to stress the country's uniqueness among the Arabs. This inclination is somewhat tempered by the occasional inclusion within the repertoire of a Palestinian or Arab dance, or by media discussions of Egyptian or other folklores; but this makes no substantive difference. On the admittedly rare occasions when it is discussed explicitly, the motif of Iraq's uniqueness comes across loud and clear. Thus, for example, in a statement marking the appearance of a journal of folklore studies, the Ministry of Culture and Information calls upon 'all writers and intellectuals . . . to take part in preserving the heritage of our [Iraqi] people [Sha'b]'.[36] Another example of Iraqi cultural awareness is provided by the party organ, in its review of a film depicting Iraqi folk dances. The writer is bitterly critical of the producers for featuring an Egyptian dancer in place of an Iraqi dancer, and for including a non-Iraqi (Egyptian, apparently) dance in Iraqi dress. 'There was no need to exhibit it,' he wrote 'as long as Iraq has its own beautiful local dances.'[37]

More common, however, are assertions that, by fostering its own folklore, Iraq contributes towards 'molding the pan-Arab identity', as Culture Minister Tariq 'Aziz put it. Indeed, the possibility that expansion of local folklore could lead to the opposite result, i.e., to greater disparity between the Arab states, is never conceded by most of Iraq's cultural commissars.[38] At most, the risk is acknowledged implicitly, as when a folklore researcher claims that preservation of folklore 'does not encourage localism and regionalism'.[39]

At the 1977 Baghdad Folklore Congress, only one delegate, the Iraqi art critique Sami Mahdi, plucked up the courage to address the thorny issue of the possibly divisive effect inherent in fostering folklore. Mahdi was not a prominent figure, but in view of the virtually oppositional views he voiced, and the fact that his speech was given publicity, he may have represented circles of influence:

> We are, as is well-known, one single Arab nation . . . we are striv-ing for unification of the Arab homeland and emancipation of its masses . . . and building up socialism in it . . . The act of reviving the popular heritage could be one of the instruments of the pan-Arab and socialist struggle, just as it could be an obstacle on its path . . . That means that our interaction with the popular heritage has to be selective and [solely] that part of it which fits this [pan-Arab and socialist] concept . . . is worthy of interest and study and revival, and whatever doesn't [fit that concept], isn't [worthy thereof].
>
> . . . The Arab nation . . . [possesses, *inter alia*] a heritage which grew up during the stages of division and separation . . . and what made it stand out even more was the invention of the modern entities [the existing nation-states] and the backwardness of pan-Arab conscious-ness and the reinforcement of separatist tendencies . . . Accordingly, any interest [in the separate heritage of any Arab country] and its consolidation, implies consolidation of the manifestation of division and the obstacles on the path of pan-Arab unity . . . We are bound to oppose and reject any variant which will ultimately lead to a fracturing of the completeness of unity and express a call to divisiveness and regionalism, and justify talk of 'special characteristics' and a quest for an 'independent entity' for each Arab state. Hence, it is vital that attention be directed [solely] to [that which we hold] in common . . . we must relinquish, and wrestle with, the heritage created by the conditions of division and separation, and which has become . . . a manifestation of uniqueness and alienation, however glamorous this heritage and [however] gratifying to the regional arrogance . . . of the [existing] artificial states.[40]

This statement could be construed as a challenge to Iraq's cultural policy which, while not indifferent to Arab folklore as a whole, focussed all the same mainly on Iraqi folklore.[41]

On the level of the individual nation-state, Sami Mahdi does not duck consideration of the thorny issue of the folklore of non-Arab minorities in the Arab homeland like that of the Kurds or the dwellers in southern Sudan. In his view, such folklore should be legitimized and preserved. Any other practice would give rise to resentment and jeopardize national unity. But any such recognition to the diverse should be given with restraint, so as to avoid reviving what is already extinct. Under no circumstances should the state be transformed into 'a mosaic that will consolidate separation and weaken the amalgamative elements' in Iraqi or Sudanese society. In this sense, his views closely resemble the aforementioned statement by Saddam Husayn, but they, too, offer no real solution. Mahdi's position diverges sharply from those of the vice-president (and the general line of the cultural establishment) in his firm opposition to an emphasis on the uniqueness of Iraq's geographical regions, such as scientific studies of children's games in one town or apparel in another. Furthermore, the writer opposes the 'revival' of extinct folklore – which, at the time, was a principal Iraqi objective. Mahdi's argument is dual: first, such a 'revival' resuscitates superstitions and backward customs, such as popular medicine (an untenable argument, since the documentation and exhibition of popular medicine does not imply its application in daily life). The second argument is only implied, but the writer nevertheless seemed genuinely troubled thereby: the proliferation of the elements which set apart the various regions would prejudice national Iraqi unity; proliferation of the elements which set Iraq apart from the rest of the Arab world would make it harder to attain 'the establishment of a united, democratic and socialist all-Arab society'.

Regardless of the soul-searching – which should not be discounted – and with regard to the balance between the local and the pan-Arab, Iraqi sources leave no doubt that the principal stress was laid upon fostering Iraq's uniqueness. This uniqueness was emphasized further by linking present local Iraqi folklore with the cultures of ancient Mesopotamia.

FOLKLORE AND THE MESOPOTAMIAN HERITAGE

A salient feature of activity in relation to folklore was its frequent reference to two distinct historical epochs: the present, or recent past; and Iraq's ancient history. Thus, Iraqi folklore was treated by cultural publicists, academics and ideologues as a more or less direct continuation of the civilizations of the Mesopotamian valley.[42]

This approach was given implicit institutional expression in the Mosul festivals, where scenes from Iraq's ancient past were depicted side-by-side with performances of folklore from the country's various regions, Mosul itself in particular.

As we have already seen, this approach was expressed with even greater clarity by the policy of the Iraqi Fashion House, which presented an unbroken continuum stretching from Sumer and Akkad to the popular costumes prevalent in the various regions of twentieth-century Iraq. On occasion, this notion was expressed explicitly. During the early days of the Fashion House, *al-Jumhuriyya* affirmed that its purpose was to illustrate 'the connection between [present day] Iraqi apparel and the civilizations of Mesopotamia', and 'to emphasize the civilizations and progress of Iraq [ancient and modern]'.[43] Admittedly, the underlying aim of the Fashion House was occasionally characterized as 'revival of the pan-Arab heritage',[44] but unless one regards any contribution to the Iraqi heritage as necessarily a contribution to the pan-Arab heritage, the Fashion House cannot claim to enrich the latter. In fact, pan-Arab considerations were totally absent from the law whereby the National Fashion House was constituted: the words 'Arab' or 'pan-Arab' (*qawmi*) are not even mentioned there, and the law refers solely to 'Iraqi heritage' or 'ancient Iraqi fashions' (Articles 1–3). And there is no mention in all the descriptions of the House's costumes of popular or ancient costumes from Arab countries outside Iraq.

Further testimony to the intention of teaching the public to associate folklore with ancient Mesopotamian culture is offered by the academic journal *al-Turath al-Sha'bi*. The journal was first published in 1969 and is dedicated to Iraqi folklore.[45] While some saw its appearance as a symptom of separatism,[46] the journal continued to appear regularly into the 1980s. During the first decade of its publication most of the articles dealt with folklore in the limited sense of the term. Folklore was defined as 'the art of the everyday' which excludes 'extinct verbal traditions, or material examples no longer in use'.[47] This definition notwithstanding, the journal also published numerous articles dealing with the cultures of ancient Mesopotamia. Thus, for example, it printed a new translation of the Gilgamesh Epos (the original translation was earlier published by the archeological journal *Sumer*);[48] translations of the 16th–17th century BC 'Hymn of Ishtar' and of 'an Akkadian tale . . . discovered in the library of Ashurbanipal';[49] studies of Sumerian apparel from the era of the Dawn of the Dynasties (2700–2500 BC)[50] and studies of 'folk festivals in ancient Iraq' (Babylon principally).[51] These writings appear to have been published in *al-Turath al-Sha'bi*, rather than in *Sumer*, due to the desire of the former's editors to exhibit their conviction that the subjects discussed appertain to Iraqi folklore. In one instance at least this view was expressed unabashedly by one of the journal's leading contributors, who offered this explanation for collating folklore and fostering it:

> We collect [our] heritage because it enriches our literature, our customs . . . and contains psychological indicators of the collective [character] of the Iraqi individual throughout the centuries, apparently reaching back to the Sumerian or Babylonian period.[52]

It may or may not have been fortuitous, but the journal sporadically published articles dealing, at varying levels of clarity, with the continuity, 'since the dawn of history', of Iraqi culture, and, as occasionally hinted, the Iraqi race.[53] Hints of this sort are extremely numerous in other journals published in Iraq.[54]

A further instance of the self-same approach – whereby the two epochs are connected in a kind of historical 'short-circuit' which bridges thousands of years of separation and oblivion – can be found in the layout of certain Iraqi museums. Special sections, devoted to folklore and Iraqi life in the early twentieth century, are often to be found flanking archeological exhibits. As Iraqi sources admitted, such a layout is not usual in the world's museums; its purpose, they affirmed, is 'to highlight the heritage of successive generations . . . to reinforce the connection between [present] and past, and elucidate it to the present generations, to enable them to benefit from the practices of their forefathers'.[55] Furthermore, it was reported in 1973 that the Institute for Folklore Crafts planned to manufacture 'artistic sculptures to recount the history of ancient and modern cultural Iraq, from the Babylonian and Assyrian periods, [by way of] the Abbasid era, up to the present day' so as to disseminate them at exhibitions, and sell them to tourists and visitors.[56] Indeed, in the late 1980s the Directorate of Folklore Heritage was already producing beaten copper plates, carpets and rugs with Medieval-Islamic and Mesopotamian pre-Islamic themes and selling them to citizens and tourists in Iraq, as well as trying to turn it into a cash earning export [Plates 1A, 1B].

Apparently with a similar purpose in mind of reinforcing the connection between present and past, the National Folklore Troupe included in its repertoire a dance-and-song entitled 'Hammurabi'.[57]

4   A Passion for Archeology

> Antiques are the most precious relics the Iraqis possess, showing the world that our country, which today is undergoing an extraordinary renaissance, is the [legitimate] offspring of previous civilizations which offered up a great contribution to humanity.
>
> Saddam Husayn at a convention of Iraqi archeologists
> (*Sumer*, 1979, p. 9)

It was not long after the Ba'th advent to power before it emerged that the new regime entertained a particular weakness for archeology. A comparison between the sums made available to the Administration of Antiquities under the 'Arif regime, and the funding provided by his Ba'th successors, shows a significant increase significantly in excess of the rise in cost of living. During three years under 'Arif (1964/65, 1965/66, 1967/68) the Administration's average annual budget was 417,263 dinars; this increased to 757,526 dinars during the first four full budgetary years of Ba'th rule (1969/70; 1970/71; 1971/72; 1972/73),[1] marking an increment of 81 percent, while the cost of living index rose by no more than 35 percent from 1964 to 1973.[2]

According to the enthusiastic reports of Iraq's archeologists, the allotment may have been far greater than indicated by the official budget. Only a few months after the Ba'th came to power, the director-general of Antiquities announced that all graduates of Baghdad university's Archeology Department would find employment with the Administration of Antiquities.[3] In 1970, he proclaimed that, since July 1968, 'the archeological projects have enjoyed all the help and assistance of the revolutionary government, due to its conviction of the necessity of redeeming the heritage'.[4] On a different occasion, he affirmed that the government's support for the Administration 'was made evident in the large sums [allotted] for its activities'.[5]

So anxious was the regime to unearth the secrets of Iraq's ancient past that no sooner was an agreement concluded with the Kurdish rebels than the government organ called for excavations to be extended to Kurdistan.[6]

Though relatively large resources were earmarked to excavations, the regime's main interest was political, not academic; as an *al-Jumhuriyya* columnist explained, the regime was bent on,

> Uncovering . . . the civilizations of the ancient forefathers . . . which is the material aspect of the culture of our [Iraqi] people and home-land . . . raising the cultural level of our toiling masses by making them familiar with our forefathers' culture which underlies our [modern] culture.[7]

From the mid-1970s and onward, these allotments may be presumed to have undergone a further substantial increase not entirely reflected in its official budget. The increase was made possible by the 1974 boom in oil revenues; but most governments would use the additional resources for a variety of purposes other than archeological excavations or the restoration of ancient sites. If the Iraqi regime nevertheless elected to effect so significant an increase in this particular field, it should be regarded as an indication of the special importance attributed thereto. In 1975, the Administration reported that its great successes in exca-vation and preservation, in museum construction and in publication of research work, were without exception 'the outcome of the material and moral support its archeological programs enjoyed from our revolutionary government . . . the enormous financial allotments had far-reaching effects in propelling the Administration forward'. Reportedly, objectives set out years ago had been achieved.[8] The largest excavation project conducted in the seventies – financed by Iraq and executed for the most part by foreign expeditions – was in the basin scheduled for inundation by the Himrin dam. Between 1977 and 1980, no less than 75 different sites in the basin were excavated.[9]

After Saddam Husayn became President in July 1979 there was another quantum leap in government spending on archeological digs and recon-struction.

A first expression of this enhanced importance of archeology was a law promulgated in 1979 which elevated the Administration of Antiquities to the rank of 'State Organization for Antiquities and Heritage'. The single director-general now became chairman of a board of directors, establishing five to seven posts of directors-general for the purpose of current administration. The law defined the tasks of the 'Organization' as 'uncovering . . . the ancient civilizations which existed in this country', 'to permit the public to view' the antiquities and their restorations, and 'organizing conferences and exhibitions in Iraq and around the world'.[10]

In the 1979 volume of *Sumer*, the director-general of the newly-founded 'Organization for Antiquities and Heritage' notified his readers that 'the budget . . . is today several times larger than previously'.[11] At the same time, the director of the Babylon excavations told an American journalist that 'whatever we want, we get . . . Not just a million or two, but anything we wish, without restrictions!'[12]

The actual work – excavation, restoration and renovation – though also devoted to Islamic sites (such as al-Mustansiriyya, the Abbasid fortress of Baghdad and the great mosque of Samarra)[13] laid the principal emphasis on pre-Islamic sites.

A different aspect of this interest in antiquities was the campaign to repatriate important archeological artifacts. In 1974 the RCC amended the 1936 Antiquities Law to permit the government to confiscate, against compensation, relics hitherto held in private possession. The law was immediately and successfully applied.[14]

With the same aim in mind, the government has, since the mid-1970s, conducted a major international campaign to coax governments, museums and universities the world over to restore Mesopotamian antiquities to their place of origin. In mid-November 1975, Iraq succeeded in eliciting a United Nations resolution calling for the restoration of antiquities to the lands of their origin. Subsequently, the regime went out of its way to explain its motives behind these efforts:

> The stele of Hammurabi awaits impatiently in the Louvre, and the library of Ashurbanipal is in the British Museum, and the Procession Street and the gate of Ishtar have yet to return, and are languishing sadly in [East] Berlin . . . their abandonment . . . in the museums of the world, and their inability to return to the homeland from which they emerged is a cultural calamity and a major crime . . . In previous periods [in Iraq, governments] did not grasp the importance of these antiquities, taking no interest whatsoever in these stolen treasures . . . but since the revolution [of July 1968], there has been great progress . . . the Iraqis and their nationalist-socialist revolution are determined to restore the treasures which are the symbol of the first and greatest civilizations in human history.[15]

Europe and the United States showed a willingness to cooperate. For example, a journalist for *al-Jumhuriyya* told his readers that French Prime Minister Raymond Barre, characterized as 'the heir of the antiquities robbers', was astounded, on visiting Baghdad in 1979 to discuss an oil deal, 'when Saddam Husayn demanded of him that the Louvre return the stele of Hammurabi'.[16]

Politically speaking the most important aspect of this search for national-Iraqi roots in ancient Mesopotamia was the educational campaign, aimed to awaken the interest of the Iraqi masses in their country's ancient history.

And while the need to rescue the sites about to be flooded in the Himrin Valley could be explained in terms of professional necessity, this campaign can be construed only in an ideological context.

In mid-1969, the editor of *Sumer* and the Director-General of Antiquities announced that the Administration planned 'to build museums and archeological centers in every province and sub-province, and at every archeological site of importance'.[17] This grandiose undertaking was never completed, but even that part which was accomplished is impressive. By the mid-1970s brand-new archeological museums had been constructed in Basra, Nasiriyya, Ctisphon-Madain, Irbil, Kirkuk, Nineveh (the 'Nergal Gate' museum) and a small museum at Baghdad university.[18] The National Museum was renovated and enlarged, as were the museums of Mosul and Sulaymaniyya. In addition, there were pledges to erect museums at Ramadi in Western Iraq, Rumaytha, Najaf and Karbala in the south.[19] In the late 1970s or early 1980s, museums were indeed built at Ramadi and Aqarquf – both lying west of Baghdad;[20] however, no information is available about Najaf or Karbala.

The museums and archeological sites (notably the Assyrian sites near Mosul, and the national museum in Baghdad and Babylon) became lodestones for pilgrimages by Iraqi citizens, and, furthermore, by delegations and leaders, from the Arab world and elsewhere, on official visits to Baghdad. These tours by dignitaries gained extensive publicity, as did the comments they made or that were attributed to them. The first subjected to this new practice appears to have been Iranian diplomats (in 1969, soon after the Ba'th takeover and shortly before the Iraqi-Iranian dispute over the Shatt al-Arab had erupted), who were taken to the ruins of Babylon to remind them of the source from which the Akhaemenian civilization drew its inspiration, Hammurabi having predated Cyrus the Great by some 1200 years. The report depicted the Iranians 'stunned by the sight they beheld'.[21] When Sudan's President Ja'far al-Numayri visited Baghdad in 1975, after a lengthy period of Iraqi-Sudanese hostility, he was taken to an Assyrian site near Mosul, where, to the gratification of his listeners, he declared: 'The antiquities I have seen are proof of the historical grandeur of this [Iraqi] people [*al-sha'b*].'[22]

Several museums drew up educational programs and held exhibitions for the benefit of students and school pupils during their summer vacations and at other times. These projects were sometimes supplemented by exhibitions of work the students and pupils had created under the inspiration of the museum exhibits.[23] The Administration of Antiquities went so far as to organize a two-month seminar for Iraqi journalists, with the aim of 'elucidating the principal characteristics of the civilizations of ancient Iraq'.[24] Special occasions, such as the conclusion of a season of excavations, or anniversaries of the party or revolution, were marked by the museums with special exhibitions, to which the public was invited 'so that our citizens shall learn about their eternal heritage'.[25] Similar activities were also pursued abroad: Iraq took pains to send roving exhibitions to Europe and Japan, to enable those countries to 'become acquainted with the civilization of Iraq in the present and past . . . and renew their awareness that the soil of Iraq has been the cradle of civilization for the past five thousand years'.[26]

A Ministry of Culture report spoke of an increase by close to one hundred percent in the number of exhibitions held annually by the National Museum between 1974 to 1977, in Iraq itself, in Arab countries, and abroad.

The various provincial museums, while specializing in antiquities uncovered in their own regions, nevertheless stressed all-Iraqi unity by exhibits from other provinces, or pictures accompanied by explanatory captions.[27]

Salient and striking as museum construction was, the restoration (or 'resurrection') of important archeological sites was doubly impressive. The reconstruction of Hatra (al-Hadar), Nineveh, Nimrod and Ashur in the north, and the restoration of the Ziggurat of Aqarquf to the west of Baghdad[28] were major undertakings. (There was also talk of reconstructing more modest sites from Muslim-Arab history, at Samarra, Baghdad and elsewhere.)

But the most ambitious project was the reconstruction of the ruins of Babylon.[29] The reason for the focus on Babylon appears to have been dual: first, self-evidently, the city's special status in Mesopotamian history and its worldwide renown; and second, its location in the Shi'i region and on the boundaries of Baghdad enabled the regime to use it as an illustration of the historical unity of Iraq's people, or at least of the country's Sunni and Shi'i Arabs (Ashur in northern Iraq has similar points in its favor, see below for the Mosul Festival).

As early as 1971, an enthusiastic professional journal published government plans relating to Babylon:

Drawing upon the faith of the revolutionary government in the revival of the enormous civilizational heritage of our country [the Administration of Antiquities] has adopted a mighty plan to build up the city of Babylon because of its far-reaching importance to human civilization . . . a plan . . . designed to rescue this city and restore it to its former splendor.[30]

After delays for reasons technical and professional, but not financial, the first stage commenced in February 1978; the second phase was scheduled for completion in 1988. The two phases comprised a large drainage project (the ruins were largely inundated by salty groundwater) which dictated the diversion of the river Hilla. Both phases of the restoration were to focus principally upon the later Babylonian period: the temple of Ishtar, 'the southern fortress of Nebuchadnezzar', the Greek amphitheatre, Ishtar's gate, Mardukh's gate and the Ziggurat. The search for the Hanging Gardens was pursued with great zeal, but the Iraqi archeologists were uncertain as to their location or form. The plan also called for the construction of three museums, to be named after Nebuchadnezzar (for finds from the later Babylonian period), Hammurabi (the earlier Babylonian period) and Alexander the Great (Hellenistic period); the Iraqi planners however saw no need for a museum dedicated to finds from the Persian-Akhaemenian period. The entire landscape in and around the restored city was to be redesigned, to revive the vistas – flora and fauna – of ancient Babylon. In view of the city's deterioration the government undertook an exceedingly heavy task. Indeed, reports dating from the years 1979–80 speak of 750 laborers fully employed in excavation and reconstruction, as well as dozens of experts; work proceeded 16 hours each day, simultaneously at eleven separate sites within the city.[31] Considerable work also appears to have been accomplished during 1981, as an Iraqi journalist testified after visiting the site:

> As we entered the gate [of the city] . . . work was proceeding at full tempo; it was as though the city's inhabitants had returned again. But these were the grandsons of those grandfathers who constructed this lofty civilization, and it is consequently no wonder that they rejoice in their labors . . .

A woman archeologist interviewed at the site, while showing academic prudence, confessed:

> It's a wonderful thing for a person to work on restoring his nation's civilizational heritage. Joy overwhelms me when I find an archeological relic, for it is part of our civilization.[32]

The cost of the enterprise was originally assessed at 10 million dinars ($30 million). The government proposed to recruit funds from around the world, being incapable of meeting such an outlay (prior to the oil price boom).[33] In subsequent years, the government took the entire cost upon itself.[34] The project was defined as 'one of [Iraq's] principal national development projects'.[35]

In the early 1980s, in disregard of the economic difficulties brought on by the Gulf War, there were reports of work in process at Babylon, as well as other sites. On a visit to Babylon early in 1983, Deputy Prime Minister Tariq 'Aziz stressed the interest in the project shown by 'the leadership of the party and the revolution, headed by President Saddam Husayn', and encouraged those engaged therein to press ahead with their efforts.[36]

As a result of the war, the first phase was not completed until the fall of 1987, whereupon the second phase was launched without delay. 'Hundreds of Iraqi craftsmen' were granted exemption from military service to allow them to go ahead with their work. In October 1987, and again throughout most of 1988, in preparation for the Babylon Festivals, 450 meters of eleven-and-a-half meter high new yellow brick walls and two gates were hastily erected, with no regard to the archeological sites on which they were built. Using sixty million such bricks, the huge work force was, in fact, building a new Babylon rather than reconstructing the ancient one. A replica of the Ishtar Gate was built, too, in full-size (though some 100 meters south east of the correct place) and restoration also went ahead on the great Ziggurat. (By 1988 two temples, including that of Ishtar of Agade, a palace and the Greek amphitheatre were properly reconstructed). Saddam Husayn reportedly gave the undertaking a 'blank check', as he wished Babylon to be 'an inspiration to his people [as it] engaged in the terrible . . . conflict with Iran'.[37] (For the Babylon International [Music] Festival, see below.) The area was developed in many ways to attract local tourism from al-Hilla and other neighboring Shi'i centers of population and from Baghdad. While no high quality hotels were built there or in al-Hilla, a first-class highway was built between Baghdad and al-Hilla which enables tourists or Baghdadis to get there within two hours. On the spot the government has provided toilets, a shaded area that can be used for picnics, a restaurant, a large recreation lake and other such amenities.[38]

Although only partially restored by the late 1970s the city's ruins were already of considerable service to the regime on various occasions. In May 1977, completion of restoration work on the Greek amphitheatre was marked when over 2,000 spectators from the *muhafazah* [province] of Babylon (principally, it seems, from the Shi'i city of Hilla) gathered in the amphitheatre to watch an Academy of Arts performance of 'Gilgamesh', 'the Odyssey of ancient Iraq'; and thus 'life returned to this eternal venue which had been silent for thousands of years'.[39]

In mid-1979, as restoration of the Ishtar temple neared completion, the party organ assured newly-wed couples that they would soon be able to spend their honeymoons at the temple, and the shrine of Ishtar would again be replete 'with all the atmosphere of love and marriage ceremonies which prevailed within it in the days when historical Babylon flourished'.[40] One can only guess at the reaction of the Shi'i *'ulama* in Karbala, a mere few miles away from Babylon, on reading of Ba'th intentions of renewing the 'atmosphere of love' in the fertility shrine situated under their windows. Be that as it may, Iraqi archeologists, and very possibly party ideologues, being familiar with the pagan fertility rite of Ishtar and its attendant reveries, must have been fully aware of the astounding implications of the suggestion put forward by the party organ.[41]

In September 1981, the first anniversary of Saddam's Qadisiyya, the war with Iran was marked in the ruins of Babylon and the city of al-Hilla by throngs of revellers in three days of celebrations under the slogan: *'Nabuchadnasr al-ams Saddam Husayn al-yawm'* [Yesterday Nebuchadnezzar, today Saddam Husayn].[42] Speaking on behalf of the president, his Kurdish deputy Taha Muhyi al-Din Ma'ruf connected the present war with earlier Persian attempts, stretching back into antiquity, 'to eliminate Iraq's independence'. Ma'ruf launched his speech with the cry:

> O the masses of our great nation, O victorious sons of Iraq, O grandsons of Nebuchadnezzar and al-Qa'qa' . . . O sons of the middle Euphrates and O masses of al-Hilla, your salute to the battle of Saddam's Qadisiyya under the slogan Yesterday Nebuchadnezzar, today Saddam Husayn establishes the link between the historical contributions of this country . . . and the heights of today and the flags of victory fluttering under the leadership of the fearless and inspired leader Saddam Husayn.[43]

In his address, the vice-president contrived, very concisely, to encapsulate four disparate elements: the Shi'i population, which for ideological reasons he addressed in a roundabout way (i.e., by addressing the inhabitants of the middle Euphrates and al-Hilla); ancient Babylon, depicted here both as symbol of the ethnic unity of the Iraqi people, and by implication, as token of its partial dissociation from the rest of the Arab nation; al-Qa'qa', hero of the historical battle of Qadisiyya (AD 635) associated with the liberation of Iraq from the Persian Zoroastrian foe, and with the Islamic golden age which preceded the death of Imam Husayn (AD 680) and the tragic rift within Islam; and Saddam Husayn, the leader of a united, modern Iraq. The vice-president went on to stress the nation's common destiny, past and present, by describing the eternal enmity, stretching back to the dawn of history, between the aggressive Persians and the united Iraqi people:

When the mighty kingdom of Akkad and Sumer was founded, as an expression of the first Iraqi internal patriotic [*wataniyya*] unity in history [sic!], the 'Elamites attacked this kingdom, and thus the first Iraqi kingdom to express the unity of the homeland was exposed to a hateful attack by the Persian 'Elamites . . . And when Iraq rose again, and the United Kingdom arose, and Sargon the Akkadian arose as the leader who united Iraq, the black [Persian] . . . lusts reawakened; but the Iraqi leader Sargon repelled them forcefully . . . [and in modern times too] your determined resolve was the mountain . . . upon which the dreams of the grandsons of Xerxes and Kisra were shattered.

And Kamal Yasin, governor of Babylon province, added:

The festival's celebration in this *muhafazah* expresses the faithfulness of this city [Babylon], which witnessed the civilizational genius of the Arab [!] man, and [which played] an illustrious role in building up the unity of the Arab nation and liberation of its lands.[44]

The two speeches are significant principally in their delineation of a link – ethnic, cultural and political – connecting the Shi'a of southern Iraq with the country's Semitic history (referred to here as 'Arab' [see below]) and its subsequent Arab-Islamic era, all of which was set in contrast with the Persian-Aryan race and civilization. The urgency of the regime's efforts in this direction, at a time of war, cannot be overrated: the ties – of family, religion and culture – connecting the Shi'i population of the holy cities (particularly the *'ulama*, including the Arabs among them) with their Iranian counterparts, and sometimes, the Tehran authorities, had been a thorn in Iraqi flesh ever since the state's constitution at the end of World War I.[45] The fusion of this traditional relationship with the Khomeini revolution lent added impetus to the quest for a basis of identification whereby to sever links between the Iraqi Shi'a and Iran. In this context, Babylon's ruins were transformed into one of the regime's principal cultural-ideological instruments, not merely for uniting Iraq's political community, but also for the concomitant effort to wean parts of the country's population away from rival external affinities, primarily to Iran.

The Babylon Festival was ultimately transposed into the Babylon International Music Festival, which took place between 22 September and 21 October 1987. Its emblem featured the profiles of Nebuchadnezzar and Saddam Husayn, and it was held again under the slogan: 'Nebuchadnezzar yesterday, Saddam Husayn today.' Throughout the month, orchestras from all over the world performed on the stage of the Greek amphitheatre, in four temples and in Nebuchadnezzar's Royal Court. Iraq's contribution included the play 'Nebuchadnezzar the Sun King', written by the renowned poet, playwright and critic, Jabra Ibrahim Jabra, and performed by the Iraqi National Troupe. Another evening was dedicated to 'songs embodying the civilization of Iraq . . . [and] the historical city of Babylon'. The ancient site also housed sundry exhibitions: books on Iraq and its ancient history, art and so on. Iraqi citizens in large numbers were reported to have visited the venue in the course of the month-long festival.[46]

The Babylon Festival of 1988 adopted the slogan: 'From Nebuchadnezzar to Saddam Husayn, Babylon arises anew [*Babil tanhadu min jadid*]!' At the opening ceremony, attended by senior party functionaries and foreign culture ministers, a brief speech by Culture Minister Latif Nusayyif Jasim was followed by the entrance, through three gates from Procession Street, of a throng of Babylonian soldiers, bearing swords and lances, and marching to drum-beats and the music of authentic antique instruments. They were headed by a float upon which Nebuchadnezzar was perched clutching a banner 'referring to the glory of Babylon of the past, and the present of the new Iraq'. The Babylonian monarch presented the banner 'to his grandson, flagbearer of the Twin Rivers, President Saddam Husayn', who was represented by Culture Minister Jasim. The soldiers were followed by children bearing candles [?] and palm-leaves [emblems of the Iraqi landscape]. Bearers of ancient Babylonian incense pots completed the procession. In an evening dedicated to Iraqi music an orchestra played an overture 'Nebuchadnezzar' by the Iraqi-Armenian composer, Beatrice Bohanesyan. The last evening was dedicated to Iraqi folklore dances from Mosul, Baghdad, and Basra produced on a high artistic level, and Iraq's most popular singer sang in a colloquial dialect a new song on the Iraqi homeland 'from the mountains of the north to the reed swamps of the south'. During the festival the ministry of information arranged an international symposium of archeologists and lawyers dedicated to Hammurabi's Code. It opened with a biography of Hammurabi by Mu'ayyad Sa'id, the Director General of Antiquities. This biography bore strange resemblance to that of Saddam Husayn. Otherwise, the symposium was academically sound, and for three successive evenings all its proceedings were broadcast on the TV, including the most professional lectures like one on the theory of evidence in Hammurabi's code and other such presentations, simultaneously translated from English, French and German. This festival lasted only two weeks, but it was no less lavish or splendid than its predecessor, and all its events could be seen on the TV screen every evening.[47]

The last Festival with a Mesopotamian component to be introduced was President Saddam Husayn's birthday. The celebrations of 1990 included people dressed in Babylonian and Assyrian robes prostrating themselves before the audience, and a tableau of a baby Saddam rocking in a cradle in the marshes.[48] This was, apparently, not so much an attempt to imply that the president was an heir to Moses but, rather that he follows in the footsteps of Sargon the Akkadian (about 2400 BC) who being an illegitimate child was found according to the Akkadian myth, by the royal gardener, after his mother, a priestess, sent him on the river in a caulked basket.

Unearthing the past became, aptly, a central theme in the Ninth Regional congress of the party that convened in June 1982, following a serious setback in the war, when Iraqi troops were driven out of Abadan and Khorramshahr. The Congress asserted that, during the Ba'th rule, 'For the first time under the [Republican] Revolution archeology has attracted great attention'. The Report mentioned in particular the salvage works at the Himrin and Haditha Basins, the 'restoration' of Babylon, Ashur and Samarra, the large-scale works conducted in seventeen other ancient cities and the current establishment of twelve new archeological museums.

In such a context it was only natural for President Saddam Husayn, when encouraging his people to continue to fight against the Iranian enemy, to invoke the full depth of the newly-found history of the Iraqi people:

You, worthy Iraqis, descendants of the people of Babylon, Assyria and the great Abbasid state, have guarded your historical glory and your brilliant present [against Iran]. You have been the true children of this great people which created great civilizations . . . You have remained free and independent.[49]

The ups-and-downs of official Iraq's preoccupation with Mesopotamia's pre-Islamic past are vividly illustrated by the life story of Professor Taha Baqir, the country's most renowned archeologist under Qasim and the Ba'th, and a long-standing enthusiast for the theory of the cultural (and, by implication, ethnic) connection between ancient Mesopotamians and modern Iraqis. Born to a middle-class Shi'i family in the southern city of al-Hilla, he completed his MA studies at the University of Chicago in 1938 and then joined the Directorate of Antiquities. In 1941 he became curator of the Iraqi National Museum (a post he held till 1953) and henceforth made no secret of his belief in the Iraqi people's historical continuity all the way back to ancient times. It was a period of growing interest by Iraqi intellectuals in the Mesopotamian heritage: as already noted, *Sumer* was founded (Baqir was a member of its editorial board), and certain artistic circles began to take an interest in the local art of ancient times. In 1953, Baqir was appointed aide to the Director of Antiquities, and in 1958, under Qasim, he became Director. Having received his full professorship in 1961, he also served as vice-president of Baghdad University between 1961–63. In 1963, when 'Arif and the Ba'th came to power, Baqir was relieved of all his posts and forced to retire, when only 50 years old. He spent the years 1965–70 in Libya. In 1970, he was recalled by the Ba'th regime, and restored to his professorship at Baghdad University. In 1971 he became a member of Iraq's Academy of Science. In 1978, upon his retirement at the age of 65, Baghdad University's Faculty of Humanities rendered him the rare honor of dedicating a special issue of its bulletin to him.[50]

5 Mosul's Spring Festivals: Mesopotamian Rites

In April 1969, Mosul provided the setting for festivities of an unusual nature. On April 10, in the presence of Commander-in-Chief and RCC member General Hammad Shihab, and under the auspices of President Ahmad Hasan al-Bakr, the city's 'First Spring Festival' was inaugurated.

Speaking on behalf of the president, the RCC and the Ba'th Regional Leadership (though not the pan-Arab leadership) General Shihab delivered an address which was pan-Arab par excellence; the other dignitaries spoke in a similar vein. The speeches were followed by a procession of large floats, the first of which, in the same spirit, bore a large map of the Arab homeland; it was succeeded by a parade of the flags of all the Arab states. Next came a float with models of Jerusalem's al-Aqsa Mosque and the Dome of the Rock, and, fittingly for a secular pan-Arab party which does not discriminate between Islam and Christianity, another portraying 'the Church of the Resurrection' (the Holy Sepulchre); both floats were ringed by a squad of Palestinian *fida'iyyin*. The procession also included floats portraying characters important in Islamic-Arab culture: one dedicated to the war hero of early Islam, Khalid n. al-Walid, others to the medieval Muslim philosophers and poets al-Mutanabbi and Abu al-'Ala al-Ma'arri, to the great Abbasid Caliph Harun al-Rashid and so on. The interesting point about this section of the procession was that all the personalities it featured were, in the first place, local heroes. They all belonged to Iraq's Islamic history and were meant to represent Iraq's exellence by emphasizing its contribution to general Islamic history. This section was followed by a float bearing 'a Ziggurat with the powerful men of Assyria'; others featured the gilded lyre and the Queen of Sumer; a model of Ishtar's Gate in Babylon; a model of the 'bride of spring', clearly appertaining to the ancient Rite of Spring; Sennacherib and 'the towers of mighty Nineveh'; the Queen of Hatra surrounded by models of that city's buildings; 'Nergal's Gate which restored us to eternal Babylon'; and a float depicting the Hanging Gardens of Nebuchadnezzar the Second. All these were characterized as 'aspects of our [Iraqi] civilization . . . from earliest times up to our own day'.[1]

Special attention was devoted to Hatra for two reasons: it is an Arab site, whose Arab character was easy to identify unlike, for example, that of Ashur; and it is of pre-Islamic origin. Both characteristics meshed well with Ba'th secular Arabism. At the conclusion of the nine-day festival, a large crowd of 7000 spectators assembled in the Hatra temple, 'the place which, hundreds of years ago, heard the priests' hymns . . . to spring and love [!]'. 'All that night,' reported a correspondent for the government daily, the visitors 'relived the history of . . . their great and ancient [Arab] nation.'[2]

Apart from the clear signal sent out all over Iraq through these descriptions in the national press that, while a great measure of continuity would be preserved and the links with Arabhood would be retained, very real changes were on the way in relation to the particularist Iraqi entity; the Mosul festival's most prominent feature was an absence of clarity with regard to the connection between Mesopotamia's principal cultures of antiquity (Hatra's civilization was shortlived and relatively without influence), and Arabhood.

The next festival, produced in the following year, was dedicated to spring, to the grandeur of ancient Iraq and to Arab-Kurdish fraternity – the latter to mark the regime's March 11 agreement with the Kurdish Democratic Party of Mustafa al-Barazani. The head of the managing committee explained the festival's aims as, primarily, 'highlighting the value, archeological and historical, of ancient Iraq's civilization and the advanced [character] of the Iraqi man [!] . . . in the generations of antiquity'. To erase any doubt that the Kurd, too, was an Iraqi man, the committee head stressed that this festival would be marked by special Kurdish activities, offering 'new testimony . . . to the integration of this people in the shade of its mighty revolution'.[3] An identical message was also delivered in non-verbal form: the procession, which included a float with *fida'iyyin* and another to mark the party's anniversary, also featured one upon which an Arab and a Kurd together bore the portrait of President Bakr. In addition, there was a renewed display of floats with scenes from Sumer, ancient Babylon (Hammurabi's Stele), new Babylon (the Hanging Gardens, the Lion of Babylon), Semiramis [Samuramat], queen of Assyria, the remains of Hatra and scenes from the Golden Age of the Islamic-Arab Abbasid period.[4]

In the 1971 festival, the historical point of departure was put back from Sumer to a float bearing a cave man who lived 100,000–200,000 years ago, and was supposed to represent the primordial Iraqi. It was followed by floats carrying *aba'una al-awa'il* ['our early fathers'], the Sumerians [who, it will be recalled, were not Semites] and the ancient Babylonians; a float representing new Babylon offered the procession's first reference to the pan-Arab theme, with 'a lesson for the Zionists' in the form of Nebuchadnezzar, at the head of his armies, bringing his Jewish captives from Jerusalem to Babylon. Next came scenes from the life of Islamic-Arab Iraq: the Islamic conquests in the Mesopotamian valley; the greatness of al-Rashid; science in the era of al-Ma'mun; the decline following Hulagu the Mongol (the Turks were not even mentioned); the revolts of 1920 and 1941 against the British; the founding of the party; the partition of Palestine (the sole non-Iraqi feature); and the revolutions of 1958, 1963 and 1968. In short, a representation of the continuity of Iraqi history and pre-history, with a certain connection to the Arab nation, chiefly through the glory of the Abbasid period which centered on Baghdad. Characteristically, while Nebuchadnezzar was glorified as the liberator of Palestine, in the overall context of the procession he appeared not as Arab but as Iraqi. This festival, which lasted seven days, saw the first displays of folklore and modern art, directed at embodying two different, though interrelated ideas: the cultural continuity between present-day Mosul and ancient Mesopotamia, and the folklore unity of the present-day Mosul region, where Arabs, Kurds, Turkomans and Chaldeans live in close proximity.[5]

April 1975 witnessed a threefold festivity: as in previous years, the spring festival was celebrated, as was the party's anniversary; but in addition, it was the 'festival to reinforce internal patriotic [*watani*] unity'. Elaborating on the festival's significance in the particular context of the crushing of the Kurdish revolt in that year, the governor of Nineveh province carefully skirted the knotty problems of the ethnic, lingual and cultural differences which divide the Iraqi people. He explained:

The soil of this province enfolds the historical unity of our [Iraqi] people [*sha'bina*] throughout the generations, for it was here that the heroic Assyrians built up the civilization of Assyria, Nineveh and Nimrud, it was here that the desert Arabs built the eternal city of Hatra, and the city of Mosul contains numerous testimonies to the glorious Abbasid period, and the mighty achievements of the period of President Bakr.[6]

In other words, for Kurds, Arabs and others, the common denominator is the stretch of land upon which they presently live, and their shared pride in its history.

At this festival, like its predecessors, descriptions of the passing floats avoided clear identification of Assyrians with Arabs: Assyrian civilization was clearly distinguished from its Arab counterpart, though both were perceived as phases in the long path of the Iraqi people. Likewise, no explicit attempt was made to identify the Kurds, the principal theme of that year's festival, explicitly with Assyria – a point likely to have evoked particular difficulty in view of the Kurds' Indo-Aryan origins.[7]

In subsequent years, all trace vanished of the war in the north, and the festival dealt exclusively with the themes of peace, patriotic unity and glorification of Iraq's majestic past and present.[8]

In 1980, for the first time in the annals of the Mosul festival, the (new) president Saddam Husayn, put in a personal appearance to greet the visitors; the government daily dedicated its entire front page to coverage of the event. In view of growing tension with Iran, and the activities of Shi'i and Kurdish opposition groups, the president laid great stress on the ideological theme of unity of the Iraqi people.[9]

In 1984, the emphasis was on the all-Iraqi character of the festival, which was designed to feature all communities: 'Arabs, Kurds, Syriacs and . . . Yezidis, who have lived together peacefully for generation upon generation.'

A newspaper explained that the spring festival would revive an ancient (pagan) tradition: 'Historians recall that in ancient Nineveh, the capital of the Assyrians, it was their custom to celebrate the spring season by a 12-day festival in April, throwing away all their cares.'[10] The continued celebration of this festival, and specific mention of its pagan origins – at a time of a war against an Islamic Republic that accused the Ba'th of atheism, and thus of great government efforts to placate religious circles in Iraq – indicates the extent to which it was cherished by the regime.

Celebration of the festival continued throughout the Gulf War: that of 1988 was launched by Husayn's deputy, Izzat Ibrahim, and held under the slogan: 'Saddam, the blossom of our eternal spring'.[11]

The year 1977 witnessed the launching of 'the First Festival of Ur', celebrated, like that in Mosul, early in April. Some connection may be surmised between Khomeini's advent to power in Iran, and the decision to make Iraq's Shi'i south (the tel of Ur lies between Suq al-Shuyukh and Nasiriyya) the scene of a festival virtually identical with that held in the mixed Arab-Kurdish region of the north. Apprehensions over an eventual rift within the Iraqi political community are reflected in the words of the proclamation:

> The city of Ur renews its ancient artistic splendor . . . [King Urnamu, 2050 B.C.] united the state administratively and politically, after it had been divided and split.[12]

The government urged artists from all over Iraq to prepare the exhibition in Ur with 'posters, paintings and artistic works drawn from history, so as to create a modern artist connected with the heritage'. Poets were called upon 'to compose works connected to Sumerian life', and readers were assured that, in the course of the festival, the Dhi Qar actors' association would stage a 'historical play' bearing a contemporary social and political message.[13]

In April 1979, a local festival of a different nature was inaugurated. The holy city of Karbala celebrated the Festival of Ukhaydar, a fortress of the early Abbasid period located on its outskirts. At this festival, the local-territorial element was intertwined with the religious significance of the Shi'i shrine where the third Imam, al-Husayn, is buried, and with Iraq's Arab identity in the face of the Iranian enemy. In his opening speech to the 1984 Ukhaydar festival, Iraq's vice-president said:

> The sword that Saddam of the Arabs is unsheathing today in the face of the hateful enemies of the nation is the identical sword drawn by the Imam Ali. The banner which the Imam al-Husayn carried is the identical banner carried today by his heroic grandson, President Saddam Husayn, and by the heroes of glorious Iraq.

For the benefit of the Sunni-Arab audience, the vice-president also emphasized the past glories of 'the vast Abbasid state' which 'flourished in Mesopotamia'. The festival's slogan was: 'The principles of the Imam al-Husayn are shining in Saddam's Qadisiyya' (i.e., the war against Iran).[14]

Saddam Husayn's ascent to the presidency was followed by the inauguration of another festival which, while dedicated to Arab culture, was nevertheless rooted very deep in the soil of Iraq: the al-Mirbad Poetry Festival, held in Basra to commemorate the ancient camel market which developed into a meeting place for Arab poets and orators. Since November 1979, poets and poetry critics from all over the Arab world and abroad had been invited to the southern city for a week or ten days of poetry readings and analysis. To drive home the concept of Iraq's pivotal role in Arab culture and in world civilization, the poets, Arabs and others, were, on one occasion at least, shown the magnificent collection of costumes – ancient Mesopotamian, Abbasid, and more modern Iraqi – designed and presented by Iraq's National Fashion House.[15] Additional local festivals were inaugurated in subsequent years.[16]

The leitmotif of all the festivals was the affirmation – almost always implicit, and very rarely explicit – of the existence of an Iraqi people, and an 'Iraqi man'; the latter having, since pre-history, generated a series of magnificent civilizations and displayed dedication in defending his native soil, from Sumer, by way of Akkad, Babylon, Assyria, the onset of the Islamic conquests, the period of Abbasid glory, right up to Iraq under Ba'th rule. Iraq was generally perceived as a cultural entity; or, perhaps, as a series of civilizations interconnected by historical memory; but sometimes, also, with a common ethnic and racial denominator (such as when Hammurabi is characterized as 'our ancient forefather') as an entity which, transcending the vagaries of time, has continually lived and created in the Mesopotamian Valley. Alongside this view is the more traditional perception which stresses Iraq's native soil, and its history, as the sole common denominator.[17]

Up to the late 1970s, the festivals trod the narrow path between Arabhood and Iraqidom; the overwhelming impression is that their organizers and advocates view a very large portion of Iraqi history as having no connection to Arabhood.[18] This view depicts Islamic-Arab culture as nothing more than one of the civilizations created by the Iraqi people. Indeed, Iraqi genius was in evidence in the creation of the Mesopotamian Valley's pre-Islamic civilizations, just as it was when the Iraqis elevated broader Islamic Arab culture to its highest peaks;[19] and this genius was still alive and well under Ba'th rule. In the words of President Ja'far al-Numayri, of the Sudan, who fully comprehended the new cultural and ideological phenomenon, 'we found in Mosul a rich civilization which contributed [greatly] to the Arab nation, as it continues to contribute, and will contribute much in the future'.[20]

Any definition of the relationship between the present-day Iraqi people and its Mesopotamian Valley forerunners, remained blurred until the second half of the 1970s; and even then, elucidation was offered, not at the Mosul festival, but by other channels. The reason for this vagueness was apparently that any precise definition of this relationship seemed liable to foil the impression that there exists a historical common denominator between Arabs and Kurds; any specific association of the Arabs with the Assyrians and Babylonians would have severed the link between the Kurds and the ancient history of the Mosul region, and, indeed, of Iraq as a whole – and it was precisely this link that the festival set itself as a prime aim to foster. On the other hand, an unequivocal severance between the pre-Islamic chapters of Iraqi history, and its Arab portions, would have greatly exacerbated the identity problems of Iraq's Arabs. Accordingly, rather than foster a precise definition of the historical link between Iraq's ancient and modern inhabitants, the purpose of the various festivals was to encourage the latter to sense pride in their predecessors' achievements, which, in the interests of all-Iraqi unity, were to be regarded as the common heritage of all of the citizens of twentieth-century Iraq. Notwithstanding the deference rendered to the Arab nation at the Mosul festivals, the latter in fact drew a distinction between the Iraqi people and the rest of the Arabs, and this could not but further cement Iraq's internal unity; the festivals were probably designed as a signal to the Kurds that Iraq was changing course away from the old concept of integrationist unity, which to them denoted nothing short of inundation in an Arab ocean. Shortly after the Iraqi army had dealt the Kurdish rebels a crushing blow, in the spring of 1975, Saddam Husayn declared:

Our people consists of Arabs and non-Arabs. When we discuss pan-Arab [*qawmi*] sentiment, and the meanings of pan-Arab action, it is incumbent upon us that the discussion be in a style and manner which will not bring the non-Arab to feel that all this has nothing to do with him, or even awaken harmful aspirations . . . Necessity requires that . . . the focus be upon the fact of Iraq being part of the Arab homeland, rather than . . . upon the Iraqi people being part of the Arab nation [!]. In this manner . . . we will not arouse the national aspect in an adverse direction among the other, [Kurdish] part, of our [Iraqi] people.[21]

What induced the regime, or, as appearances would suggest, a certain circle within the ruling elite, to choose Mosul of all places as the launch pad for its 'Mesopotamian offensive'? One can only surmise. First, it may be assumed that cultural policy that could be interpreted as implying separatist inclinations could not be practised in Baghdad without arousing too much opposition. Provincial Mosul, with its numerous important archeological sites, offered a far more suitable arena for such a novel experiment; it was the press, radio and television which brought the tidings to the notice of the Baghdad public. Second, Mosul, the crossroads of almost all of Iraq's minorities and communities – Sunni-Arabs and Kurds in particular – was a suitable stage for a display of the unity of all sections of the people. The Mosul Festival was first held in 1969; earlier that year the Iraqi party convened its Seventh Regional Congress, which resolved to seek a peaceful solution to the Kurdish problem. One of the Congress resolutions called for 'a direct relationship between the Kurdish and Arab masses', and urged the party to reinforce its links with 'Kurdish organizations – progressive, patriotic, political and professional', so as to bypass the 'traditional leadership' (denoting support for Jalal Talabani's group as against Mustafa Barazani).[22] In this context, the Arab-Kurdish culture festival of Mosul offered a means of forging such a 'direct relationship' with those Kurds willing to collaborate with the regime.

Finally, a number of facts point to Saddam Husayn's personal association with the Mosul festival. First, it was he who, during the second half of the 1970s, and doubly so after becoming president, gave an unabashedly powerful momentum to the Mesopotamian myth. This was reflected *inter alia* in the proliferation of territorial festivals, of which the most outstanding was that of Mosul. Second, during the first year of his presidency, he personally attended the Mosul festival, where Bakr had never put in an appearance. Further, the personages who inaugurated the various festivals were all Saddam Husayn's intimates, or who took a neutral position between him and Bakr, and were not identified with outspoken adversaries of Husayn, such as 'Abd al-Khaliq al-Samarra'i and his like.[23] And upon Husayn becoming president, the festival was elevated into an all-Iraqi event. With that, the festival's celebration, which acquired a fairly high public profile, must have required at least the tacit consent of other members of the leadership, and thus the Mosul Festival cannot be regarded as Saddam Husayn's 'private enterprise'.

6 Mesopotamian Symbols in Official Iraq

In April 1970, the RCC decided to alter the names of eight of Iraq's sixteen *muhafazat* [provinces]. Most of the new names signified a blend of connotations – Iraqi, pan-Arab and Islamic. Thus, for example, the province of al-Ramadi west of Baghdad was renamed al-Anbar, after a Euphrates city of antiquity which was stormed in AD 634 by Khalid n. al-Walid; the Abbasid Caliph al-Saffah made it his capital, and so it remained until its displacement by Baghdad. But these salient historical events were not the reason behind the name-change; a news agency report explains that the city was the site of 'the renowned battle [which led to] the uprooting of al-Baramika by the Abbasid Caliph Harun al-Rashid'.[1] Such a presentation is a gross exaggeration. If indeed the event took place at al-Anbar, it was here that Harun al-Rashid, in an act of great ferocity, wiped out a family of Persian origin which, having served him well for many years as his viziers, helped introduce Persian administrative traditions into the Abbasid Empire.[2] Be that as it may, the new name adopted reflects the wish to obliterate Persian cultural and political influences that, in 1970, were quite strong in the two holy cities of Najaf and Karbala.

The province of Kut was renamed Wasit, for the city founded between Basra and al-Kufa by al-Hajjaj n. Yusuf al-Thaqafi in the Muslim year 82 (701 AD); it served throughout the Umayyad period as the capital of *'Iraq al-'ajam* ('Persian Iraq'), i.e., Khozestan. This choice may have been a hint at Iraq's claim to sovereignty over Khozestan-Arabestan; alternatively, the ancient name may have been chosen merely to provide historical continuity.

The new name of Qadisiyya granted to the province of Diwaniyya was of far more clear-cut significance. Qadisiyya was characterized as the site of the 'decisive battle between the Arab armies and the Persian army, which put an end to Sasanid rule over Iraq [in AD 635]'. In the same vein, al-Samawa province was now called al-Muthanna (n. al-Haritha, one of the leaders of the Muslim-Arabs who conquered Iraq from the Sasanids).[3]

The name of Nasiriyya province was changed to Dhi Qar. Dhi Qar was the location where the Arab tribe of Bakr n. Wa'il battled a coalition of other Arab tribes and regular Persian troops. In view of the fact that the

61

battle took place prior to the Islamic conquests, the resort to its name is significant in its support for the Ba'th secularly-oriented claim that Arab national consciousness predated the rise of Islam, as well as in its emphasis on a further impressive Arab victory over the Persian foe. Al-'Amara province was renamed Maysan (this being the early medieval name of the province). In this province the Muslim-Arab war hero, al-Muthanna, inflicted a crushing defeat upon the Persians in the year AD 633; in AD 686, the Umayyad Commander Mus'ab n. Zubayr routed there the army of the Shi'i rebel al-Mukhtar al-Thaqafi. Both events conveyed an important historical lesson for the people of Iraq.[4]

All these name changes, while relating to Iraq's Islamic-Arab or pre-Islamic periods, still referred clearly to the country's Arab history. Two further names, however, endowed Iraq's administrative map with full historic depth. Mosul province was renamed Nineveh. The government organ told its readers that the city of Mosul had, in fact, been built by the offspring of the people of Nineveh (the Assyrians). The change therefore bridged the gap of centuries, implying that the province's current inhabitants (the Kurds apparently included) were blood relatives of the Assyrians (in disregard of the fact that the new city stood on the ruins of a Sasanid city). A few years later a new province was created between Nineveh and Baghdad under the name of Salah al-Din. This province included the town of Tikrit, where both the Medieval Kurdish-Muslim hero Salah-al-Din and many of the ruling elite under the Ba'th (including President Bakr and Vice President Saddam Husayn) were born.

Finally, al-Hilla province was renamed Babylon. The public was told that this was the city of Hammurabi, father of the famous code, and of Nebuchadnezzar, the conqueror of Jerusalem, who ruled over the entire region 'from the Gulf to Egypt'.[5]

A number of smaller administrative units [*nahiya*] also gained 'Mesopotamian' appellations: one *nahiya* in Dhi Qar province was now called Akkad, and another in Babylon province was likewise renamed Babylon. A *nahiya* in *qada* al-Hamdaniyya near Mosul, was called 'Nimrud' for the Assyrian city whose ruins it contains; likewise, the *qada* which encompasses Hatra (al-Hadar) was named after that city.[6] (A *nahiya* located in al-Muthanna province, the location of the Sumerian city of Uruk, had long borne the Arabic version of its name, al-Warka. The same is true in regard to another *nahiya* in the southern province of Qadisiyya called 'Sumer'.)

Thirteen years after the renaming of the provinces, the president could, by mere mention of the new names, play on his countrymen's sense of history:

Oh brothers ! Sons of Baghdad and Maysan and Dhi Qar and Nineveh, Salah a-Din and Najaf and Karbala, and Sulaymaniyya and Arbil, al-Anbar and al-Muthanna . . . and Babylon . . . and al-Qadisiyya . . . you are the sons of the Tigris and Euphrates, sons of the [biblical] tree of knowledge and of Noah's Ark which cast anchor on your soil,[7] sons of the civilizations of the Mesopotamian valley which cast their light upon humanity when humanity was in darkness, you the sons of 'Ali and al-Husayn . . . and the grandsons of Salah al-Din . . . behold, their swords are with you . . . will the grandfathers abandon their grandsons when their grandsons are fighting for justice?[8]

In the summer of 1980, a decade after having renamed the provinces, the RCC endowed the new National Assembly (parliament) Building with the name 'Hammurabi Building', so as to establish the link between the Iraqi law-maker of ancient times and his modern successors.[9] In the course of the 1970s numerous additional Mesopotamian names made their appearance in Baghdad. Thus, for example, one of the city's eastern suburbs, lying at the end of Palestine Road, is called 'Sumer'. Another neighborhood, Babylon, lies within a bend of the Tigris, near Baghdad University. To the north of the city, east of the Tigris, the neighborhoods of al-Quds (Jerusalem) and Ur border on one another.[10]

A random survey of Iraqi policy in the 1970s regarding the design of symbols finds Mesopotamian elements here too. In some instances, it is unclear when the emblem was put into circulation; in one or two cases, they were leftovers from the previous regime which remained in use – further evidence that the Ba'th regime, in fostering the Mesopotamian myth, often merely reinforced an existing trend.

The Ba'th takeover was followed by formation of the 'General Federation of Iraqi Women', for which a special emblem was designed, depicting a huge frontal eye in the profile of a young girl. The self-same technique, wherein the face is portrayed in profile with an eye seen frontally, was common among the artists of Mesopotamia (and Egypt likewise). Mesopotamia's contribution was the unnatural size of the eyes.[11] The girl's hand emits a three-pronged jet of water, a symbol of the eternal flow of the Tigris and Euphrates which was very common in Mesopotamian art works from the Sumerian period onwards.

A law promulgated in 1976 regulated the markings of products fashioned from precious metals. The stamp for high-carat gold bears the form of the winged bull from the palace of Ashurbanipal, in Nimrod (about 865 BC), which is housed in the British Museum. Platinum products bear a bearded ox-head taken from a mythological bas-relief at Tel al-'Ubayd near Ur (2450 BC); products of low-karat gold are stamped with a Ziggurat.[12]

In preparation for the Seventh Summit Conference of the Non-Aligned States, which Baghdad was to host in September 1982, a special competition picked an emblem designed by the renowned Shi'i sculptor Nizar al-Hindawi, which would figure upon all the statements, publications, gifts and souvenirs associated with conventions of this nature. The emblem consisted of a palm tree whose design was totally identical with that common in Mesopotamian wall-reliefs (where the palms bear 7 or 9 fronds). In this case, there were seven fronds, in token of this being the seventh conference of its kind. In the artist's own words, the emblem was:

> an original symbol of Mesopotamian civilization. This is the tree the Iraqis have admired, from the Sumerians and Babylonians up to our own times . . . The ancient Iraqis drew the palm with seven fronds. The symbol seems to have been [particularly] cherished by the Assyrians.[13]

Another sphere where Mesopotamian and other local elements are in ample evidence is in coins and bills, as well as postage stamps. From 1980, and possibly some years earlier, all Iraqi coins, from 10 to 250 fulus, bear a large palm tree, and rows of palms along the Shatt al-Arab. Since the 1980s at least, the five dinar bill depicts Hammurabi as he appears on his renowned stele. One 10-dinar bill shows the winged bull from Nimrod, and another bears the portrait of Abu 'Ali al-Hasan n. al-Haytham (Alhazen, about AD 965–1039). He was a famous Arab mathematician and scientist; although a long-time resident of Fatimid Egypt, he was born in Basra, where he spent the first thirty-odd years of his life. A 25-dinar bill has, on one side, Saddam Husayn in field-marshal's uniform, against the background of the Medieval battle of Qadisiyya; on the other, it shows the Gate of Ishtar in Chaldean Babylon.

The year 1968 witnessed the appearance of three 'Mesopotamian' stamps depicting the Ziggurat of Ur, statues in Nimrod, and a scene from Babylon. In 1971, a special stamp commemorated Mosul's Spring Festival. The next year, another stamp marked the Festival of Palm Trees, and the Holiday of the Dates. The stamp issued in 1974 to mark the second anniversary of oil nationalization included oil rigs and industrial installations – and, totally out of context, an Assyrian lion, a Sumerian prince and the Ziggurat-like minaret of Samarra's Malwiya Mosque. In 1977, a special stamp commemorated the Festival of Abu al-Tayb al-Mutanabbi (the Arab philosopher and poet, AD 915–965 renowned for his prolonged sojourn with the desert Arabs, though born in Kufa and spending much of his life in Iraq). A stamp was issued in 1979 in memory of Jawad Salim (1920–1961), Iraq's most famous sculptor and founder of a school of plastic art which was heavily influenced by ancient Mesopotamian art forms. That same year, a similar honor went to the pan-Arab intellectual Sati' al-Husri, who was Syrian-born but spent his most creative years (1921–41) in Iraq, where he formed the educational system.

There were also other stamps, but the Mesopotamian and other local motifs were paramount. As in other spheres, here too history did not begin with the Ba'th. Babylonian, Sumerian and Assyrian art works had been depicted on Iraqi stamps since 1923, though to a much lesser degree than under the Ba'th.[14]

A totally different sphere also bears traces of Mesopotamian and local-Islamic inspiration: a casual glance at the entertainment column of any Baghdad daily will reveal a Sheherezade Bar and Grillroom; an al-Rasheed Oberoi Hotel; an Uruk restaurant; a Semiramis and Nimrod night clubs; an Ishtar Sheraton Hotel; a Babylon Oberoi Hotel with al-Warka (Uruk) Grillroom and a Hanging Gardens rooftop bar, and a Hammurabi Gardens Coffee House. In Mosul's Nineveh Oberoi Hotel *masguf* (grilled fish) is served in the Ashur hall and the Ishtar restaurant offers a 'popular new menu'. The sports columns of the papers report of a handball match between the Assyrian club and the Babylon team in al-Mansur field; the Iraqi merchant fleet has launched 'Hummurabi'; the ministry of culture has established a Babylon cinema studio, and government-owned factories are producing Ishtar refrigerators, freezers and stoves.[15]

A further field where Mesopotamian influence comes into play is in orders of distinction. As far back as the reign of Faysal I, the highest order of distinction was the five-rank Order of the Twin Rivers. Its form is not specified, but the name indicates influences neither pan-Arab nor Islamic.[16] Under the Ba'th, the order was separated into two categories, civilian and military, again with five ranks each. The central element is an eight-pointed star with a close resemblance to the emblem of Ishtar. The Qasim period instituted the highest order of distinction, the Order of the Republic, which appears to have carried over into the Ba'th regime. The central element of the order is a replica of Iraq's national emblem under Qasim: the sign of the Mesopotamian sun god.[17]

The closing phases of 'Arif's rule witnessed the introduction of a special and very costly decoration: the Rafidayn (twin river) Necklace. Its first link bears the design of a Mesopotamian palm tree; the second, the Sumerian lyre; this is followed by a link with the head of Sargon the Akkadian, as depicted on an ancient stele, and the next bears a likeness of Hammurabi's stele. Other links depict the Assyrian winged bull, the Babylonian lion, Ishtar's Gate, a dome-and-minaret 'symbolizing a Muslim mosque', the spiral minaret of Samarra's al-Malwiya mosque, al-Mustansiriyya College, the minaret of Mosul's al-Hadba mosque, an oil rig, a dam and Jawad Salim's Revolution Day Monument.[18] The necklace remained unmodified under the Ba'th; the regime even took pains to publish a renewed and detailed description of it.[19]

Finally, Mesopotamian themes and names of personalities connected with the Abbasid golden age in Iraq as well as with the history of the Shi'a also filtered into military appellations. Thus, for example, the Popular Army had Baghdad detachments named for the Abbasid Caliphs al-Ma'mum and Abu Ja'far al-Mansur; a Shi'i unit from Najaf was named for Muslim n. 'Uqayl (AD 642–683, cousin and supporter of al-Husayn n. 'Ali), and there is the al-Imam al-Husayn unit from Dhi Qar.[20] There is also a unit called 'The [Hanging] Gardens' recruited, not surprisingly, in Babylon province,[21] and a Hammurabi unit from Najaf province.[22]

The regular army has a unit called Hammurabi; another unit was named for Nebuchadnezzar, and another for Gilgamesh.[23] And there is an army unit for the Seventh Shi'i Imam Musa al-Kazim (buried in al-Kazimiyya, Iraq) carried over from the monarchy.[24]

In the same way, when Iraq produced its first medium range (650 km) surface-to-surface missile, it called it after the third Shi'i Imam, al-Husayn. The second missile (950 km) was called after the Third Imam's brother, al- 'Abbas (both are buried in Karbala). The third missile (2,000 km range), still in development stage in 1990, was named Tammuz, and Iraq's first tank (apparently a version of a Brazilian-made tank) was given the name Lion of Babylon.[25]

The process of inculcating a Mesopotamian awareness finds its most striking expression far from the sight of the masses: to be precise, in legislation, or rather, in 'the reasons for enactment' which offer a preamble to new laws. A law promulgated early in 1980 and dealing in the highly sensitive matter of personal status, imposed various restrictions on the prerogative of a husband to proclaim his wife *nashizan* [rebellious]. The explanation states that the law was enacted:

> in harmony with the principles of the Islamic *Shari'a* which conforms with the spirit of the times, and in accordance with the principle of justice and the objectives of the Ba'th party . . . and the ancient Iraqi constitutions, particularly the Hammurabi constitution which devoted . . . great attention to the family so as to preserve the familial ties.[26]

Much more tangibly Iraqi-centered were laws that, in addition to their quest for a cultural and historical common denominator for the Iraqi people as a whole, also sought to guard it against excessive assimilation with other nations, Arab inclusive. Thus, for example, the first Interim Constitution of 1968 stipulated that 'to be appointed prime minister, deputy prime minister or minister', a person 'must be Iraqi, of Iraqi parentage and related to a family resident in Iraq since . . . at least 1900 and holding Ottoman [as different from Iranian] nationality';[27] the 1970 interim constitution required that 'a member of the Revolutionary Command Council [RCC], a vice president of the republic, and a minister, must be an Iraqi, born in Iraq, to parents likewise born in Iraq'.[28] Similarly, while the first Interim Constitution stipulated that 'non-Iraqis may not own agricultural land', the 1970 interim constitution further restricted non-Iraqis by denying them ownership of *all* real estate.[29] In the same vein, the first law of the National Council (parliament) stipulated that each of its members must be 'an Iraqi by birth, both of whose parents are Iraqi by birth'.[30]

Similar restrictions were subsequently imposed on at least some of the country's professional associations.[31]

Finally, in 1985, at a crucial juncture in the war with Iran, Iraqi territorial nationalism was rammed home in unprecedented fashion when the Citizenship law was amended by the addition of an oath of allegiance that echoed of Blood and Soil and Iraq Above All:

> I swear by Almighty God and by Iraq's pure soil, water and skies, that I shall guard Iraq against any foreigner that would engage in aggression against it, or plan to enslave it, or conquer it, or turn it into his vassal, and that I shall defend it by all means, so that its banner remains high with no other banner higher, and its sovereignty elevated with no other sovereignty eclipsing it, and may God witness my words.[32]

These laws do not necessarily imply Iraqi isolationism. Indeed, when the first such laws were introduced in 1969–70, Iraq was pursuing a most aggressive pan-Arab policy. However, they denote that, since 1969–70 at least – as signified by inauguration of the Mosul Spring Festival and promulgation of the first Iraqi-centered legislation – the Ba'th party no longer held to its traditional view whereby Arab unification would have the existing Arab peoples vanish into a unitarian smelting pot. Arab unity was increasingly seen as an association of clearly-defined nations in loose federation, wherein Iraq would play a leading role. Thus, these laws and the cultural developments accompanying them should be seen as evidence of an emerging Iraqi self-awareness and self-assertion, and a beginning of a shift from traditional Ba'th egalitarian and integrative pan-Arabism into a hegemonic and Iraqi-centered pan-Arabism with strong undertones of Iraqi egotism (see the Conclusion).

7 Art With Local and Mesopotamian Components

TERRITORIAL INFLUENCES ON MODERN IRAQI ARTISTS

From Badr Shakir al-Sayyab, the pioneer in modern Iraqi poetry, to Jawad Salim and Khalid al-Rahhal, the two pillars of modern Iraqi art, Iraqi writers and artists tried to find their inspiration in the rich legacy of their country's long history. The present Iraqi government goes out of its way to give the encouragement of the arts almost as much priority as that of the military logistics, even under the prevailing circumstances of war. (Khalid al-Kishtayni of the Iraqi Culture Center of London, in a lecture, Exeter, July 1981)

Since the early 1950s, Iraqi painters, sculptors, playwrights and poets have been delving into ancient Mesopotamian culture and Iraqi folklore. In the plastic arts, two groups emerged between 1950 and 1953; some of their founding members were still active in the late 1980s. The first, the Avantgarde Group (also called the Group of Primitive Art), was founded in 1950; according to official Ba'th publications, it sought inspiration in 'primitive [Mesopotamian] Iraqi art and Iraqi folklore'. The group was led by the painters Fa'iq Hasan (Baghdad 1919–) and Isma'il al-Shaykhali (Turkey, 1927–). Under Ba'th rule, the group remained in existence, growing substantially and acquiring great prestige, with some of its members winning lucrative posts. (In 1986, for example, al-Shaykhali was director-general of the Culture Ministry's Department of Plastic Arts.) The second group, the Baghdad Modern Art Group, evolved around Iraq's most famous modern artist, the Communist Jawad Salim (born in Ankara, 1920; died in Baghdad, 1961), and his colleague, Shakir Hasan (Baghdad, 1926–). According to the same publications, this group 'sought to express . . . modern life while keeping in perspective the artistic heritage of ancient Iraq'. Other members of the group still active under the second Ba'th regime were Nuri al-Rawi (1925–), Mahmud Sabri (1927–), Tariq Mazlum (1933–) and 'Ata Sabri (1913–).[1]

Utterly spontaneous under the monarchy, the territorial trend received official blessing from the regime of General Qasim. The most extravagant example was the commissioning of Jawad Salim to fashion the

Fourteenth of July Statue (later known as the Monument of Liberty [*Nasab al-Huriyya*]). Situated in Liberty Square (*Sahat al-Tahrir*) in central Baghdad, it is a huge work, comprising a bronze bas-relief on a concrete wall ten meters high and fifty meters long. According to the official publication issued upon its inauguration, the monument was 'purely Iraqi art, whereby the Iraqi epic theme . . . [is] expressed in an Iraqi style, a mixture of contemporary manner and age-old tradition'. The description goes on to defend its execution in bas-relief, rather than in three-dimensional sculpture, 'since the greatest Babylonian, Assyrian and Arab sculpture had always been largely of this kind'.[2] The architect who designed the wall upon which Salim's figures were attached reportedly 'derived his inspiration from the Great Gates of Assyria and Babylon'. A study of the monument shows that, along with a blend of Cubism and Socialist Realism, it does indeed reflect Sumerian, Babylonian and Assyrian influences. [See Plate 2.] As described in the official guide, its elements include an Iraqi peasant whose head has 'an ancient Assyrian look, to indicate the cultural continuity of the land of the two rivers'. Aptly pointing to the Assyrian tradition, the publication notes that 'the emphasis is on the tough hands'. [See also the muscular hands and legs of the soldier, Plate 2B.] The farmer's strident leg stance is clearly influenced by the manner wherein Naram Sin, the king of Akkad, is depicted in his famous victory stele (and configurations of other contemporary figures): where the king's left leg tramples a vanquished enemy; the farmer's leg, as befits Socialist Realism, rests on a shovel. [See center of Plate 2A.] The same monument features numerous other influences of Mesopotamian art. For example: the bull above the peasant is in bas-relief, but, akin to the heads of the winged bulls guarding the entrances to Assyrian palaces, the head is three-dimensional. Overhanging the soldier at the center of the monument is a disc which, according to the publication, represents 'the sun . . . one of Iraq's oldest symbols. Here, the revolution's first sun rose'. The disc does, indeed, bear some resemblance to the emblem of the Akkadian sun god. [See Plate 2B.] Likewise, many of the monument's figures face sideways, their shoulders are depicted frontally, and their feet again point sideways – typical features of traditional (or ancient) art. Similarly echoing ancient Mesopotamian practice, principal figures are depicted in great detail, while secondary ones (i.e., servants in ancient works, here – children) are delineated only in general outline. [See Plates 2A and 2C.]

Under the Qasim regime, Salim, Hasan and their colleagues were succeeded by a somewhat younger age-group including some now regarded as Iraq's most prominent contemporary artists: Khalid al-Rahhal (1928–87), Muhammad Ghani Hikmat (1929–   ), and Isma'il Fattah who, in 1986, was Chairman of the Iraqi Association of Plastic Arts. The 'Arif brothers halted all government aid to the local trend as such, but it persisted nevertheless, even if less conspicuously, and was joined by new artists such as: Diya al-'Azzawi (1939–), Salih al-Juma'i (1939–) and Hamid al-'Attar (1935–). Under the Ba'th regime, Mesopotamian and local trends came to bear upon a younger generation of artists who embarked upon their careers in the 1970s and 1980s. The author has traced Mesopotamian influences in the works of over forty-five Iraqi artists active between the early 1950s and late 1980s; the actual number may be substantially larger.[3] Under the Ba'th regime, artists whose work reflected Mesopotamian influences received official blessing in the form of favorable reviews in the daily press and artistic journals, where they were lauded for the historical depth of their creativity and held up as models for emulation in the creation of a school of Iraqi art. A different and more tangible form of patronage were lucrative posts in the Ministry of Culture, or the commissioning of large-scale art works. Many artists also had special exhibitions sponsored for them by official bodies. A particularly conspicuous example of such an exhibition was held in 1978 by the General Institution for Archeology at Iraq's National (archeological) Museum, to mark the Ba'th party anniversary. The aim of the exhibition was to foster 'the deep continuity between the artistic creation of pre-historic eras, the Islamic era, and our modern sculptors'. The exhibition's slogans included 'Thy walls, oh Babylon, shall never fall again!' or 'Babylon calls upon you to work for it!' The most prominent artist displayed was Muhammad Ghani, whose works were hung alongside authentic Mesopotamian relics; critics stressed 'the great resemblance'. Ghani himself was characterized as 'an artist who combines the power and hope of the present with the movement of the past' by 'enriching his practice with the practice of the civilization of his homeland'. The new generation of Iraqi sculptors were urged to emulate him in creating art which was 'patriotic, and deep-rooted'.[4]

An example of work commissioned by the Ba'th regime is Mukhlid al-Mukhtar's bas-relief adorning the Babylonian Hall at Baghdad's Saddam international airport. The eighteen-square-meter marble relief reportedly depicts 'Babylonian sites and emblems' and pictures 'derived from the ancient artistic heritage of Mesopotamia, in modern design'.[5] Another such example is Sa'd al-Shamari's sixteen-square-meter bas-relief at the Irrigation Ministry, which adopts a typically Assyrian style to depict the continuity of irrigation in Iraq, from Sumer up to the technology of the modern age.[6] Yet another example is Ghani's bronze statue of the Babylonian legislator-king Hammurabi, who is depicted in three dimensions (in contrast with his two-dimensional presentation on the famous stele). The large sculpture (4.20 meters high) was emplaced at the entrance to parliament to remind Iraqi legislators of their forerunner.[7] More subtle Mesopotamian influences may be detected in the large (some seven or eight meters high) statue entitled *Nasab al-Masira* (the journey monument) which was fashioned by Khalid al-Rahhal, like Ghani a disciple of Jawad Salim who shared, in his youth, his mentor's Communist leanings. According to the sculptor, the monument, which was dedicated to the Ba'th party, is heavily influenced by Iraq's ancient heritage:

> As a result of my work in the Iraqi National Museum, which was really my first school, and my work in archeological excavations, I have learned many secrets of our civilization . . . I decided to build a monument that would glorify this civilization and the struggles of our [Iraqi] people through the ages . . . until July 17 [1968]. I proposed it to the officials and received from them total support and assistance.

The monument is comprised of three figures standing on a very high, boat-like pedestal. (The boat apparently symbolizes the party. In one of his speeches Saddam Husayn equated the party to a boat, and called upon all Iraqis to board it.) One figure is that of a boy who symbolizes the young Iraqi generation. The boy is looking at the National Museum, this being 'a testimony that we have a civilization and history by which we are inspired and which lit our long road'.[8] [See Plate 3A.] A close scrutiny of the bronze bas reliefs on the walls of the monument reveals a Mesopotamian bull, standing above a fallen warrior in a position that closely resembles that of the Lion of Babylon standing above a human body, the half naked figure of Ishtar [see Plate 3B], and an Assyrian lion hunting a deer (no photograph available).

Of the various works commissioned, the most imposing, depicting the Hanging Gardens, is located in al-Zawra park in central Baghdad. Designed by Salih Jasim, this is his impression of how Babylon's Hanging Gardens may have looked. Extending over 3600 square meters, it is built Ziggurat-like in four stories, with wide staircases ascending to the third floor. The staircase is flanked by sculptured lions, copied from Babylonian art. The surrounding walls are bedecked with three thousand square meters of glazed ceramic bricks featuring Babylonian lions and other designs derived from the Gate of Ishtar and other archeological remains. The gardens are rich with flowers and greenery. The third level housed a fountain sending up 20-meter columns of water in seven different hues 'like the seven colors of the sun's spectrum'; its water was drawn from the first level, in obedience to Herodotus' account of Nebuchadnezzar's designers 'lifting the water from the pond'. As described by visitors who toured Baghdad in the 1970s, it was indeed a magnificent sight, but it fell into disrepair during the 1980s.[9]

A conviction of the need to integrate old and new was frequently expressed by the artists themselves. A disciple quoted Jawad Salim's wish that his Fourteenth of July Monument, which he believed to be 'the first created by an Iraqi hand and Iraqi mind many hundreds of years after the last Assyrian monument', be viewed as 'a lasting symbol of the Iraqi man'.[10] Going even further, al-Rahhal, in an interview to the government daily, admitted his conviction that the Iraqi people are the direct offspring of the Sumerians of old, and confessed that this belief had shaped his intellectual world. *Inter alia*, he said:

> There are things in Iraq that haven't changed, they are the taste of bread, and love, and water. I was 16 years old and I worked in the Temple of Art, in the Iraqi Museum, and I completed [my work:] the Sumerian Princess. I used to spend . . . most of my time outside the museum [after work] studying the faces of the women sour-milk vendors [from south of Baghdad] for they represent the continuity in today's life of the Sumerian face: the same eyes, sharp and broad, and the brows running together, and the nose, and the cut of the features! In this fashion, reality always provided me with models for my work.[11]

Iraq's painters and sculptors reflect these Mesopotamian influences in various ways, and to varying degrees of clarity. As already noted, some of their works are nothing but a fairly accurate copy of an antique art piece, with minor modifications such as a marked enlargement of scale in a bas-relief, an exchange of the material wherein the work is crafted (wood, bronze or marble, replacing limestone), three-dimensional sculpture in place of a bas-relief; alternatively, the ancient art work, in more or less original form, is integrated in a larger creation. This is the case, for example, in the bronze bas reliefs attached to the Monument of the Journey mentioned above. This is also the case with an oil painting representing Iraq's younger generation (students, male and female; a soldier; Arab and Kurdish peasants) against the background of the lion hunting scene from Ashurbanipal's Palace.[12] A similar combination of ancient and modern figures – though the bas-relief as a whole is fashioned in Assyrian style – can be found in the aforementioned work emplaced at the Ministry of Irrigation. A further example is Nizar Hindawi's 'The Nationalization', which seeks to glorify the 1 June 1972 oil takeover; the painting depicts all the social sectors of the Iraqi people: proletarians, peasants, students, and soldiers and there is

even a Shi'i *mujtahid* complete with black *'amama* [religious headdress]!
The figures all raise their arms in fervent pathos against a background of
oil rigs, smoking factories and similar charming vistas. At the very center
of the picture is Hammurabi's stele; but the god and the king featured upon
it, instead of facing one another as in the original, jointly direct their gaze
outward, towards the oil rig, in a kind of gesture of joy and gratitude.[13] A
similar approach, though on a far higher artistic level, may be seen in the
beautiful sculpture of a boy standing by his sitting old mother at the foot
of a tall, stylized Hammurabi Stele (the inscription on the Stele is in Arabic
not in cuneiform). While the mother, symbolizing the Old Iraq, is looking
down with an air of desolation, the son, the New Iraq, is raising his eyes
hopefully to Hammurabi's figure engraved in bas relief at the top of the
Stele. [See Plate 4.] A further such example of old-and-new combined is a
picture in the manner of Socialist realism, by an unknown artist, depicting a
modern Iraqi landscape with workers and peasants merrily engaged in their
labors or dancing, the center of the picture being occupied by a Sumerian
girl with oversized eyes and brows running together above the nose [for
features that are similar to these, appearing in a Sumerian Sculpture of a
young girl, see Plate 10C], wearing the famous Sumerian headpiece from
Ur with its three gold stars and rows of gold leaf, and clutching a loaf of
bread in her arms.[14] Another example, regimented to a lesser degree (or
not at all!) is Hamid al-'Attar's plaster relief entitled 'Gilgamesh', with
ancient motifs and figures (the latter considered by many scholars to be
Gilgamesh and his travelling companion Enkidu); the work also features
Ishtar's star, the whore from Uruk who managed to transform Enukidu
from wild beast into man, and other Mesopotamian symbols. Both figures
and symbols are stylized, largely reflecting the artist's own interpretation,
and the entire work is uniquely original.[15]

A similar approach is evident in Ibrahim Rashid's coal drawings. One
depicts the debris of war, and, fluttering overhead, a quasi-centaur, winged
and eagle-headed, derived from the eagle-headed protective genie featured
in numerous Assyrian reliefs. [See Plate 5A, and cf. Plate 5B.] Another of
his drawings renders the famous 'dying lioness' of Nineveh in a futuristic
interpretation which represents the beast's head movements as a series of
partly-interposed images. [See Plate 6A, and cf. Plate 6B.] Integration of
a different sort may be found in the resort of some artists to cuneiform
as a decorative element, or the occasional combination of cuneiform with
Arabic letters. [See Plate 7A.][16] A particularly beautiful example in this
respect is the emblem of the Babylon Festival [see Plate 7B]: the cuneiform
on the left-hand side reads, in fact, in Arabic, *Mihrajan babil al-duwali*
[Babylon International Festival].

With regard to perspective, most of the works which borrow from Mesopotamian art apply the principle of 'conceptual realism' or 'abstract rationalism', wherein the traditional artist sought to depict his subject's most typical aspects as familiar to the beholder, rather than as actually seen by the latter from any chance perspective. The intention was to present symbols, readily identifiable and universal – rather than create of a convincing visual illusion. Consequently, the subject is viewed simultaneously front-and-side, or sometimes side-and-above (as, for example, when a river is shown from above, while the fish within it are depicted from the side). Thus, many paintings and reliefs by modern Iraqi artists present human figures with the face in profile, eyes and shoulders frontal, and the feet again in profile. Similarly, the pictures are without depth or perspective, in the sense that 'up' denotes 'behind' or 'distant'; a figure that appears 'distant' is no smaller than one at the bottom of the picture that is 'close'. A typical example is exhibited in Baghdad's Medical City, where Muhammad Ghani's marble relief displays various scenes of medical care and research, modern in content but traditional in technique. The detail [see Plate 8A] shows figures and objects from different vantage points. For example, the upright figures are presented as though the artist is on the same horizontal plane; but when it comes to the patient on the stretcher, or the two patients reclining on the lawn, they are seen from above. Similarly, the nurse's shoulders are well-nigh frontal, while her feet are in profile; and her hands and general posture closely resemble Mesopotamian figures from the end of the Old Babylonian period. Likewise, the reclining patient (top right) and the tree branch above him closely resemble the famous bas relief depicting a reclining Ashurbanipal (669–626 BC) in his garden and his seated queen [compare to Plate 8B].[17]

In many instances, modern figures adopt postures identical or very similar to those in Mesopotamian works, whether with hands angular like Assyrian kings, or clasped in the manner typical of Sumerian princes standing in composure or prayer. This is the case, for example, with the worker seated in a chair at the center of a painting by an anonymous Communist artist, reproduced on the cover of the March 1982 issue of the party's monthly *al-Thaqafa al-Jadida* issued in Europe. [See Plate 9A.] However, whereas Sumerian pictures have the fingers of the left hand outstretched, here the left hand extends into a clenched fist, as though the worker's revolutionary elan holds him ready at any moment to leap from his seat. [Compare to Plate 9B.] The picture's other Mesopotamian elements include the Gate of Ishtar in the background, engraved with two Akkadian sun emblems (together with the Communist party slogan: 'A free homeland and a happy people!'). Also present is a local element:

the minaret of Samarra's Malwiya Mosque. In addition, whereas the picture's perspective is horizontal, the water at its forefront seems to be viewed from above. The Kurd to the right and the Arab to the left are both portrayed in traditional manner (eyes and shoulders frontal, face and feet in profile). The worker's head, bald and perfectly rounded, closely resembles that of the Sumerian ruler Gudea of Lagash; in other features typical of Sumerian sculpture, all the figures have very large Sumerian eyes and perfectly rounded eyebrows almost meeting above the nose. Indeed, these latter 'Mesopotamian' elements figure frequently in modern Iraqi art: disproportionately large eyes with perfect and very well-marked eyebrows also characterize Ghani's Sheherezade, and her king, Shahryar, for example. [See Plates 10A and 10B.] Her huge, empty eyes, with the perfect bow of the eyebrows nearly touching above the nose, and her hair parted in the middle, make her almost a carbon-copy of the famous girl's head from the 3rd millennium BC, found at al-Warka (Uruk). [See Plate 10C.]¹⁸

In his Shehrezade and Shahriyar, Ghani combined a medieval subject matter (figures from Arabian Nights) with some ancient Mesopotamian influences.

Another group of Iraqi artists specialize in primitive sculpture. The first to engage therein was Mun'im Furat (Baghdad, 1900–72). However, while Furat denied any external influence (thereby implying that the Sumerian elements in his art, which he did not disclaim, were in fact inherited directly from his Sumerian ancestors), some of his successors admitted to being inspired by early Mesopotamian sculpture, whose influence is generally very easy to trace. [See Plate 11, and cf. Plate 9B.] Most of these artists came from poverty-stricken homes, had never studied art and could not afford to engage therein full-time. Under the Ba'th, however, they were awarded government posts, and since the mid-1970s have had special exhibitions arranged for them.¹⁹

Finally, Mesopotamian influences are evident also in the building style of public buildings, at least in Baghdad. Thus, when a new Sheraton Hotel was built in the capital in the late 1970s, it was called Ishtar Sheraton and its entrance was designed to resemble the Ishtar Gate (now in East Berlin), all covered with an imitation of the famous glazed colored ceramic tiles depicting walking animals. In the case of the Ishtar-Sheraton one animal, the dragon, is repeated many times. [See Plate 12A.] To give the tourists a more realistic feeling that they are, indeed, residing in an Ishtar guest house, the interior decorator placed a well-performed, very sensuous modern version of the goddess Ishtar in the lobby. [See Plate 12B.] Likewise, the Babylon Oberoi Hotel is reminiscent of a Ziggurat.

Alongside these Mesopotamian-inspired monuments, the streets and squares of contemporary Baghdad also teem with statues and monuments that draw upon Iraq's medieval-Islamic history. Thus, for example, one may find in front of the National Library a beautiful, larger-than-life bronze statue of the medieval, Iraq-based poet and philosopher al-Mutanabbi by Muhammad Ghani (1977); a large bronze statue by Isma'il Fattah al-Turk, depicting the famous medieval artist Yahya al-Wasit (completed 1972) is placed at the entrance to Saddam Art Centre; Muhammad Ghanis' large monument depicting Kahramana, 'Ali Baba's wife, pouring boiling oil (in fact, cool water) into the forty jugs, where the forty robbers are hiding, serves since 1971 as a public fountain in one of Baghdad's large squares; and there are other such reminders of the 'Abbasid golden age, such as a five-meter bronze sculpture by Khalid al-Rahhal, depicting the head of the 'Abbasid Caliph Abu Ja'far al-Mansur, who established Baghdad ('the Round City') in the eighth century. The latter was designed in 1976 to serve as 'a link between [Baghdad's] illustrious past and its bright present'.[20] One of the most interesting monuments is a larger-than-life bronze sculpture by Isma'il Fattah of the famous Baghdad-based poet Abu Nuwas (AD 757–814). The latter, well-known for his love and wine poetry, is depicted sitting on a high pedestal, holding in his left hand a massive wine chalice. [See Plate 13.] This sculpture, created in 1972 was, apparently, meant to remind the public of the Ba'th secular credo. (Less conveniently for the Ba'th, Abu Nuwas was born in Ahwaz, and wrote in Persian as well as in Arabic).

Classical Islamic influences are evident in monuments that were built during the Gulf War, and in particular those connected with Iraq's fallen soldiers. The most impressive of the latter is Isma'il Fattah al-Turk's magnificent Martyr Monument (*Nasab al-shahid*), unveiled on 30 July 1983, to celebrate the Ba'th Revolution Day of 1968. [See Plate 14.] At the heart of the monument are two forty meter high and fifty-five meter wide separated halves of a mosque's dome, built at the center of an open circular area of more than 400,000 square meters. The two parts of the dome are covered with blue glazed ceramic tiles. At the center of one of the halves there is a symbolic tomb draped in the Iraqi national flag. The second half has a fountain at its center, symbolizing 'the generous sacrifice of the Iraqi people' (but also bringing to mind the traditional combination of a mosque and streaming water). There are other Islamic components in this awe-inspiring monument: on a huge marble slab at the center there are Quranic verses inscribed in the ancient Kufi script. The white circular platform with the two azure blue halves of the dome at its center is surrounded by an azure blue moat which provides an historical lesson: it is meant to remind the visitor of the Battle of the Moat (which the Prophet won due to his military ingenuity and unorthodox tactics). According to the official version, 'the partition and aperture between the two halves . . . symbolize the course to heaven along which the spirits of all martyrs are bound to travel'. A pre-Islamic connection is not missing either: the open space was chosen because 'in the past many famous monuments such as Ziggurats, obelisks, pyramids and the Spiral Minaret of Samarra were constructed in this manner'.[21]

TERRITORIAL INFLUENCES IN POP-ART DURING THE WAR

The onset of the war with Iran gave rise to a new genre of popular art: paintings and posters, but mostly drawings in the daily press depicting the unity of the Iraqi people and its organic connection to its territory. The unity of all Iraqis is expressed, sometimes, by depicting Kurds and Arabs united in the defence of their homeland [see, for example, Plate 28]. More often, however, this is done through the use of Iraqi soldiers, children or women, intertwined with motifs that can be easily identified with Iraq's landscape, thus symbolizing the contemporary unity between the Iraqi nation and territory. Another way of creating a fusion between people and territory is through the integration of the present-day people and the ancient or medieval history of the land. Very often the contemporary Iraqi people are represented in the person of the President, Saddam Husayn, in a variety of Iraqi historical settings. Thus, for example, one painting presents him embracing Sa'd n. Abi Waqqas (hero of the historical battle of Qadisiyya) above a scene of combat, ancient and modern. Another painting shows him commanding both the ancient and the contemporary Battles of Qadisiyya [see Plate 15], and yet another shows Saddam accepting the Mesopotamian heritage, embodied in a palm tree, from a Babylonian figure that resembles Shamash, the Sun God, as he appears on the Stele of Hammurabi. In fact, the president himself stands in a position reminiscent of that of Hammurabi, facing his god on the famous Stele. The background, cuneiform with medieval and modern Arab writings, symbolizes the cultural continuity of the Iraqi people. [See Plate 16.] In a different picture, on display at the entrance to the ancient site of Babylon, a helmeted Saddam is towering above a Babylonian scene [Plate 17]. In another, Saddam in Arab headgear and gown, is riding into battle on an Arab stallion, at the head of columns of Babylonian warriors who emerge from the Gate of Ishtar. [See Plate 18.] In yet another work, the president is supported in his battle by a phalanx of Sumerian warriors, taken directly from the Vultures Stele of

Telloh[22] [see Plate 19], and in another he is building the New Babylon, aided by Nebuchadnezzar [see Plate 20]. Occasionally Saddam Husayn is also depicted as leader of all the Arabs, but only from an Iraqi-centered point of view. This is, for example, the case with a drawing showing him standing on the territory of Iraq, surrounded by a lush grove of palm trees and defended by guns pointing east (towards Iran), and, in a gesture reminiscent of Sumerian and later Mesopotamian figures pouring water to quench the thirst of a pleading Arab girl (the Arab nation), positioned at the center of the map of an arid Arab homeland. [See Plate 21.] Probably the most interesting (certainly the most complex) of these popular works, tying together the president as the embodiment of the contemporary Iraqi people, and the ancient and medieval history of Iraq, is a drawing that appeared on a full page of the party daily *al-Thawra* in honor of Saddam Husayn's birthday. The drawing [see plate 22] by Wisam Murqus depicts President Husayn, wearing Arab 'abaya and headgear riding his Arab horse in a position reminiscent of popular Shi'i paintings describing 'Ali, the First Imam, riding to battle, only Saddam Husayn is holding the Torch of the Ba'th Revolution instead of Dhu al-Faqar, 'Ali's famous sword.[23] The horse is jumping above a primitive boat, representing Udpishtim's Ark, sailing in the heavy waters of the flood (according to the Epos of Gilgamesh, the ark was, in fact, cubical, rather than boat-shaped). On the shore, at the bottom of the drawing, a new weed is sprouting, symbolizing spring and fertility, and the Sumerian-Babylonian god Tammuz (Dumuzi) is re-born, emerging to the sunlight from the Underworld where he had spent the winter. As Saddam Husayn, too, was born in the spring, the allusion is that Saddam Husayn and Tammuz both symbolize spring and rejuvenation (and perhaps they are in fact one).

A leading territorial motif is the Iraqi palm tree, which one 'weekly drawing' in *al-Thawra* depicts as a woman-warrior (implying women's equality) bearing human Iraqi children. In another, the entire Iraqi nation is shown emanating from a palm tree. In other drawings Iraq's palm trees join in hurling fire and tossing hand-grenades at Khomeini [see for example, Plate 23], and Iraq's mountains are fighting against Iran [see Plate 24]. In a somewhat different drawing, an Iraqi soldier is shown actually sprouting forth from the country's soil, protected in his patriotic battle by an Assyrian Winged Bull. [See Plate 25.][24] In yet another one, an Iraqi tree is growing a contemporary woman-soldier and an ancient Assyrian warrior, both standing ready for battle (thus impling both the unity of man and landscape and that of past and present). It also depicts a dove-of-peace resting in a tree symbolizing Iraq's wish for peace. [See Plate 26.] Many of these popular works have various motifs intertwined:

palm trees and palm fronds, cuneiform, Assyrian kings and warriors, Picasso-style peace doves, Iraqi soldiers with women and babies (as a boost to the national birthrate).[25] Finally, one comes also across artistic attempts to demonstrate the unparalleled contribution of the civilization of Mesopotamia to the world of today. [See Plate 27.]

While it is difficult to determine with any degree of precision the relative importance to Iraqi artists of Mesopotamian and other local influences, the existence of the latter, and moreover, their significance, can hardly be questioned. To put matters in a correct perspective, it should be pointed out that there are other influences, too, chiefly Islamic influences, Socialist realism and European modernists chief among whom is Pablo Picasso. The influence of European modernists is very prominent in the work of most Iraqi artists, of whom almost all – with the sole exception of the 'primitive' sculptors – spend at least a few years at European academies. Socialist realism permeated through the Soviet-Iraqi political and ideological dialogue, as well as the Marxist background of some leading Iraqi artists, but it seems to be on the wane in the 1980s. However, as has been shown, Mesopotamian influences can be clearly detected in the works of many Iraqi artists, frequently to their own admission; moreover, these influences feature in the work of artists generally regarded as the most important in present-day Iraq (e.g., Salim, Rahhal, Ghani, Furat, al-Shaykhali, Mazlum, al-Rawi, al-'Azzawi, al-Fattah and others). Further, an unbroken continuity is evident, from the early 1950s, long before the Ba'th came to power, right up to the late 1980s; the number of artists borrowing from Mesopotamian art shows no decline – on the contrary, they appear to be on the increase. Another factor contributing to the resilience of the 'Mesopotamian' and 'local' schools is the adherence thereto of artists hailing from both the Sunni and Shi'i communities (the latter include Furat and his daughter, Kazim Khalil Sa'id, Hamid al-'Attar, Hindawi and many others) as well as a number of Kurds and Turkomans. Accordingly, the phenomenon, far from being narrow-based or sectarian, appears to be all-Iraqi. Finally, this style is pursued not by Ba'this alone, but also by artists who are non-political or ex-Communist (the Communist party has always had its reservations regarding pan-Arabism; its members are accordingly drawn to the emergence of a local Iraqi culture.)

Finally, as already noted, the influences of Mesopotamian art are complemented by another local tradition: medieval Islamic art. This applies particularly to the Medieval painter, al-Wasiti, who was born in Iraq and spent most of his life there.

It should be recorded that, since becoming president, Saddam Husayn has adopted a number of the regal customs of Mesopotamia. One such is affixing plaques like that in Haifa Street, which notes that the street and its buildings were 'completed in the era of the Leader President Saddam Husayn'. In the same vein, special bricks were introduced into the new walls of Babylon at two meter intervals, inscribed with the testimony that Babylon was rebuilt in the era of President Saddam Husayn .

The last large-scale monument erected in Baghdad that may be considered as pop-art was conceived during the war; connected to it was Saddam Husayn's Victory Arch, completed in mid-1989. The Arch [see Plate 29] consists of two titanic hands, widely believed to be blown up replicas of Saddam Husayn's own hands down to his fingerprints holding two gigantic Islamic swords that meet forty meters above a large parade ground. Around the places where the two hands rise from the ground there are two heaps of Iranian helmets, some of them pierced by bullets and shrapnel.

The Victory Arch conveys an unmistakenly aggressive message, implying that, even after its alleged victory in the war under President Saddam Husayn and the Ba'th party, the Iraqi people continue to live on its sword.

To give the Arch full historical depth, on the fringe of the parade ground [see at left of Plate 29] one can see small-scale replicas of Babylon's Gate of Ishtar and a ziggurat. To complete the historical sequence, on Victory Day of August 1989 the President, riding on a white horse under the arch, was wearing the same ceremonial attire that King Faysal I wore during official state ceremonies. Indeed, the absence of the founder of the modern Iraqi nation-state from Baghdad's streets and from the national pantheon was noticed by the president who, in his youth, helped topple the monarchy. On 21 June 1989 the Iraqi press announced that a replica of the Italian-made bronze equestrian statue of King Faysal I (erected in 1930 and torn down by angry crowds on 14 July 1958) would be re-erected in its original site. Ironically, this is a square bearing today the name of Gamal 'Abd al-Nasir.

The symbiosis between the regime and its artists has not been a voluntary one. An artist who wishes to stay in Iraq and create has little choice but to tow the official line. This is particularly the case with those who engage in the creation of outdoor art. The fact that the party line included a Mesopotamian component, however, may have made it easier for artists who were inspired by Mesopotamian art long before the Ba'th came to power to tow this line. Be that as it may, from the regime's viewpoint the co-optation of Iraq's artists has proved extremely successful; at the beginning of the 1990s Baghdad is replete with buildings and large-scale monuments and sculptures that span the ages from Sumer to the Ba'th, and there is no escape for Baghdadis from the historical and contemporary personalities, scenes and symbols which the ruling regime considers essential for their national education. The educational message, however, extends beyond the mere interpretation history; the numerous monuments everywhere create an impression of official omnipotence and convey a sense of tremendous central power and purposefulness.

Artistically speaking, the results of the Ba'th cultural campaign in the realm of the plastic arts are mixed. Even though created in the service of a dictatorship, many of the works performed under the Ba'th by leading artists like Ghani, al-Rahhal and Fattah are, in themselves, beautiful works of art. Two years after the cease-fire in the Gulf, however, far more numerous in Iraq as a whole are unattractive monuments, conceived and performed hastily by indifferent or mediocre artists at the behest of an insatiable president. Saddam's Victory arch, for one, is both aggressive and ugly. In another public square in the capital the municipality commissioned six bulky and unattractive bronze statues of the leaders of the May 1941 anti-British revolt. And in Basra, on the Shatt al-Arab, the government sponsored over 80 bronze statues of all the senior officers who died defending the Southern city. All are dressed in the same uniforms, all have the same blank expression on their faces, and all point east, towards Iran, accusingly.

Finally, in mid-1990 Culture and Information Minister Latif Nusayyif Jasim announced yet another huge assignment given Iraq's artists by their president; erecting statues for 'all the kings and caliphs who ruled over Iraq before Islam and after it'. This presidential order, Jasim confided to a throng of artists summoned on short notice, 'comes to immortalize . . . all those who took part in building Iraq and defending it' throughout the ages. When completed, Jasim went on to explain, 'this civilizational project will turn the past into a tangible present for . . . the coming generations, so that it would become a moving force for the sons of glorious Iraq to continue to sacrifice for, build and defend their homeland'. All this, the minister concluded, was 'part of the re-writing of history, according to the approach defined by . . . Saddam Husayn in the early 1970s'.[26]

It is left to be seen whether this mass-production of bronze kings and caliphs would, indeed, create great art.

8 Mesopotamian Inspiration in Theatre and Poetry

Although there were some very early beginnings in Iraq directed at a limited audience, the first Mesopotamian-inspired play aimed at an all-Iraqi audience and with a clear political message that involved all-Iraqi patriotism (as well as other ideological elements) was probably 'The Walls' (*al-Aswar*), written by the leftist Khalid al-Shawwaf in the mid-1940s and published in 1956.[1] It evolved round the social and national struggle waged by a worker ('*Iyar*'–May), 'a patriotic officer,' and 'the masses of slaves and peasants' against the corrupt Babylonian King Belshazzar and his court, as well as the religious establishment that through 'magic', 'falsification', and 'lies' serves the upper classes. While the court is exploiting and oppressing the masses and is immersed in the pursuit of worldly pleasures, the Persians, aided by the Jewish moneylender Izykil, invade and conquer the city of Babylon. This low point in Iraqi history becomes the starting point of the Iraqi patriotic struggle for national independence, led by the worker and the patriotic officer.

This play may have served as a source of inspiration in later years to playwrights who combined Mesopotamian scenery, Iraqi identification, and secular and socialist values. Such a play was 'Tammuz Rings the Bell', probably written before the Ba'th takeover, which blended Babylon with Assyria. The Communist playwright 'Adil Kazim and producer Sami 'Abd al-Hamid reproduced the palace of Nimrod, 'tyrant of Babylon'. Tammuz, 'the symbol of life and fertility in the Babylonian legends', is here a young revolutionary, the 'symbol of the brave leadership'; Tammuz is ringing the bell of Iraq, thus 'awakening [it] to life and revolution'. Presented by the Group of Contemporary Theatre in late 1968 and early 1969, the play was defined by the critic of *al-Thawra* as 'a positive step on the way of our new Iraqi theatre', and was the first of many such productions in Ba'thi Iraq.[2]

In 1972 the press reported two more plays set in ancient Mesopotamia: 'Urkajina', set in Sumerian Lagash, and 'The Flood' (al-Tufan), the latter by 'Adil Kazim, set in Uruk. Both demonstrated what was termed as 'committed thinking' in the treatment of 'contemporary Arab society'. In 'The Flood', written in the mid-1960s, Kazim made use of the epos of Gilgamesh as a setting for 'a class struggle between the simple people and the rule of the priests'.[3] It seems, then, that the pre-Islamic era was chosen not only to provide a local Iraqi setting, but also to enable the playwright to launch an indirect attack against the religious establishment.

For its world fame, as well as for its dramatic qualities, the epos of Gilgamesh was very popular among Iraqi playwrights. The theatre critic of the Communist weekly *al-Fikr al-Jadid* counts in 1977 no less than four different plays based on that legend; in fact, there were more.[4]

There are only two such plays, however, of which we possess sufficient information to give an account of how the Mesopotamian legacy was resurrected and put to use in the service of Iraqi *wataniyya* and other party ideals. One such highly politicized interpretation was written by Salah al-Qasb and probably staged in 1976. Following Enkidu's death Gilgamesh roams around the world looking for 'immortality – the revolution.' He wanders in countries and continents where people are being oppressed and he shares their sufferings: in Chile, Palestine, Africa, Lebanon and Rhodesia. Finally, he returns to Iraq. There, he gives his blessing to a child born in the National Archeological Museum, among the relics of Iraq's glorious past. The child, the new Iraq, is born on the July 1958 revolution and comes of age with the Ba'th revolution of July 1968. To this general message of Iraqi identity and anti-imperialism, the writer adds more sophisticated political messages. First, Palestine does not rank any higher than other oppressed countries. Second, although Gilgamesh, the Iraqi revolutionary, identifies with the sufferings of the oppressed around the world, he returns to Iraq to build a socialist revolution there and thus to revolutionize the world (or the Arab world) through a successful example that eventually would radiate its influence, rather than through an immediate Trotsky-like 'world revolution'. This is in line with Saddam Husayn's concept of 'socialism in one Arab country' that emerged in the late 1970s.[5] Finally, the growing displeasure of the Ba'th with the Communists and the USSR during the second half of that decade is evident in that the play completely ignores the fact that the revolution had already succeeded in some parts of the world, namely, the USSR and the socialist camp. In the words of the Communist critic, who treated the play more like a political platform than a work of art,

> the practice of the revolution in Iraq, which Salah equated with the immortality of Gilgamesh in the land of the Twin Rivers . . . received great support from the socialist countries. Is it right, then, that we should build immortality, imagining that we are cut off from the progressive world? . . . Salah's interpretation of the immortality of Gilgamesh, though revolutionary, remains [thus] incomplete.[6]

A very different interpretation of the same epos was directed by the inde-fatigable Sami 'Abd al-Hamid with two different groups, both considered leading repertories in Iraq, in four broadly different productions, from a small hall to a large open amphitheatre, and all this in just under two years. The text was much more faithful to the original legend, and it was less political and more philosophical. The director confided to his readers that for many years he had intended to produce such a play, yet it became possible only 'when the demand to resurrect the [Iraqi] heritage became acute'. This may be a fair account of the collaboration between Communist-inclined (and other non-Ba'thi) intellectuals and the regime in the promotion of Iraqi *wataniyya*.

By slightly bending the ancient legend, the director expressed his views on such major issues as socialism, religion, sacrifice and idealism. Thus, for example, the beginning of the search for immortality is seen as the moment of Gilgamesh's transformation from an egotistic tyrant to a revolutionary idealist and a philosopher. Instead of following the original plot, where the gods produce a journey companion for Gilgamesh to save the city Uruk from his tyranny, the director turns to the audience and asks them to produce Enkidu, 'by which I tried', as he explained, 'to create an interpretation by which it is the people [and not the gods] who create the hero'.

In the same vein, the people shelter Gilgamesh against the wrath of Ishtar and successfully oppose her will. When it came to the scene where the snake steals the enchanted weed of immortality from the sleeping hero, the director decided to deviate from the original plot, which he regarded as 'mythological and metaphysical', and instead his hero brings the weed to Uruk and shares it with his people, as would befit a materialistic and socialist hero. The play also treats such questions as democracy and authoritarianism through the relations between Gilgamesh and the people of Uruk. The role of women in society is treated through the negative role played by Ishtar, who tries to tempt Gilgamesh, and the positive one played by the whore, who turns Enkidu from an animal into a human being. There are also other issues that come up, like friendship, class struggle and the meaning of eternal life. A great effort was made to recreate the Babylonian environment through elaborate costumes and scenery.

The most spectacular performance of 'Abd al-Hamid's 'Gilgamesh' was the one given in the Greek amphitheatre in the ruins of Babylon. It was performed on a huge stage with 63 participants and included the crossing of rivers and wandering through forests. The audience, some 2000 strong, came from Hilla and the nearby villages of the Babylon district.

The most provocative performance of the play was its staging in

Damascus in June 1979, when the Iraqi-Syrian unity talks were in full swing, reminding the Syrians of Iraq's historical and cultural seniority.[7]

Although details are not available to us, there is frequent mention of more plays that were inspired by Mesopotamian history and mythology. In 1975, for example, the theatrical group of Karbala presented a play based on the period of Hammurabi, entitled 'The Stele'. Reportedly, it was 'inspired by . . . the creative ability of our [Iraqi] man that manifested itself in [Hammurabi's] enactment'.[8] Later there is mention of a play based on an ancient Sumerian text, 'The Lamentation of Ur', and of other plays inspired by similar themes.[9]

It is difficult to assess the relative weight of such 'Mesopotamian' plays in Iraqi theatrical output. Some indications, though, may be found in an account of the Iraqi theatrical season of 1977–78. Out of twenty-two productions staged by the seven leading groups, only two were Mesopotamian, both of Gilgamesh. However, this was the only play to be produced twice in the same year.[10] This fact, together with the expensive production at Babylon and the representative task that the play was given in Syria, indicate a high degree of official support and thus may serve to illustrate how the regime promoted *al-Iraqiyya* through Mesopotamian-inspired theatre.

Under the Ba'th regime, numerous movies, documentaries and features have been dedicated to Iraq's medieval and more distant past. The most important film focusing on the Islamic period is dedicated to the historical Battle of Qadisiyya. Produced during the war with Iran this is a poignant anti-Iranian film and, at the same time, it gives a generally accurate account of the evens that led to the battle and the battle itself. It stresses the common denominator of the Islamic-Arab as well as the Iraqi setting. As for 'Mesopotamian' films, in addition to documentaries the ministry of culture produced a few cartoon films (the Epos of Gilgamesh and others) and they are frequently shown on the Iraqi TV.

Even more conspicuous than productions of Mesopotamian inspiration, contemporary Iraqi theatre is also notable for plays dealing with local issues, such as the struggles of the Iraqi peasantry, comedies in regional dialect and the country's modern history. When Tariq 'Abd al-Wahid was asked why his plays were all dedicated to historical themes and personalities which are local (i.e., Yunis al-Sab'awi) as opposed to Arab, the young playwright (1944–   ) replied: 'A child, in getting to know people, first becomes familiar with his family. As he grows up, he gets to know his relatives, and then his region.'[11] Coming from a Ba'thi playwright, such a view represents a major ideological revolution.

As in art and theatre, poetry also witnessed the first appearance of Mesopotamian motifs in the 1950s. It was Badr Shakir al-Sayyab

(1923–64), the most prominent modern poet in Iraq – indeed, in the entire Arab world, to cite a widely-held view – who began in 1956 to introduce figures from Mesopotamian mythology into his poetry; the subsequent phase of his work is referred to by literary critics as his 'Tammuz period', for the god Tammuz and the goddess Ishtar who became its central images at that time. In the mid-1960s, under al-Sayyab's influence, or at least, following in his footsteps, Mesopotamian themes emerged in the poetry of 'Abd al-Wahhab al-Bayyati (1926–   ) a further member of the leading trio of modern Iraqi poets. The third is Nazik al-Malaika (who did not employ Mesopotamian themes in her poetry). Some major critics would make it a quartet by adding the name of the Kurd Buland al-Haydari. Haydari (1926–   ) and another prominent poet, Shadhil Taqa (1928–74), also incorporated Mesopotamian mythology into their works, though in a far less conspicuous way than al-Sayyab and al-Bayyati.

What was the common denominator of all these poets, that could explain their shared inclination towards Mesopotamian mythology? There was nothing uniform in their social or denominational origins: al-Sayyab was a Shi'i from a small village near Basra, Jaykur; al-Bayyati is a Sunni from Bab al-Shaykh, one of Baghdad's poorer quarters; al-Haydari is a Kurd from a middle-class family, and Taqa, likewise middle-class, came from Mosul's Sunni-Arab community. In political affiliation, Taqa was a veteran Ba'thi (in 1974, shortly before his death, he served as acting foreign minister). Al-Sayyab, al-Bayyati and al-Haydari had in their youth been close to the Communist party. This gives their fascination with pre-Islamic Iraq a partial explanation which, however, is not sufficient: al-Sayyab, for example, left the party (or was expelled) in the mid-1950s, when he joined the Arab Nationalist movement (*al-Qawmiyyun*); thus, his initiation into writing poetry with a strong local-Iraqi component coincided with his adoption of the pan-Arab credo. Al-Bayyati for his part never formally joined the Communist party, finding various opportunities to stress his independence; and al-Haydari has dissociated himself from political activity since the second half of the 1960s. Overshadowing the trio's Communist affinities seems to be the fact that they moved in the same social and intellectual circle in Baghdad during the late 1940s and early 1950s – a time when secular Iraqi intellectuals increasingly leaned towards borrowing from the cultures of ancient Mesopotamia, although such a bent could be interpreted as, and in the 1960s indeed became, a mark of Iraqi isolationism. In addition, they were all born after the establishment of the monarchy and went through its educational system, which introduced the study of pre-Islamic Iraq into the curricula. Al-Bayyeti, al-Haydari and Taqa were still in school when, following the 1941 Rashid 'Ali anti-British revolt the education system went through a metamorphisis one of the results of which was a heavier emphasis on Iraq's pre-Islamic eras.

Al-Sayyab's poetry resorted to motifs from various world mythologies: Greek, Christian and others; since 1956, however, those most conspicuous in his work were Mesopotamian. Moreover, he generally employed them within the context of Iraqi political events, or as a vehicle for his pantheistic view of Iraq's landscapes, particularly those of his native south. Thus, for example, a young maiden, crucified and quartered by the Communists during the suppression of the March 1959 Mosul uprising (the Iraqi Communists supported General Qasim in his struggle against the pan-Arabs), was depicted by him as 'Ishtar, the fair-haired virgin'; Tammuz was the nail driven into her womb, to displant fertility with death; Babylon's Hanging Gardens were a symbol of the forlorn dream of a happy Iraq.[12] In another poem, Qasim was Cerberus, and Iraq became Babylon; the revolution betrayed by Qasim was the dead god Tammuz, whereas hopes of rebirth, love and beauty were embodied in Ishtar, 'the sad goddess, the frightened goddess . . . from her blood, the grain shall be fertilized, the god shall grow'.[13]

In 'The City of Sindbad,' – referring to Basra, the city in which al-Sayyab spent most of his youth – one finds a combination of the landscapes of southern Iraq, the horrors of the Qasim era, and Christian and Muslim but most conspicuously Mesopotamian symbols:

> . . . / as if ancient Babylon, surrounded by walls / comes back to life / in her high iron domes / a bell is ringing, like the wailing / in a grave, and the sky a field of carnage / her hanging gardens, its young crops are heads / cut by the sharp axes / . . . / Is this my city? Are these the ruins/ upon which it was engraved: 'let life live'? / . . . / Is this my city? The daggers of the Tatars / are plunged above her gate, and the open desert is gasping / around her roads, and the moon does not visit her / Is this my city, with all these delves / with all these bones? / . . . / . . . And in the villages/ a thirsty Ishtar is dying with no flower on her forehead / . . . / . . . and the palm trees / on her river bank are crying.[14]

In a poem dedicated to his home village in southern Iraq, al-Sayyab equates himself with Tammuz-Adonis who was killed by a wild boar, and who is waiting to be resurrected by Ishtar:

> The wild boar's fang is tearing my hand / and the blaze is plunging into my liver / and my blood is gushing forth, flowing / . . . / 'Ishtar,' garments are fluttering / and the grass is flickering in front of me / . . . /

> if only light would flash through my veins / to illuminate the world for me / if only I would rise and return to life / . . . / I wish my veins were vines / and Ishtar would kiss my mouth / . . . [15]

In his 'City Without Rain' it is most likely that the awakening of Tammuz refers to the July 1958 revolution, the mounting hope and the ensuing disappointment (although it may also be seen in a more general way as referring to the Arab nation and the hope for its revival after its long slumber).

> [He] woke up from his slumber of clay under the vine twigs / Tammuz woke up, returned to green Babylon to attend it / the [celebration] drums of Babylon are about to beat, then / the whistle of wind in her towers and the moanings of her sick descend upon her / and in the chambers [of the temple] of Ishtar / the clay incense pots remain empty, with no fire / . . . [16]

In a personal, non-political poem dedicated to his son, and expressing his pantheistic philosophy, the Mesopotamian gods are embedded into memories of his own childhood and that of his son, generating an atmosphere of tranquil joy:

> Daddy, daddy / your voice flows to me in the darkness like fresh rain / flows out through slumber while you are asleep in bed. / From which vision did it come? From which heaven? which place? / I keep swimming in its drizzle, swimming in fragrance / as if the valleys of Iraq / opened windows from your dream to my sleeplessness: every valley / that Ishtar endowed with blossoms and fruits as if my soul / in the soil of darkness is a seed of wheat and your echo is water / . . . / Tammuz returned with each spike of grain dallying every wind / . . . [17]

Al-Bayyati resorts to mythological symbolism, with Mesopotamian motifs the most prominent, to express the poet's alienation from the modern world, and his despair of the dream of an ideal society. As he himself explained in numerous interviews, and in prose relating to his poetry,

> the poet is trapped in a world which, replete with torment, misery and poverty, lacks spirit and is obsessed with materialism and greed for power. Even in those places where the socialist revolution has triumphed, the poet – a revolutionary idealist incapable of condoning compromise, and even less, of coming to terms with the revolution's

deviations and its disfigurement by pseudo-revolutionaries – finds himself 'in exile in time and place'.[18]

While not expressed outright, al-Bayyati's poetry exudes a sense of great personal isolation: the alienation of the modern intellectual, a left-leaning atheist in a conservative, religious milieu; and an abandonment of all hope of its revival by transformation into a thoroughly modern and progressive society. To him, Babylon represents humanity's spiritual grandeur in the remote past; simultaneously, it is a symbol of the metaphysical city, of an ideal society, of man's emancipation and of an unfulfilled dream. Ishtar is the goddess of love and rebirth – hope of a new era; her touch would re-ignite the dying embers of revolution (alternatively, will instil new life into the Iraqi people, or that Arab nation which al-Bayyati pronounces 'dead');[19] but even she will remain forever a lost dream, a faded painting on a crumbling wall.

/ Oh stars/ Babylon under the tent of night / upon its ruins wolves are forever howling / and the soil fills its empty, sad eye- holes / Babylon, under the foot of time / is awaiting resurrection; Oh Ishtar / rise, fill the jars / and moisten the lips of this wounded lion / . . . / and bring down rain / in these gloomy ruins!/ but Ishtar remained on the wall / her hands mutilated, her face covered with dust / and silence and grass / . . . / Oh, beloved one! / go back to the legend / an ear of corn, a sun without noon / a woman of smoke a broken jar / Tammuz will not return to life / ah, alas! / Babylon under the dome of night / . . . / I screamed upon its ruins: Ishtar! / the walls cracked / and the moon sank down on the ruins / and the rain fell. . . . [20]

In 'The Picture and the Shadow' there is a faint breath of hope for the downfall of the world of 'Cement and Iron and Banks' and 'the return of the soul' by which al-Bayyati may mean love, idealism, sacrifice, striving to end human suffering, and real dedication to the cause, as distinguished from power lust and hypocrisy, so widespread among ex-revolutionaries who became 'professional politicians'.[21] In addition, however, the passage could be read as an expression of hope for the return of the Iraqi soul or, as some would have it, the Arab soul:

If only the pieces of this torn picture were pieced together / then the burnt-down Babylon would rise / shaking ashes off her rags / and a butterfly and a lily / would spring from the hanging gardens / and Ishtar

1A. Al-Wasity illustration for al-Hariri's 32nd *maqama*, reproduced in a wall carpet by the Ministry of Culture and Information, The Directorate of Folklore, 1987.

1B. A reproduction of a hunting scene from an Assyrian bas relief, in a wall carpet by Irbil Carpets.

2. The Monument of Liberty by Jawad Salim, 1961, Liberation Square, Baghdad. A bronze bas relief on concrete.

3. Monument of the Journey by Khalid al-Rahhal, erected in 1980, National Museum Square. Bronze and bronze bas reliefs on concrete.

4. A Child, a Mother, and Hammurabi's Stele (inscribed in Arabic) by Muhammad Ghani. Bronze and marble, mid-1970s, Baghdad.

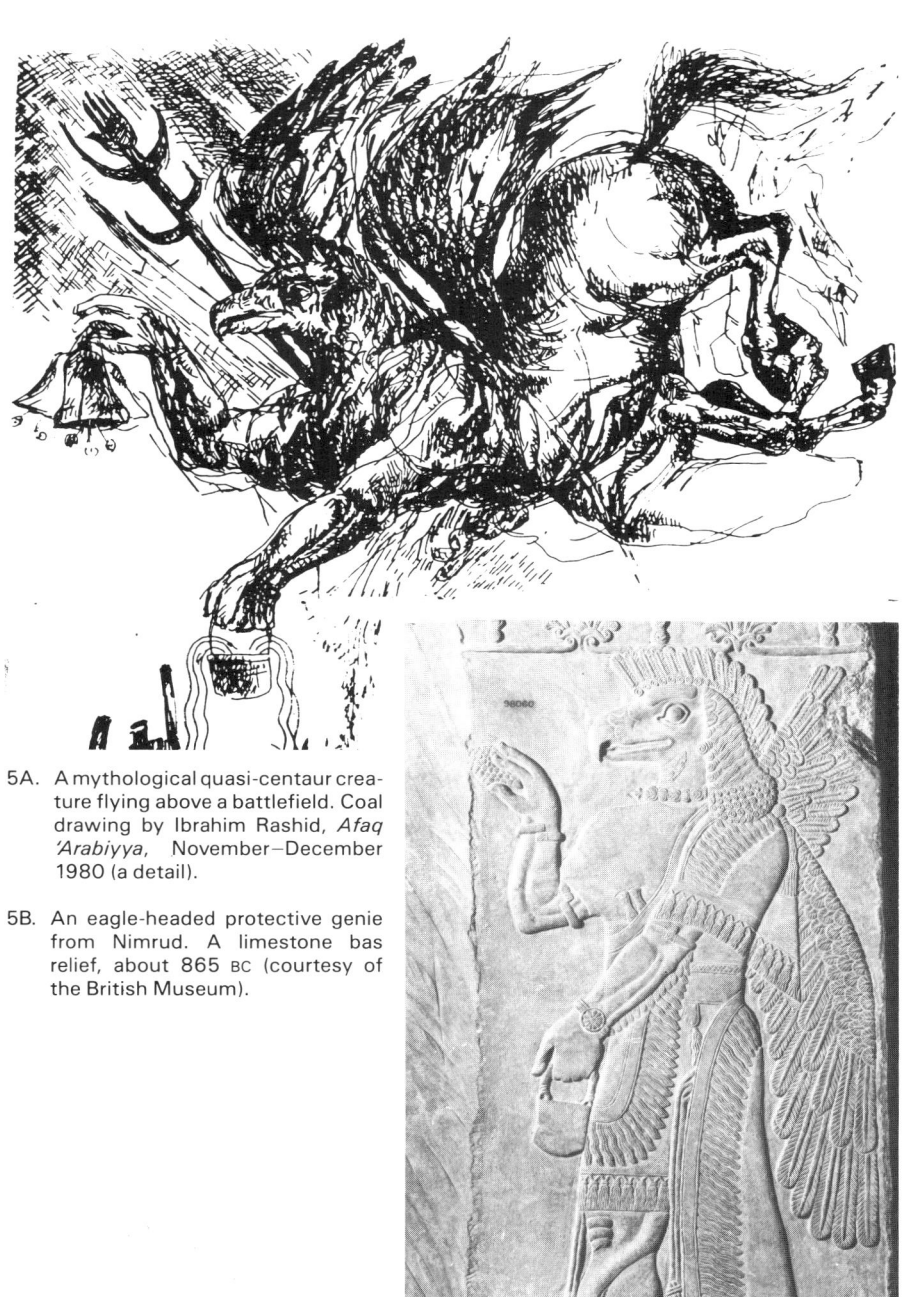

5A. A mythological quasi-centaur creature flying above a battlefield. Coal
drawing by Ibrahim Rashid, *Afaq
'Arabiyya*, November–December
1980 (a detail).

5B. An eagle-headed protective genie
from Nimrud. A limestone bas
relief, about 865 BC (courtesy of
the British Museum).

6A. Coal drawing by Ibrahim Rashid, *Afaq 'Arabiyya*, November–December 1980.

6B. The Dying Lioness, Ashurbanipal's Palace, Nineveh, circa 645 BC (courtesy of the British Museum).

١

أحبني آشور بانيبال

مدينة بنى لحي وبنى من حولها الاسوار

ساق اليها الشمس بالاغلال

والنار والعبيد والأَسرى ونهر الجنة الفرات

7A. An Illustration by Hashim al-Samarji, for 'Abd al-Wahhab al-Bayyati's *Diwan*, Vol. III. (Beirut, 1975), p. 135.

7B. Saddam Husayn and Nebuchadnezzar on the emblem of the Babylon International Festival (note the cuneiform-like inscription on the left-hand side) by an anonymous artist.

8A. A bas relief describing medical treatment by Muhammad Ghani, Italian marble, early 1970s at Medical City, Baghdad (*Madinat al-Tibb*).

8B. Ashurbanipal and his queen in the palace garden. Alabaster relief from Nineveh, circa 645 BC (courtesy of the British Museum).

9A. Iraqi National and Proletarian Unity, *Al-Thaqafa al-Jadida*, March 1982.

9B. Gudea, Ruler of Lagash, in a posture of reverence, 22 BC (courtesy of the British Museum).

10A. Sheherezade by Muhammad Ghani. Bronze, 1970s, Abu Nuwas Street, Baghdad.

10B. Sheherezade by Muhammad Ghani, bronze, 1970s, Abu Nuwas Street, Baghdad.

10C. A Girl's Head, 3rd millennium BC, Al-Warka (Uruk).

11. Primitive sculpture by Hamid Madi (1927–   ), limestone. Source: *Naif Art in Iraq* (Baghdad, 1982).

12A. (*above*) The entrance to the Ishtar-Sheraton Hotel, Baghdad.

12B. (*left*) An anonymous sculptor's version of the goddess Ishtar, standing upon a sun emblem (instead of her own eight-pronged star), Ishtar-Sheraton Hotel lobby, Baghdad.

13. The medieval poet Abu Nuwas by Isma'il Fattah al-Turk. Bronze, 1970s, Abu Nuwas Street, Baghdad.

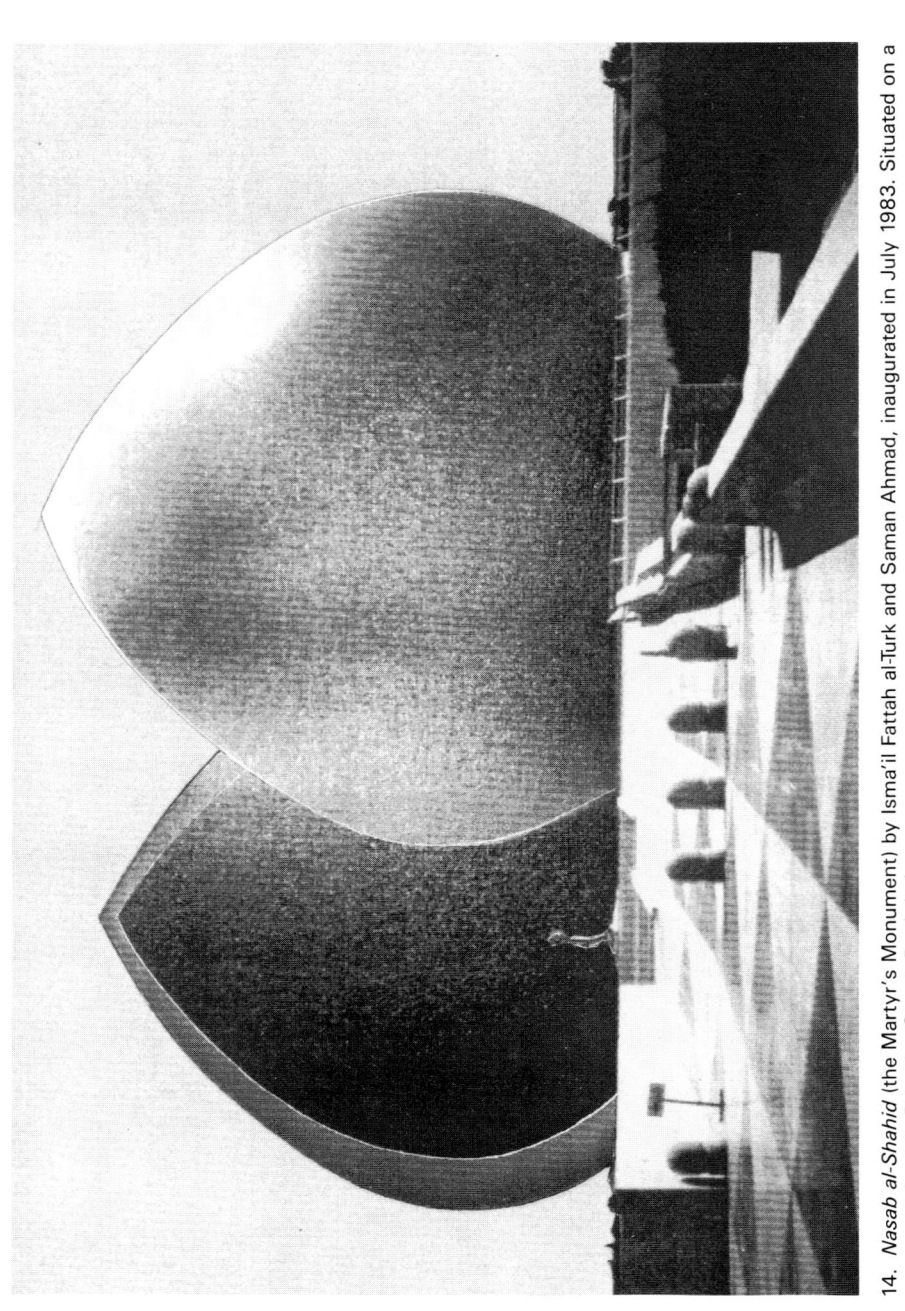

14. *Nasab al-Shahid* (the Martyr's Monument) by Isma'il Fattah al-Turk and Saman Ahmad, inaugurated in July 1983. Situated on a semi-island, in Palestine Street, Baghdad.

15. Saddam Husayn commanding the Old and New Battles of Qadisiyya in a large outdoor oil painting by Muhammad al-Hayuri (?), Baghdad.

16. (*above*) Saddam Husayn receiving the Mesopotamian bequest from a Babylonian figure. Anonymous artist, oil on canvas (*Alif Ba,* 8 January 1986).

17. (*left*) An outdoor painting of Saddam Husayn towering above a Babylonian scene by Zaydan al-Ni'ma (?), situated in Babylon, 1987.

18. Saddam Husayn leading Babylonian troops to battle by Husayn al-Jarmat (?), *al-Iraq*,
     17 July 1987.

19. A Sumerian Phalanx rushing to aid the Iraqis in their war under Pres. Husayn by Ibrahim Rashid. Coal drawing, *al-Thawra*, 29 February 1984.

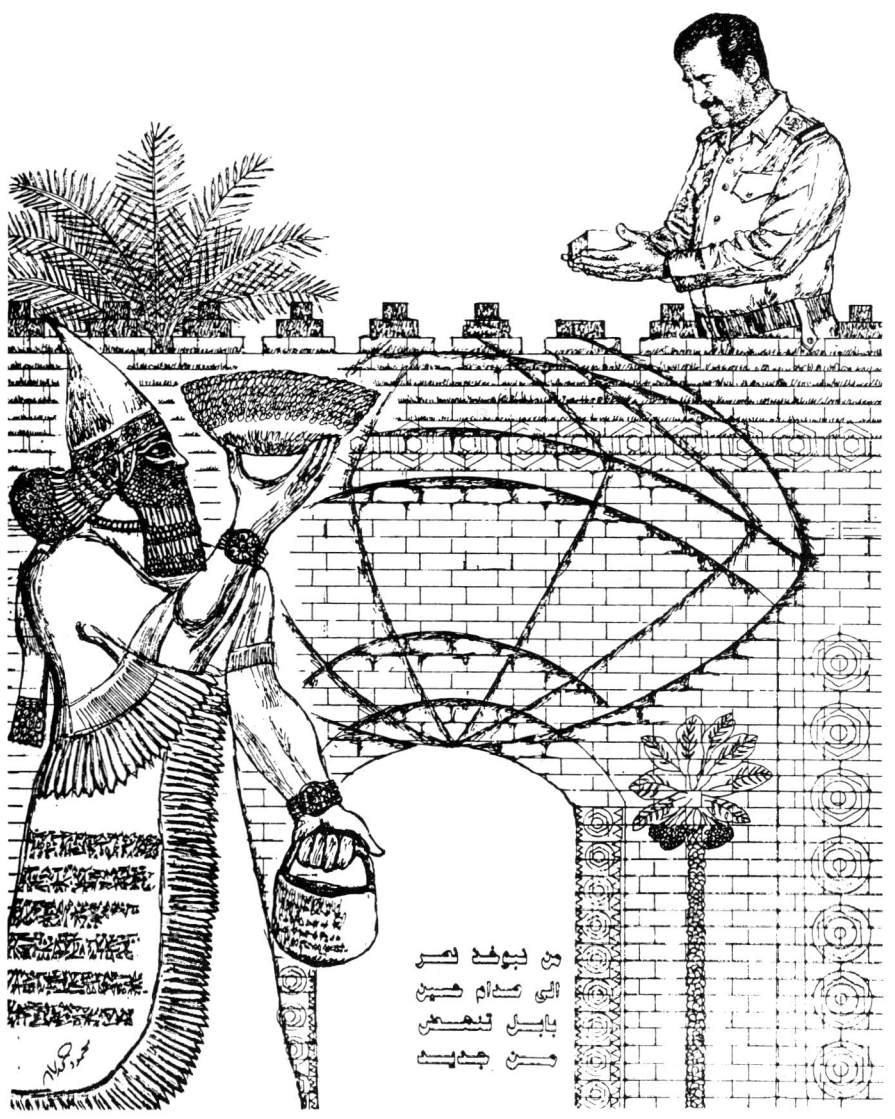

من نبوخذ نصر
الى صدام حسين
بابل تنهض
من جديد

20. 'From Nebuchadnezzar to Saddam Husayn Babylon is rising again', by Mahmud Hamad, *al-Thawra*, 20 September 1987.

بريشة الفنان محمود حمد

21. Mahmud Hamad's drawing in *al-Thawra*, 29 April 1987.

22. A drawing of Saddam Husayn, the god Tammuz reborn, and springtime by Wisam Murkus, *al-Thawra*, 28 April 1986.

23. The Iraqi Palm trees are fighting Khomeini (*al-Thawra*, 16 February 1986).

24. The Mountains of Iraqi Kurdistan are fighting Iran. Wisam Murqus, *al-Thawra*, 28 June 1987.

بريشة الفنان وسام مرقس

25. Assyrian winged bull protects the Iraqi warriors. Wisam Murqus, The Weekly Picture, *al-Thawra*, 18 November 1984.

26. An Iraqi tree growing modern and ancient warriors defending Iraq by Mahmud Hamad, *al-Thawra*, 14 September 1987.

لوحة الاسبوع

بريشة الفنان محمود حمد

27. Mesopotamian culture as the fountain of present-day world civilization by Mahmud Hamad, *al-Thawra*, 12 July 1987.

28. Arab-Kurdish unity: both nationalities share common roots and a common cause, defending the Iraqi homeland against Iran. Wisam Murqus, *al-Thawra*, 15 March 1987.

29. Saddam Husayn's Victory Arch: two hands holding swords above a parade ground. Anonymous artist, bronze and stainless steel, 1989, Baghdad.

would smile / on her bed, playing with her lyre / and Osiris would return
/ . . . / If only they were pieced together then a spark would flare up / in
these vanquished temples / and the graves of cement and iron and banks
would shake and rock/ and the morning rooster would cry in Tehran /
and Man would be born/ from the froth of the sea and the bottom of the
waves / . . . / and the soul would return and light would return / and the
buried would be resurrected. / . . . / and the wall of falsehood would be
destroyed.[22]

In 'One Thousand and One Nights' images that seemingly emerge from
the Arabian Nights like 'the enchanted, winged black horse' and Alladin's
lamp are intertwined with scenes and figures from ancient Babylon (and
with modern realia), creating an obscure, surrealistic atmosphere and
suggesting a cyclical order of things in history:

I fly every night on my black, winged, enchanted horse / to a country
you never visited . . . / . . . / I am carrying Alladin's lamp / drowning
in the singing, pale, sad morning / I am extending a ladder of voices / on
which I am ascending to Babylon / as a singer and as a wizard / searching
in its hanging gardens for a blue flower / for the words of the temple's
priest . . .

This search for the rebirth of the everlasting, ideal world, however, is
destined for failure and despair.[23]

In '*Marthiya Ila 'A'isha*,' 'A'isha is no other than Ishtar, and the
poem is intended, according to an Iraqi critic, to be 'a new form of the
language and stance of the Sumerian poem "The Descent of Ishtar to the
Underworld."'[24]

In 'The Descent of Orpheus to the Underworld', despite the Greek
heading (that implies failure and tragedy), al-Bayyati again conveys pes-
simism and desolation mainly through Mesopotamian symbols. The legendary winged bull, the mysterious survivor of the ancient civilization
of Assyria, flies high above as a reminder of a long-vanished greatness
and symbolizing the distant hope for resurrection, but the world remains
engulfed in 'death and autumn leaves'. The poet is alone in his dreary cave,
trying to bring about the revolution, or the birth of a new age, but in vain:
resurrection, though it arrives, is twisted and deformed, and the legendary
bull cannot revitalize the decaying, modern world:

The prayers of the wind in Ashur, and the Knight in his iron armor /
is dying without being defeated in the war / and is blown away . . . /

under the walls of night, and the legendary bull is flying / ramming the sun with his horn . . . / . . . / all your wounds bled to death at the dawn of the dynasties [the early Sumerian era] and in the ice age / Why, then, are you alone in the cave? / carving the legendary bull on the walls with fire, wrapping yourself in the rags of a fugitive / . . . / in vain you are screaming, since the night is long / . . . / ah, how desolate are my nights on the walls of Ashur with death and the leaves of autumn / while I am ascending from her underworld toward the light and the distant dawn / dead, resurrected in iron armor / Oh, the legendary bull, flying over the smoke of the large cities / . . . / you are screaming in vain, because the world is dying among the objects and stones and flesh / and the civilizations are dying / . . . .[25]

In his collection 'Poems of Love On the Seven Gates of the World', in 'The Birth and Death of 'A'isha in the Ceremonies . . . Written . . . on the Tablets of Nineveh', it is Ashurbanipal's unrequited, ill-fated love through which al-Bayyati conveys his sense of alienation and hopelessness,[26] and there are more examples of such use of Sumerian, Babylonian and Assyrian motifs in his poetry.

What induced both these poets to adopt Mesopotamian mythology? The riddle finds no adequate answer in any of their own explanations. Al-Sayyab's recourse to Mesopotamian symbols is partially elucidated by his claims of poetic rationale, a desire to camouflage his criticism of the Qasim regime, and a reluctance to adopt pre-Islamic Arab mythology (so as to duck a confrontation with the religious establishment).[27] But this does not explain why he picked on Ishtar and Tammuz as his principal motifs, rather than, say, figures from Greek or Christian mythology which, it will be recalled, he had employed up to 1956, and with which he was thoroughly familiar. Al-Bayyati likewise avoided a specific identification of his poetry with local-Iraqi nationalism; like al-Sayyab, he must have been wary of accusations of isolationism. But, in an astonishing interview to *al-Jumhuriyya*, al-Bayyati confessed that the metaphysical ideal city figuring in his work 'at times, it is Babylon, at others, Thebes', but, in fact, it is Baghdad:

The true Baghdad, and Baghdad the fable, is concealed within my words and my poetry; once, it's Nissapur, and another time it's Babylon, and the other names [of cities]. All the names of cities mentioned in my poems terminate in the name of Baghdad, flowing towards [the city] and draining into it.[28]

Elsewhere, al-Bayyati admitted that his poetry was designed to reveal 'the pages of the man who has lives in this ancient land [Iraq] to which we belong', 'this great man [which is] nearly five thousand years old' whose offspring ultimately fell beneath the hooves of the Mongolian invaders. '[It was] the mute misery between the ruins, and the quest after . . . the man of all the civilizations and epochs [of Iraq and mankind] that induced me to stretch out my hand towards [the primordial] dawn.'[29]

In total contrast to al-Bayyati, al-Sayyab rarely spoke about his poetry. However, his works contain very numerous expressions of his love for Iraq, and of his anguished yearnings for his country whenever he was abroad, whether in exile or on his travels.[30] Whatever the reasons, conscious and sub-conscious, for the ubiquity of Mesopotamian themes in their poetry, al-Sayyab and al-Bayyati started a poetic tradition in Iraq.

Under the Ba'th regime, critics make frequent reference to the profound affinity linking al-Sayyab and al-Bayyati to the soil of Iraq and its ancient civilizations. Al-Sayyab has been commemorated in numerous ways, including a poetry festival in his name, and a large monument of him erected in Basra overlooking the Shatt al-Arab, and his family enjoys a pension. As for al-Bayyati, he was recalled from his Cairo exile after the Ba'th revolution, and awarded a senior government post by the new regime.[31] In later years he left Iraq, and in the 1980s he was living in Spain, but he still visited Iraq and contributed from time to time to Iraqi magazines. Younger poets have tried to follow in the footsteps of the two masters, but in contrast with the continuity evident in the plastic arts, no new al-Bayyati or al-Sayyab has yet surfaced. (The poets have however been supplemented by writers and novelists, the Ba'th period has brought publication of numerous stories employing Mesopotamian themes.) Iraqi poetry today is largely (though not entirely) regimented; while much of the work of al-Sayyab, al-Bayyati and al-Haydari may be regarded as politically committed or 'engaged', it is vastly unlike that of their younger colleagues. The latter have, under the Ba'th regime, made Babylon's Hanging Gardens, Ishtar's Gate, Ashur and Ur into very concrete historical sites, rather than ethereal symbols of hope, despair, loneliness, alienation or unrequited love; their purpose is to mobilize the masses and instil them with pride in Iraq, in its legislators and scientists of antiquity, as well as the warriers and architects of its mighty empires, from Sumer by way of the Abbasid period and to Salah al-Din; the young poets aim to ennoble the present, and assure the ancient-but-new Iraqi people of a glorious future under the omniscient leadership of their dynamic and youthful president, Saddam Husayn, heir to Nebuchadnezzar, Sargon, Hammurabi and Harun al-Rashid. Their poems are often interwoven with Mesopotamian and other local elements, until the ancient history of Iraq becomes at one with the country's soil, water and landscape. Thus, Khalil al-Asadi, writing in the daily of the Defence Ministry:

> . . . Peace . . . that is in your hand / since the dawn of all civilizations, goes with you / sowing in the fields of history deep love for a future that will be proud of you forever ! / Oh sublime Iraq, how noble you are ![32]

Another poet, writing to reassure the people after Iraq's loss of al-Faw, addresses Saddam Husayn:

> O my President ! / I have heard a nation's voice speaking from Babylon: / O the valiant and proud of the army's heroic corps / March on the enemy / . . . and fight his scattered remnants / . . . and purge the mountains and the plains /[33]

At the same time, Dr Muhammad al-Hallab wrote:

> O the redeemed homeland / in your hills / on your soil / the world's civilization is being built / and the resolve of your people [is awakened] anew / To you is all I write / . . . Since one thousand years / or more / we lived / on the remnants of the glory / of al-Rashid's Baghdad / and on the exploits / of Sa'd and al-Qa'qa''s Qadisiyya / . . . and it was said: Ashur is here / and there al-Walid had passed / Since a thousand years or more / Time expected the new birth / Till April brought [Saddam Husayn's birthday and] / the new dawn . . . / a grandson was born . . . to al-Husayn / the Hawk of al-Rashid's Baghdad / Good tidings to you ! / O Arabs / O Nebuchadnezzar / O Babylon / O Land of Sumer / O Akkad / good tidings ! / The baby is born / The daring knight / . . . and this is a day of festivity/.[34]

Subsequently, after the liberation of al-Faw, a Kurdish poet marked the president's birthday with a typical blood-and-soil poem:

> Al-Faw . . . was a prisoner / . . . the sacred soil of al-Faw was blazing, groaning / the grass refused to grow green / the roses and flowers refused to blossom / but the soil's baptism with sacred Iraqi blood restored its sanctity and brought forth in its salty land narcissi / . . . the Iraqi soil taught us that he who drinks the water of the Twin Rivers and inhales the sweet air from Kurdistan's mountain peaks to the papyrus groves of

al-Ahwar [in the south] . . . will not sleep . . . as long as one inch of his soil is prisoner / . . . The very grains of soil would turn into bombs / the oaks and palm trees / would become missiles . . . / . . . and the . . . sun that refused to shine on an imprisoned city . . . will [now] light the roads of victory and present the warriors and their leader, the symbol of lofty Iraq, Saddam Husayn, with flowers.[35]

There are other works, more poetical and less political, like 'Enkidu's Dream' and 'Ishtar of the Ruins' by the Shi'i poet, Faysal Jasim, or 'A Babylonian Inscription' by another young Shi'i, Salah Hasan, wherein the influence of al-Sayyab and al-Bayyati is paramount – also 'Ishtar Creates Rain' by Salam Sirhan, or 'Ali al-Husayni's 'The Sorrows of Utunapishtim'.[36] But these poems are less conspicuous than their skin-deep, highly-politicized counterparts.

Even al-Bayyati himself, writing from the remote vantage point of Madrid, produced a poem which, while superior to most of what the Iraqi press publishes, is little more than an attempt to imitate his own great works of the past.[37] In 1989, however, he published in Cairo a new *Diwan*, *Bustan 'A'isha*, dedicated to the eternal 'A'isha-Ishtar, and to the agony of the post-revolutionary era, under 'the robbers of the revolutions'. In a poem named 'Cities of Fear', al-Bayyati writes:

Cities that live on rumors / lies / empty talk / and on human blood and the lost right/ sleeping in fear on the gate of the small tyrants . . . /[38]

Of the regimented poetry, by far the best is the text of the new national anthem composed by an able poet and veteran Ba'thi, cultural commissar Shafiq al-Kamali. Written with great technical skill, the anthem very concisely encapsulates the full scope of the Ba'th's new national credo: in addition to expressions of Iraq's uniqueness and pride, and its claims to Arab leadership, the text also elaborates on the themes which in the early 1980s were designed to serve the Iraqi people as focus for their political identification and its collective historical memory.

Homeland that spreads wing to the horizon / And clad itself in civilizations as mark of honor / Blessed is the Land of Two Rivers, homeland wherein / splendor and resolve, majesty and grandeur / This land is a flame and splendor / and loftiness that dwarfs the sky / Lofty mountain at the peak of the world / And the pride implanted within us by these lowlands [in the south] / Babylon inside us, Ashur is ours / and with us history is filled with glow / among mankind we alone / combine the wrath of the sword and the forebearance and sagacity of the prophets / When we ignited the Arab sand with revolution / and bore the banner of liberation as thinkers / Since al-Muthanna assembled the horses with light hand / and Salah al-Din covered the [sand] with lances / Oh the flying columns of the Ba'th, Oh the lion of the thicket / March like horror towards the decisive victory / and resurrect in our land the age of Harun al-Rashid / our heroic people, glory and eruption / and fortresses of might that the comrades build / you will always be to the Arabs a shield, Oh Iraq / and suns that turn the night into morning.[39]

9 The Changing Features of the Past: Re-writing History

ANCIENT MESOPOTAMIANS AND CONTEMPORARY IRAQIS

In coaxing the people of Iraq into viewing themselves as somehow related to Mesopotamia's ancient inhabitants, the Iraqi media were confronted with a difficulty. Since important sections of the country's intellectual community did not consider Babylonians and Assyrians to have been Arabs, any outright identification of the Iraqi people with the ancient Mesopotamians could be construed as undercutting the Arab character of the former. While such an interpretation was of no concern to the Qasim government, it was a different matter for a pan-Arab regime. Consequently, so long as the ancient Mesopotamians were not Arabized – a process initiated only in the late 1970s – proponents of the new trend usually resorted to equivocal allusions. But despite this intentional blurring of the issue, some outlines did emerge, exhibiting a continuum that extends between two extreme poles. One of these is the conservative view which justifies Iraqis in taking pride in their country's past, but only insofar as it served as a cradle for a succession of great civilizations. At the other pole, one finds the conviction, expressed with varying degrees of clarity, that modern Iraqis are the offspring, and sole legitimate cultural heirs, of the Sumerians, Babylonians, Assyrians and their civilizations. Between these poles lies a broad range of shades and hues, of which we will deal here only with the most coherent.

Not surprisingly, the conservative approach, in its purest form, was expounded in the internal organ of the pan-Arab leadership of the Ba'th party:

> From the beginning of history, ancient civilizations like the Assyrian, Chaldean, Babylonian and the Arab [Islamic] one, particularly during the Abbasid era, flourished in Iraq and actively participated in developing and advancing human societies.[1]

Other sources, while showing a greater attachment to, and pride in, the history of the land, remained essentially true to this approach, academically

97

self-evident and ideologically acceptable to even the most orthodox of pan-Arab Iraqis. An example of this hue is the following:

> Our beloved homeland, Iraq, the cradle of many civilizations and cultures . . . where many nations . . . and religions lived from the time of the Sumerian and Akkadian civilization.[2]

At the other extremity, one finds the view that the Iraqis are the heirs, cultural and racial, of the earlier inhabitants. As early as 1969, this view was expressed, obliquely yet unmistakably, in a report of a study of the Arabs of Asia, conducted by a Soviet professor. His conclusions, whereby the Iraqis possess 'a national character', and are distinguished in physical appearance from their Syrian and Lebanese brethren, are rendered in full, without the slightest effort towards their refutation.[3]

Ideologues and researchers, when referring to Sumerians, Babylonians etc., have made frequent resort to equivocal terms like 'the Iraqi woman', 'the Iraqi man', 'our great ancestors'; or, at times, 'our ancient grandfathers' (*ajdaduna al-qudama, aba' una, al-judud*) and similar expressions indicative of a blood-relationship.[4]

After ideologues and intellectuals had hammered in the Arab character of Mesopotamia's ancient peoples, it became much easier, and accordingly, much more prevalent, to identify modern Iraqis as their direct offspring. Thus, it was not exceptional to come across an article, published on Revolution Day 1979, which expresses a profound sense of the perennial unity between land and people through the ages. Referring to Tammuz [July], the month of the Ba'th revolution, a party ideologue wrote:

> If we look at the events of the month of Tammuz in our country, we find that many revolutions occurred in it, resulting in the welfare of our people [!]. This includes the first liberation movement aimed against foreign rule in Iraq, when the Sumerian King of al-Warka', Utu-hegal . . . 2116 BC revolted against the foreign . . . invaders . . . [which led] to liberation and independence for the dwellers of Iraq . . . One may say that Tammuz is the month of good fortune for the Iraqis because it is [also] the month of the God Tammuz . . . [5]

Not surprisingly, it is the Christian Chaldean intellectual magazine, *Bayn al-Nahrayn*, that exhibits the deepest sense of unity – cultural, spiritual and even ethnic – between modern Iraqis and Mesopotamians, considered by the editor to be the same people [*sha'b*]. Furthermore, this magazine regards the Arabs with a measure of estrangement; in relation to the Iraqi people, they are perceived almost as a different nation, like Turks, Persians and even Mongols.[6]

Somewhere between these two extremes lies the position stressing the strong bond, cultural rather than racial, which links most civilizations that flourished on Iraqi soil. A particularly forthcoming example of such an approach was provided by an Iraqi intellectual who stressed both the continuity of Iraqi cultural genius and its unique quality:

> [Foreign occupation] of the Middle East and North Africa . . . did not sever the bond between the . . . Babylonian civilization and the Islamic one . . . Hellenism, which arrived here with Alexander, . . . did not influence the region's basic civilizational structure as deeply as seen by most historians . . . [This way a] civilizational continuum was created, influenced by external events [but] not to the degree of a rupture.

According to the afore mentioned intellectual, the philosophy of the Medieval thinker al-Mutanabbi could serve to illustrate this unbroken cultural continuity. He was said to have been 'expressing feelings which accumulated in the depth of his heart, . . . [yet] their real age dates back to Babylon and Nineveh'.

Summing up, the author wrote:

> Iraq is the land of intellectual activity and the homeland of the resolute and powerful ones . . . The people of Iraq are people of vision and piercing sagacity, and with sagacity and vision come exploration and research.[7]

The above are just a few of many other articles which appeared throughout the 1970s with a view of Iraqi history as a cultural continuum.[8]

MESOPOTAMIANS AND ARABS: A DICHOTOMY, 1968–77

The 1960s and the first half of the 1970s witnessed only a few attempts to bestow an Arab pedigree upon Akkadians, Babylonians and ancient Mesopotamia's other Semitic peoples; characterizations of Mesopotamia as an Arab heritage were rare and far between.[9] This probably stemmed from a realization that such a claim was difficult to substantiate academically, and that, in any case, such an attempt would foil the campaign in one of its main goals of creating a common past for all Iraqis: Arabs, Kurds and others.

In almost all instances of its discussion within the ideological context of Iraqi *wataniyya*, ancient Mesopotamia, with the exception of Hatra, was treated as an Iraqi, not an all-Arab, heritage. The parades of the Mosul Spring Festival, which embraced both pre-Islamic and Islamic eras, offer a particularly instructive example of this dichotomy. In commenting on the significance of the various floats, the journalists of *al-Thawra* and *al-Jumhuriyya* referred to Sumerians, Assyrians and Babylonians as Iraqis, not Arabs. These parades portrayed the Iraqi people as an entity 5000 (or, in one instance, 200,000) years old, traversing numerous civilizations (of which the Islamic-Arab, while very important, was only one) but retaining its special character.[10]

When some parades portrayed Nebuchadnezzar as liberator of Palestine, the implication may have been that he was an Arab; but if so, the absence of any explicit mention thereof left readers to make their own inference. The Arab affiliation of the modern Iraqi people was, of course, never placed in doubt. Nevertheless, most of the sources which sought to promote the Mesopotamian identification, presented Iraq's near-eternal people as the only link connecting the modern Arab nation with the great civilizations of Akkad, Babylon and Assyria (and, on occasion, even Sumer). Viewed from a different angle, Islamic-Arab civilization, and Arabism as a whole, seem to appear as the latest incarnation of the new-old Iraqi people.

An examination of the equation's other side, namely, sources devoted to promotion of the Arab heritage, discovers a complementary perception. In numerous academic and semi-academic articles published throughout the 1970s, only the history and civilization of the Arabic-speaking tribes and small kingdoms immediately preceding the Islamic era, or, more often, those of the Islamic-Arab era itself, were regarded as an Arab heritage.

This is evident, for example, in the terms of reference of Baghdad University's Center for the Revival of the Arab Scientific Heritage. Had Babylon been considered Arab, its science could not have been overlooked. However, the terms refer to the 'influence of the achievements of Arab scientists in the Middle Ages on the development of sciences . . . in Europe'; they recall the need to collect and research 'manuscripts', but with no mention of cuneiform or tablets, and none whatsoever of Babylon.[11]

In other cases, in discussing the history of the Arabs in Mesopotamia, there was recourse to Assyrian, or even Sumerian, sources, to prove that Arabs were indeed present there from very early times. They were, however, clearly distinguished from Assyrians and other ancient peoples, though some kinship and close historical contacts were usually claimed.[12] A reminder that many Iraqi intellectuals did not regard the Mesopotamians as Arabs appeared in the country's leading intellectual magazine, which was designed for an all-Arab audience no less than a domestic readership. At the 1977 11th Congress of Arab Writers, a leading Iraqi critic, seeking to justify al-Sayyab and al-Bayyati in their use of Babylonian and Assyrian themes, claimed the latter as part of the 'Arab heritage'. In a sharp response, another critic made the sarcastic point that, while his adversary may have proved 'that all Arabs are Semites', he had failed to offer convincing evidence that 'all Semites were Arabs'.[13]

BRIDGING THE GAP

Following upon almost a decade of ambivalence regarding the relationship between the Arab and Mesopotamian components of the modern Iraqi people, Saddam Husayn, in an address to the Bureau of Information, apparently sought to defuse suspicions that Iraq was covertly embarking upon a secessionist course; to endow the Mesopotamian trend with pan-Arab legitimacy, he advised Iraqi historians to reconsider the history of their nation:

> The history of the Arab nation does not start with Islam. Rather, it reaches back into ages of remote antiquity . . . All basic civilizations that emerged in the Arab homeland were expressions of the personality of the sons of the [Arab] nation, who emerged from one single source.

Simultaneously seeking to justify Iraq's efforts to foster its local culture, ancient and modern, he added:

> [even] if these ancient civilizations had some indigenous attributes, [it should be said that] the local personality is nothing but a part of the more general and total pan-Arab character.[14]

The most obvious way of substantiating the Arab character of Mesopotamians lay in referring to certain archeologists, who point to the Arabian peninsula as origin of all or most Semites, in pre-historic as well as historic times. This theory was known to some Arab intellectuals and well known to school teachers (and, apparently, to pupils) in monarchist

Iraq, when Saddam Husayn and his generation were schoolboys.[15] The Mesopotamians should, accordingly, be regarded as Arabs (or Arabians). This was, indeed, the precise course adopted by most of those who sought to Arabise the ancient Middle East; in the words of the veteran archeologist, Taha Baqir:

> This fact does not leave room for doubt that, historically, the correct name for these people . . . called Semites is . . . the people of the Arab peninsula or simply Arabs.[16]

From the viewpoint of pan-Arab ideology, this approach entails at least one great difficulty. Its first aspect is that to claim all Semites as Arabs on the grounds of a common geographical habitat in antiquity, comes very close to (and is almost inseparable from) the thorny contention that Arabism derives from a common racial origin. The second aspect of the difficulty is that, whatever their origins or pedigree, Akkadians, Babylonians and Assyrians spoke languages mutually distinct and quite unlike Arabic. Claiming them as Arabs revives a question widely debated since the 1920s, i.e., who is an Arab?

Mindful of the great racial diversity of the Arabic-speaking people, pan-Arab thinkers, including Ba'thists, have traditionally steered clear of giving Arab nationalism a racial definition, preferring to define it in terms of a common language and culture and a shared history (dating back only a few hundred years before Islam) – what 'Aflaq termed 'a living memory' of that history, and a love of the nation.[17]

When the Arab character of the ancient Egyptians came up for discussion, this theoretical issue posed a problem, as was conceded by Baqir, and by Dr Ahmad Susa, a Jewish convert to Islam who became a member of Iraq's Academy of Science and wrote a large work on the subject:

> [The Semites] emigrated [from the Arabian peninsula] and mixed there [in Egypt] with the negroes of the Nile Valley, and from them and the original dwellers [of the Nile Valley], the Egyptians, as we know them in history, emerged.[18]

If indeed, the Arab character really derives from a common geographical or racial source, the reader may therefore conclude that the Egyptians can be regarded, at best, as half-Arab.

A Jordanian member of the pan-Arab leadership, Munif al-Razzaz, tried an approach more in line with traditional pan-Arab thinking. Although agreeing that their 'Arabian' origin created some bond between the ancient Semites and the Arab nation, his emphasis lay elsewhere. In his view, the ancient peoples of the present-day Arab homeland, and their civilizations, should be regarded as part of 'Arab history' (as distinct from the 'Arab nation') because, even prior to the Muslim conquests, all these peoples closely resembled one another, and the Arabs, by virtue of three civilizational factors. These were: the influence of the desert, the linguistic affinity between Hamitic and Semitic languages, and 'the everlasting drive in their civilizations towards monotheism'.[19] (Factually at least, if not necessarily as characteristics of an Arab affinity, the first two are valid; the third, however, is far-fetched, as the Babylonians were hardly noted for a striving towards monotheism.)

Another way of identifying all Arabs (and not Iraqis alone) with the region's ancient civilizations, was by claiming a virtually direct and unbroken transmission of cultural heritage. The more obvious substantiation of this claim, resorted to by many participants in the campaign to Arabize the ancients, was to point out, as did Taha Baqir, that the Islamic-Arab civilization, in its spread in the Middle East, created a 'crucible in which the various nationalities, races and stocks melted together . . . and a civilizational unity was created – the first one of its kind in the history of man'.[20]

In his effort to substantiate the claim that the 'Arab Islamic civilization was the legitimate heir to the [ancient] civilizations', Baqir sought to prove that those of Mesopotamia were linked with the inhabitants of the Arabian peninsula's eastern shore by unbroken ties – cultural, economic and political – which, he and others claimed, started in the Sumerian era, carrying through to the new Babylonian (Chaldean) period. Although implicitly admitting that these ties were ruptured when Babylon fell to the Persians in 538 BC, Baqir contended that the rupture was incomplete; in addition to whatever heritage Islamic-Arab civilization drew from the Greeks, or from ancient Mesopotamia via the Greeks, there was much, mainly in mathematics and astronomy, that they inherited directly from their Mesopotamian predecessors, via Aramaic- and Arabic-speaking cultures that sprang up in what is now the Arab east, creating a cultural bridge that spans the problematic millennium (538 BC to AD 635)[21]

The common birthplace (or racial source) is thus seen as merely the starting point of a long, common history in the course of which a common heritage was created and transmitted. However, this transmission, which Baqir located east of the Mediterranean, again left out the Egyptians and North Africans, until the Islamic conquests.

As already noted regarding the theory of the Arabian peninsula as the common source, its difficulty has a second aspect, that of language. Phoenician and Assyrian, for example, are recognized by Ba'thi intellectuals as quite distinct from Arabic, as well as from one another.[22] Presumably due to his realization that this made it very difficult to regard the ancient Semitic peoples as full-fledged Arabs (if one chooses to stick to the traditional definition of Arab character), Razzaz qualified his advocacy of the 'Arabian' theory:

> It is not easy to say that all those who migrated from the Arab Peninsula and established civilizations around it are Arabs and that we should accept it without comment. If we did this we would have been unavoidably accused of clannishness [*ta'assub*] and of historical fabrication[!]. This, because although the Assyrians, Canaanites and Chaldeans are connected with Arab history, we do not allow ourselves to say they were Arabs . . . The Arabs are [only] one of [many] branches of the great civilizational development that emerged from the Arab Peninsula and spread through the neighboring countries.

Nevertheless, since 'this [Arab] branch, after Islam and the Koran, was able to absorb all the [other] branches', denoting that 'the fountain is one and the estuary one', Razzaz too regarded 'what preceded the Arabs' [!] in the Arab homeland to be 'a part of Arab history'.[23]

Being possessed of much greater resolve to Arabize the Mesopotamians, Ahmad Susa and others were impatient with such academic reservations. Susa's aim was, essentially, to prove that the language spoken in the Arab Peninsula, primeval homeland of all Semites, was virtually identical with Arabic. This way, differences between, for example, Arabic and Babylonian, could be played down, as the latter could be seen merely as a dialect springing from the former.[24] Referring to some Western authorities, Susa pointed out that literary Arabic is the living language closest to proto-Semitic, or as he would have it, proto-Arabic. Then, to leave no doubt that the proto-Semitic language was very close to today's Arabic, Susa quoted J. Philby to wit:

> The Semites . . . were most certainly Arabs who spoke Arabic and immigrated from . . . the southern Peninsula . . . after palaeolithic times.[25]

In the absence of any similar claim regarding Hamitic languages or Berber, the ideological difficulty of the Arab character of the ancient Egyptians and North Africans, essentially unaddressed, inevitably re-emerges. Viewed from the academic angle (a valid one, since the drive to Arabize the ancients rests largely on academics, and is meant to impress the reader with its academic integrity) the chief difficulty lies in the lack of agreement among linguists and historians on the 'family tree' theory which lies at the heart of the whole campaign, and which posits the emergence from Arabia of successive waves of Semitic peoples, starting with the Akkadians and ending with the Muslim-Arabs.[26] In an effort to endow the Arab nation with an unmatched past, but also to settle accounts with some orthodox religious circles, Susa claimed an 'ancient Arab civilization' existing in the Arab Peninsula 20,000 years ago; it was 'a river civilization no less important than the civilization of the Nile Valley and that of Mesopotamia'. According to Susa, all this points to a single conclusion:

No Semites and no *Jahiliyya*, but [rather] Arab character and advancement that existed in the Arab Peninsula since man knew nationalism [!] [*qawmiyya*] and civilization 20,000 years ago.[27]

There can be little doubt that this particular pride in the pre-Islamic period was designed to rebuff traditional Muslim circles who probably viewed the revival of pagan cultures with some apprehension.

While active and systematic participation in the effort to Arabize the ancients was confined to a small number, their articles and books are widely read, and their views are also disseminated by other means. Consequently, since 1978–79, most sources concerned with promotion of the Mesopotamian heritage have presented it in no uncertain terms as Arab, eventually making this line well-nigh omnipresent.[28]

Once the ancient Mesopotamians were officially regarded as Arabs, removing the ideological difficulty involved in the dichotomy between them, Iraqi politicians, artists and poets could relate to the history of the modern Arab-Iraqi people as a single, unbroken continuity. Thus, for example, a decade later, in an interview to the Egyptian press, First Deputy Prime Minister Taha Yasin Ramadan was able to praise his president as a personality unique in all the long and illustrious history of the Iraqi people:

The Iraqi president Saddam Husayn became a symbol to the Iraqi people . . He is no longer simply a president that may be sacrificed, even if this were the price for peace, as claimed by Iran. This, because the Iraqi people correctly believe that throughout its whole long history, ancient and modern, beginning with Babylon, Assyria and Chaldea, and ending with Arab-Islam, it never had such a leadership that captured all the people's hopes as is the case now with the personality of President Saddam Husayn.[29]

Establishment, or acceptance, of the concept affirming the Arab character of all the ancient peoples who lived in what is today the Arab East did not prevent Iraqi authors from taking pride in their own particular local history. If anything, the Arabization of the Mesopotamians made it easier to stress Iraq's uniqueness, and, occasionally, even seniority, within the Arab family. This applies to ancient times, but occasionally spills over into the conviction that the historical mission discharged by ancient Iraq also extends into the present and future, entailing the obligation to serve, or lead, as the case may be, the Arab nation, and, frequently, to make major contributions to civilized humanity as a whole.

A natural target for a superiority contest was Egypt, the other great and famous culture of the Middle East of antiquity. Ahmad Susa's book sets an example to other Iraqi intellectuals on how to bring out Iraq's historical uniqueness, and how to compare the cultures of Egypt and of Iraq. Of twenty-five chapters in his *Arab Civilization*, twelve are devoted to the pre-historical era in the Arab Peninsula, eight to Mesopotamian history, three to the Peninsula's small pre-Islamic Arab kingdoms, and only one to Egypt. Furthermore, in Susa's view the Egyptian culture does not compare favorably with that of Mesopotamia. As seen by Susa, Mesopotamian civilization, in the course of over two thousand years, was repeatedly wiped out and resurrected.

> This gave it continuity and purity of origin [*asala*], as different from the ancient Egyptian civilization which . . . ended with the end of its ancient era. [The fate of the Egyptian] was similar to what befell the Sumerian civilization, which perished as a result of the triumph of the Semites . . . in Mesopotamia.

Conveniently citing a British authority, Susa added:

> It is easy to understand the reason why the dwellers of the plains of the Euphrates excelled over their competitors, the dwellers of the Nile plains. This, because everything in Egypt is easy . . . The Nile . . . was and still is flowing in perfect order and sedateness, bearing every year balanced quantities of sediments, and thus it does not create difficult problems for those who live on its banks . . . However, the situation in Iraq is different . . . The sweeping floods . . . need to be overcome . . . Then, [Iraq's] winter is very difficult while its summer

is extremely hot and long . . . This is the harsh school in which the dwellers of Babylon grew up, and this is what created in them this sharpness of perception and great intellectual capacity.[30]

Within this context, Susa is convinced that 'the civilization of the Arab nation, the mother of ancient civilizations . . . which necessarily will flourish again as happened in the past' and will shine upon the rest of the Arab world, is that of Mesopotamia, not that of the Nile Valley.[31]

The conviction that its long, unique history charges Iraq with special pan-Arab responsibilities in the present and future, was expressed in ideological and political rather than academic contexts. It first surfaced in an explicit form in the RCC communique following the Camp David Accords that launched Egypt, temporarily at least, on a separate course, thus sparking a grave crisis in pan-Arab opinion but simultaneously opening new vistas before veteran contenders for Arab leadership:

It is clear that the Arab arena is waiting for a veteran knight, capable of confronting the challenges . . . of scattering the darkness and . . . frustration. The eyes of the Arab people everywhere are turned towards your glorious revolution in this [Iraqi] region . . . It was imperative that your party . . . and revolution should step forward to [under]take all the historical responsibility, [and carry] the weight of Iraqi history, ancient and modern, in defending the dignity of the [Arab] nation . . . Iraq always had a well-known interest in the struggle against Zionism and in the liberation of Palestine, since the era of the Assyrians and the Babylonians, and in the age of Saladin, as well as in the 1948 war and the October 1973 war, until this very day . . . [32]

Heralding an Iraqi willingness to bury the hatchet with Syria and re-embark on pan-Arab activity after six to seven years of relative seclusion, this communique bore at least one further message: this time, Iraq would refuse to 'immerse itself in the pan-Arab' and lose itself in the process. Another implied message in this unusual statement set Iraq's price for cooperation in the newly-opened Palestine front, and for unity talks with Syria: recognition of Baghdad's leadership. In the late 1960s, under President Bakr, it was admittedly not uncommon to encounter Iraqi attempts to seize upon the Palestine issue and the ideological theme of the 'Arab revolution' for a settling of accounts with rival Arab regimes. Speaking in the context of the liberation of Palestine, President Bakr himself referred to Iraq's elevation 'to the stage of pan-Arab action' and to Iraq's 'historical duty'.[33] However, there are two major differences between this and the

Ba'th stance in the late 1970s: first, in 1968–69, Bakr's commitment to the Palestinian cause (or his quest for Iraqi pre-eminence) made him ready to risk his country's wellbeing, whereas in 1979, the deputy-chairman of the RCC Saddam Husayn exercised his scale of priorities to rule out an immediate military campaign:

> If you say 'we wish to defeat . . . our Zionist enemy', it is imperative that you build [first] an Iraq that will be scientifically, economically and militarily strong . . . [34]

Moreover, since 1978, the concept of Iraq's leadership in defence of the Arab nation has acquired breathtaking historical depth:

> From here Nebuchadnezzar set forth and arrested the elements that tried to degrade the land of the Arabs . . . and brought them chained to Babylon.[35] Your grandfathers went to Palestine when it was occupied, and deliverance came from here, from this [Iraqi] soil . . . Palestine is a trust with you, despite the respect we feel towards our Arab brothers whom we hope will all have a leadership role [?] . . . the liberation of Palestine lies, first and foremost, on your shoulders . . . You should aspire not only to build a strong, flourishing Iraq, but also . . . to a conspicuous pan-Arab leadership role in the liberation of the whole Arab nation.[36]

This new historical dimension represents a major change in the Iraqi Ba'th perception of their country's role in the Arab world.

As Iraqi sources concede, the turmoil in Tehran which ultimately brought Khomeini to power has threatened Iraq's political community with dismemberment.[37] In view of this menace, it was only natural that, in a tour of the Shi'i south, and in many subsequent speeches delivered around the country, Saddam Husayn, while stressing Iraq's uniqueness and primacy within the Arab nation – so vital during unity talks with Syria – should emphasize the common past, long and unrivalled, which bound all Iraqis, and the brightness of the common future awaiting them if they stuck together.

> The Iraqi people turned in the shadow of the July 17 revolution into one cell, one tree . . . stretching from Zakhu [in the north] to al-Faw [in the south] . . . In Iraq there are capacities that enable it to become a radiating center in the Arab homeland . . . It is essential that we wrest the historical opportunity [to play] the historical role performed by our grandfathers in the service of the nation and humanity.[38]

> Iraqi history teaches us that your grandfathers [*ajdad*] were always the source of the right ideas and of science, and this is how they were before . . . [the rise of] Islam [and Sunni-Shi'i schism]. It is well known that long before [the rise of] Islam, Hammurabi's laws set an example to others, and that the civilizations of Babylon, Assyria and Sumer were the cradle of world civilization. This is how you Iraqis were five thousand years ago. Today you are called upon to revitalize this eternal heritage by establishing a new civilization . . . for Iraq, . . . the Arab nation and the world at large.[39]

> After hundreds of years, history is turning full circle to come back and settle again in Iraq . . . This is your historical opportunity.[40]

Similar expressions of pride in Iraq's past, Islamic and pre-Islamic, and future, and a conviction of the centrality of Iraq's leadership role in the Arab world, have been fairly common since the late 1970s. An example of this trend are the closing lines of Iraq's new national anthem: 'May you always be to the Arabs shelter, O Iraq/And suns that turn the night into day.'

At the end of the Gulf war, Iraq's newly-found military prowess, and chiefly its missile technology and chemical weapons, served as yet another justification for its claim to Arab leadership. 'Scientific advancement and . . . military power . . . elevate the position of states in the world', explained a Brig. General in the government daily, and due to its success in launching the Tammuz missile, he promised that Iraq too would play a greater role on the regional and world arenas. 'Iraq of the New Man', added another commentator in the same daily, 'is the robust wall of the Arab nation and . . . its long arm'. 'The historical leader, President Saddam Husayn', argued the ministry of defense daily, is Iraq's successful contribution and 'the ideal example' for 'the Strategic Leader' awaited by the Arab nation. And the party daily, exuberant over the reportedly successful launch of the Tammuz I, called the missile 'Tammuz of the sacrifice and benevolence and revolution . . . from Ishtar's Tammuz [in antiquity] to our contemporary, glorious Tammuz'. The 2000 km missile, concluded *al-Thawra*, is 'a new ray of light beaming, shining, from our leader's forehead . . . to the whole world'.[41]

PERSIANS, JEWS AND IRAQIS

Since the early years of the 'Mesopotamian' trend which has characterized the second Ba'th regime, Iraqi intellectuals tend to regard their country's Persian, Achaemenian, Hellenistic, Persian-Sassanid and Turkish-Ottoman eras as periods of foreign occupation to be excluded from the legitimate history of their homeland, and, much more clearly, of their people.[42] This inclination is doubly poignant in relation to the period of domination by Persia: after all, Persia (like Greece and Turkey) still exists, and its culture therefore cannot be claimed; moreover, it remains a close neighbor and a formidable foe. Accordingly, Persia's contribution to Mesopotamian civilization is often characterized as negative, particularly since Khomeini's rise to power and the September 1980 onset of the Gulf War. As seen by Iraqi scholars, politicians and ideologues, the Iraqi-Persian confrontation is 5000 years old. It started when an expansionist ruler in Elam 'and his greedy priest Khomeini' coveted territories held by the Sumerian prince of al-Warka [Uruk]. It resumed in the third millennium BC, during the reign of Sargon I, when the 'foreign, greedy' Elamites attempted to seize portions of Akkad; it extended into a long series of Iraqi-Persian confrontations including Cyrus' conquest of Chaldean Babylon, the Sassanid occupation of Iraq and its liberation by the Muslim-Arabs in the battle of Qadisiyya, Persian anti-Arab movements under the Umayyads and Abbasids (such as the Shu'ubiyya and others) and finally, the wars between the Persians and Ottomans (the latter being perceived, in this context, as defenders of the local Iraqi population).[43] This approach, of seeing Iraqi-Iranian relations as spanning thousands of years, is certainly uppermost in the minds of party officials. so much so that, when replying to Iranian Foreign Minister Velayati's claim that 'Iraq is a new country whose life time spans no more than 40 years', Foreign Minister 'Aziz replied contemptuously:

> 'The Iranian mind and thinking is very sick and the Iranian leadership is suffering from schizophrenia. The one familiar with history finds that Iran has been for longer periods of time a part of Iraq . . . Has he forgotten that Iran . . . was part of the Kingdom of Assyria and Babylon?'[44]

Since 1980, the same approach has been adopted towards Iraqi-Jewish relations. The flip side of the concept whereby the Iraqi king Nebuchadnezzar 'liberated' Jerusalem is the notion that the Jews consequently supported Cyrus when he besieged Babylon, and in fact opened the city's gates to him.[45] As pointed out above, this notion made its first appearance in modern Iraq in the late nineteenth century, in Catholic Christian circles, and it was picked up by Muslim-Arabs much later, in the late 1940s and early 1950s, but it appeared in a clearcut political context only after the Israeli raid on Iraq's nuclear reactor. Seeking to explain Israel's fear and hostility towards Iraq, *al-Jumhuriyya*'s commentator did not rest content with Iraqi-Zionist confrontations since World War I and the Balfour Declaration; instead, he found a far more convincing explanation for the raid in the fear entertained by Prime Minister Menahem Begin that 'Nebuchadnezzar's spirit' would return to life.[46]

In 1989 the semi-official Dar al-Ma'mun Press published a lengthy study by the well-known Iraqi intellectual Sa'd al-Bazzaz, endeavoring to research Israeli's involvement in the Gulf War. 'Unlike any other land', Bazzaz claimed, Iraq has occupied a position in Zionist ideology where in a profusion of 'historic and religious factors has accumulated.' Zionist thought in this respect is 'the result of nearly two thousand [meaning, rather, over 2500] years of history', dating back to 'the most traumatic incident in their entire history . . . the Babylonian captivity'. This, and what they believe to be a divine promise to give them the land between the Nile and the Euphrates, drove Moshe Dayan as al-Bazzas confidently discloses to his readers, to declare in June 1967: 'We have taken Jerusalem . . . and are now on our way to Yathrib [al-Madina where Jewish tribes lived until the days of the Prophet] and Babylon.' This 'Babylonian complex' is directed 'vehemently' against the Iraqi people, it 'being the heir to the Babylonian heritage'. Finally, while Iranian Jews serve as a bridge between Iran and Israel, says al-Bazzaz, Iraqi Jews, who 'represent a true link with the descendents of those Jews who had suffered the Babylonian capitivity', are thus spearheading the anti-Iraqi hostility inside Israel.[47]

Even an intellectual as level-headed as Foreign Minister Tariq Aziz suggested that Israel's aid to Khomeini is a continuation of Jewish support for the Persians 'during the invasion and occupation of Babylon'.[48] The belief that Iraq is the victim of an extremely durable and intimate Iranian-Jewish coalition may explain the strange phenomenon wherein Iraqi politicians occasionally express their belief that Israel's influence on Iran is so great that it could induce it to start and end wars at will.[49]

10 The Mesopotamian Myth, Pan-Arabism and Islam

Although the new trend won the day at the official level, it is impossible to tell to what extent it actually penetrated the hearts and minds of the vast majority of Iraqis. Superficially, at least, it faced two major obstacles. First, it clashes with traditional pan-Arab concepts; second, it clashes with Islam.

As formulated between the 1920s and 1960s by persons like Husri, 'Aflaq and even the Iraqi Ba'th ideologue Sa'dun Hammadi, pan-Arabism was essentially egalitarian (in the sense of refusing to recognize the superiority of any particular Arab country over its sisters by virtue of its ancient past) and amalgamative. Indeed, 'Aflaq and President Bakr referred only to Iraq's present achievements under the Ba'th, rather than its pedigree or past glory, even when calling for Iraqi leadership of the Arab nation (which 'Aflaq had done only since the late 1970s and which, moreover, they perceived as a phase, rather than as an eternal Iraqi mission).[1] After all, the Arab peoples were ultimately expected to merge and disappear within the pan-Arab melting pot. Those Iraqis committed to traditional pan-Arab concepts may thus find the new notion hard to swallow. But then, even among pan-Arab politicians and intellectuals, pride in their homeland's particular role, Islamic and pre-Islamic, and the wish to restore their country to its past glory, is not such an aberrant phenomenon in modern Iraqi history. Thus, for example, King Faysal I of the Hijaz, in his August 1921 coronation speech in Baghdad, sought to win the support of his new Iraqi subjects to whom he was virtually unknown by harping on the strings of local patriotism:

> Oh noble Iraqis, this land has been in past generations the cradle of civilization and prosperity, and the center of science and knowledge.[2]

In his speech to Baghdad's Chaldean community, he declared:

> I have faith in the Iraqi nation, the sons of those grandfathers, that they will return to [the glory of] . . . their grandfathers.[3]

The famous Iraqi poet Jamil Sidqi al-Zahawi, one of the two leading poets in Iraq during the first half of the twentieth century, echoed these notions in his lines: 'After exhaustion and relapse / Baghdad will return to its glorious past.'[4]

Over a decade later, Dr Sami Shawkat, Director-General of Education, addressing high school students upon inauguration of a program of military training for them, said:

> Iraq's ambition [literally 'hope'] extends to all the Arab countries . . . On the banks of this formidable [Tigris] river . . . Harun al-Rashid established his throne and . . . ruled over 200 million people. We shall not deserve to be proud of him and claim that we are his grandsons if we do not rebuild what he constructed. The spirits of al-Rashid and al-Ma'mun want that Iraq would have, within a brief time-span, half a million soldiers and hundreds of airplanes . . .
>
> To power [then], O youth, raising high the banner of [King] Faysal [I], heir (*khalifat*) of Harun al-Rashid.[5]

In another enthusiastic speech, he urged:

> Let each one of us . . . repeat Harun al-Rashid's words when talking to a cloud that passed above Baghdad without raining: 'Go, rain, wherever you wish, because the yield of your rain will necessarily end up in my treasuries.'[6]

And again:

> Within the next fifty years, Iraq will be a formidable state that will dictate its will to the nations of the Middle East and decide their future as it did under al-Rashid and al-Ma'mun, or else it will succumb to imperialism and exploitation.[7]

It may be argued that Shawkat was 'merely an intellectual'; but he was put in charge of education in Iraq, and for his book to be published in Baghdad, it must have won official approval. Furthermore, he was a member of al-Muthanna club, a meeting place for anti-British intellectuals, politicians and senior army officers, and his views may be presumed to have been shared by other club members (who included Lt. Col. Salah al-Din al-Sabbagh, the moving spirit behind Rashid Ali al-Kaylani and his anti-British revolt of 1941). That such was indeed the case may be implied by the draft of the 'Covenant for the League of the Defenders of Arabism', which al-Sabbagh discussed at his home in April 1938, with General Taha al-Hashimi (who would become prime minister February through April 1941) Amin al-'Umari and Yunis al-Sab'awi (all of whom were associated with the club). The 'Covenant' called for application of Iraq's military might (à la Bismarck or Garibaldi) for the unification of the Arab nation.[8]

Similar notions, though expressed in a far less aggressive manner, feature in a book written in 1954 by the then-prime minister, the Kazimayn-born and American-educated Dr Fadil al-Jamali, earlier Director-General of Education and Minister of Education. Jamali wrote that, as scientists conceded, Iraq is 'the earliest cradle of human civilization', which commenced in 5000 BC at Tel Hasuna. Mesopotamia endowed mankind with writing, law, astronomy, land and sea transportation, art, religion and geometry which pre-dated Euclid. Under the Abbasids, Baghdad became 'the world main capital', and the retarded West 'turned to our country to see the light'. Present-day Iraq, Jamali argued, 'is the [legitimate] heir of the civilizations of Hasuna . . . Sumer, Akkad, Babylon, Assyria, Chaldea, Greece, Persia, and that of the Arabs, who never left Iraq from earliest history to our day'. As Jamali saw it, Iraq also fulfilled another great humanitarian mission; the Assyrian King Shalmanesser who defeated the Israeli King Yehu 'was the first Iraqi king to work towards the liberation of Palestine from the Israelites'. He was followed by Sargon II, who exiled the Israelites to northern Iraq; but 'the decisive move was made by Nebuchadnezzar, who took the Israelites prisoners in the 6th century B.C.'. Jamali's pride in Iraq's past great services to mankind is intertwined with his belief that it now has a similar 'mission' to discharge, the liberation and unification of the Arabs.[9] The book's importance is not confined to its composition by a serving prime minister – in itself highly significant – but also in the fact that the author was a politician whose success stemmed chiefly from his prudent occupation of the dead-center of the political and ideological consensus prevailing in Baghdad at any time. Rather than being a one-man manifesto, his book should thus be regarded as evidence of the political atmosphere reigning in the Iraqi capital in the early 1950s. It also means that Saddam Husayn and his circle, in their turn, built upon existing foundations of Iraqi-centered pan-Arabism.

This seemingly novel approach to pan-Arabism being well-rooted in Baghdad (though, clearly, not in traditional Ba'th philosophy) it could be suggested that, as long as the new trend remains within some sort of pan-Arab framework, Iraq's secular pan-Arab community may find it easier to accept than may appear at first glance.

However, Islam's attitude to glorification of Mesopotamia's ancient pre-Islamic cultures is entirely different. To Islamic eyes, these cultures all come under the loathsome characterization of *jahiliyya*, i.e., a state of paganism, ignorance and barbarism.

Bearing this in mind, it should not be very difficult to guess what may be the attitude of the *ulama* towards the revival of an ancient culture wherein a central role is played by figures like Ishtar and Tammuz.[10] Furthermore, even figures like Nebuchadnezzar, or Sargon, widely acclaimed as conquerors of Judea and Israel, would be problematic in the eyes of those versed in Islamic tradition. Although in some places, Nebuchadnezzar gains favorable reference,[11] in more than one source he and Sennacherib are seen as the scourges of God – necessary but cruel and inhuman.[12] In at least one source, Nebuchadnezzar is viewed as a blasphemer who suffers divine retribution through being transformed into a she-ass, and Sennacherib is depicted as dishonest.[13] Pagan Mesopotamian figures, however, are problematic not only from the viewpoint of Islamic *hadith*, which may be known only to scholars, but also, as reported by an Iraqi pro-Ba‘thi intellectual, from that of ‘the overwhelming majority’ of Iraqis who knew something at all about ancient Mesopotamia.

The monumental statues which remained standing at Hatra were to them [the peasants] the heathen people of King Nimrod, who rejected the prophet Abraham and in punishment, Allah turned them into stone. ‘I saw with my own eyes engraved on their chests Allah’s curse on them, inscribed in God’s own writing which only the angels could read.’[14]

So said an old peasant woman from the Mosul area, probably referring to the many Aramaic writings engraved on the stones of Hatra.

To place matters in their correct perspective, however, it should be pointed out that Iraq’s religious Shi‘i opposition to the Ba‘th regime withholds all mention of the Mesopotamian component of the regime’s ideology and culture. Shi‘i religious activists have evaded the subject in their publications between 1979 and 1989. Disregard of so conspicuous an official trend can hardly be regarded as fortuitous. It may be assumed, therefore, that the Shi‘i opposition is reluctant to indulge in overt opposition to a trend they believe to be popular with educated Iraqis, Shi‘i no less than Sunni.

The Ba‘th regime, for its part, is anxious to convince the more conservative segments of the Iraqi population that, the party’s longstanding commitment to separation of religion and state notwithstanding, the nation’s leaders, as individuals, staunchly adhere to their Islamic faith. In fact, so anxious is the regime to exhibit its Islamic convictions that the line separating the piety of individual leaders and the religious identity of state and regime is, more often than not, blurred beyond recognition. Such is the case when, for example, the media, in addition to presenting the war with Iran as a continuation of ethnic Iraqi-Persian conflicts dating back to pre-Islamic times, depicts it as a Second Qadisiyya – a war between Muslim-Arabs and heathen Persians. Similarly, the president's frequent and highly-publicized visits and prayers at the tombs of Ali and al-Husayn, as well as other shrines and mosques, Sunni and Shi'i, are designed to reassure more traditional Iraqis that, despite evidence to the contrary, their leaders (and, by implication, their country) are not going secular. As a rule, the new national blend Saddam Husayn and his colleagues offer their people in the late 1980s is more conspicuous for its Arab and Islamic (generally, Arab-Islamic) elements, than its Mesopotamian component. But since the mid-1970s this component has become prominent enough so that it can no longer be overlooked or shrugged off. Despite its belated appearance, relative to other elements of modern Iraq's national identity, this component appears sufficiently resilient to persist as long as Iraq remains under its present regime, and, very possibly, under any other secular or semi-secular regime as well. In addition to its infiltration of art and politics, the new creed appears already to have seeped into education: reportedly, Iraqi children from primary school upwards are taught that their civilization is 'at least 8000 years old'. Students at the university have to take Iraqi history classes that start from Sumer.[15] In addition, whereas the late 1970s and early 1980s saw the new theme brought up, on the political level, almost exclusively by Saddam Husayn, in the second half of the 1980s, it was picked up by numerous party officials lower down in the hierarchy.[16] Yet, as long as a thorough field study is not possible, it is impossible to evaluate to what degree the new trend has hit roots among the vast majority of the Iraqi people, and most importantly, among the Iraqi intelligentsia.

11 A New Vision of Arab Unity: From Integration to Confederation

A major aspect of party doctrine that had to be modified to suit the needs of the new age was its vision of the political shape of the future united Arab state. Traditional party doctrine held it that, when all the Arab countries unite, a huge melting pot would be created in which the various components, the existing nation states, would be effectively fused and turned into one, new amalgamated society. This vision became extremely problematic once the Ba'th regime set forth to re-mold the national consciousness of its citizens. A five thousand year old nation (or 'people', *sha'b*) as the Iraqis were encouraged to see themselves, can not be expected to disappear overnight even if it does so in the warm embrace of a loving Arab nation; near eternal history precludes or at least implies near eternal future. This issue, however, was so sensitive that it was a full decade before the regime turned to address it.

During the early years of Ba'th rule in Iraq, a discussion of the ultimate political form of Arab unity was extremely rare.[1] To understand how the Ba'th envisaged the political mold of such unity, we must, therefore, refer back to a document adopted before 1968. The preamble to the resolutions of the October 1963 Eighth pan-Arab Congress contains a quote from 'Aflaq's book, *Fi sabil al-Ba'th*, where he defines unity as creative interaction between the regions undergoing unification, and within each such region per se.

> Unity does not bring the part (*al-juz'*) to lose its character; rather stressing it and deepening it and granting it . . . truth and . . . roots . . . placing the part in its living place, as a portion of the entirety.[2]

While apparently affirming that there shall be no amalgamative unity, and that the 'parts' are to retain their existence, this statement obscures more than it elucidates. 'Aflaq was strict in his use of the term *juz'-ajza'* for 'country' apparently so as to discourage any clinging to the current division of the Arab world. Elsewhere, indeed, he is more precise in delineating the degree of legitimacy he was willing to grant to particularist nationalism: 'We say "the Egyptian people", or "the Syrian people", in a sense approximating to our expression "the people of Alexandria", or "the people of Asyut".'[3]

For a clearer understanding of how the party foresaw the future of the existing states, we must directly consult the resolutions of the Sixth pan-Arab Congress. Generally considered the ideological fountainhead of the 'neo-Ba'th', as foreign observers dubbed the Syrian party after 1966[4] (Lebanese sources habitually referred to 'the Regional [*al-qutri*] Ba'th') these resolutions were consequently seen as a departure from the traditional line. However, their critique of the party's course notwithstanding, there can be no doubt that they were regarded as legitimate and binding by the Ba'th's ''Aflaqite' wing also. Testimony thereto is abundant in Iraq's post-July 1968 dailies, where contemporaneous ideological articles were illustrated, in the upper corners of the page, with quotes from these resolutions, with the source cited.[5] Further evidence is the fact that the Baghdad-based Ba'th adopted the leftist view featured in the *muntalaqat*, on the touchy and controversial issue of which classes to categorize as 'revolutionary'.[6] The *muntalaqat*, in their criticism of the UAR experiment, affirm that future unification called for consideration of the facts, without 'ignoring or leaping over them'. The prolonged divisions within the Arab world had generated 'variegated regional conditions and disparities in economic development' which were reflected in the social, cultural and political spheres. Accordingly, 'it will be proper for the unified structure initially to take these conditions into account, so as to be able to overcome them and gradually eliminate them'. This would be achieved by 'interaction between the countries, which is the sole way to amalgamation (*sahr*)'. Unity was thus to be 'achieved by stages', and it could be deduced that the first stage would be federative, with equal rights for each country. The alternative was 'imposition and annexation' (as in the case of the UAR) and that was doomed to failure. This portrayal of the first stage may also be seen as criticism of the path followed by Michel 'Aflaq, Salah al-Din al-Bitar, Akram Hawrani and other Ba'th veterans who agreed to a hasty integrative unification between Egypt and Syria in 1958.[7]

But a very different picture emerges when the discussion turns to the ultimate form of unity:

> The classical form of federation may possibly be suited to a state with numerous nationalities, or it may merely be a stage and a step towards complete unity. That is because, if the federative union turns

into the culmination of unificatory development, it will become a framework preserving the vestiges of regionalism (*iqlimiyya*) which conform with bourgeois interests and bourgeois logic . . . At the same time, the popular substance of unity requires application of decentralization, or self-rule, which may be seen as the practical application of socialist democracy . . . however, decentralization in local and regional affairs does not have to rest upon the present map of the Arab homeland . . . because *the present entities are not eternal or natural entities, but rather, false entities, simultaneously new and artificial.* Consequently, *the new framework for decentralization of government shall be determined by the conditions of production and the modes of economic and social construction.*[8]

Dr Sa'dun Hammadi, the most important Ba'thi ideologue of Iraqi extraction, was sharply critical of important sections of the *muntalaqat* (as well as of the thinking of the old guard "Aflaqite' pan-Arab leadership, to which he himself belonged) with regard to the organic link between unity and socialism, and the class characteristics of unity's proponents and opponents. Yet, he was in unreserved agreement with the above characterization of unity's ultimate form:

The Arab states, broad in expanse . . . and disparate in their local circumstances, require a regime suited to their conditions . . . [which is] federal unity (*wahda ittihadiyya*) . . . [however] the federal form need not necessarily follow the present geographical divisions . . . [instead] the federal regime shall rest upon economic . . . foundations, for the purpose of fostering regions with particular problems, or according to administrative considerations. It is not essential that Iraq and Syria [as such], for example, should be [preserved in their present form as] two members of this federation, but rather . . . larger or lesser [territorial units].[9]

I have not found a different view, or an utterance open to an entirely different interpretation, in the writings of Ba'th thinkers from the 1960s and early 1970s. On the contrary: in relation to the unity issue, the terminology in use during this period points to an amalgamative form or at least to the disappearance of the existing states. Thus, 'Aflaq and his colleagues refer to their vision in terms of 'the united democratic Arab society', of 'a unified, independent state', of a process of amalgamation or 'smelting down' (*insihar*) in 'the crucible of the single nation' which will leave no residue of 'regionalism' or 'local nationalism' (*al-iqlimiyya*), and so on.[10] A response in a similar vein was proffered by Dr Ahmad 'Abd al-Sattar al-Jawari, minister of state for presidential affairs; while delivering a speech in Kuwait, he was questioned about Iraq's demands for adjustments in its border with its southern neighbor, to which he replied: 'It is unthinkable that Iraq should raise an issue of this nature with any Arab state. For Iraq is a state which, in principle and totally, does not at all believe in borders [between Arab states].'[11] Regardless of the stark hypocrisy of this proclamation, there can be no doubt as to the ideological principle underlying it.

Like other radical positions adopted by the party in its early years, this doctrine underwent profound and substantive modification in the late 1970s and early 1980s.

In March 1979, when hopes surged of unification with Syria, Vice President Husayn granted an interview to one of Iraq's mass-circulation weeklies, to present the Iraqi view on the form of unification:

> The world is moving towards mobility and flexibility in administration. In the unified state, we are required to work out advanced formulae of democracy and greater flexibility in administration, together with the earnest application of unitary relations in practice, not [merely] in form. We have no wish to prejudice unity or shackle the people in inflexible formulae . . . Unity . . . should not skip over objective regional realities, just as it should not give way thereto . . . Unity is not a project of pasting together regional conditions . . . In other words, it will rest upon a decentralized administration which is among the signs of the times.[12]

It should be noted that, unlike the resolutions of the Sixth pan-Arab Congress, Husayn's mention of decentralization did not refer to new regions to be delineated by economic and social considerations; rather, he referred to the two existing states, Iraq and Syria ('regions', *aqtar*, in Ba'th vernacular) within their present boundaries.

Saddam Husayn added a further tier in July 1981:

> We do not say that Arab unity is a state of affairs wherein the local and patriotic [*al-wataniyya*] characteristics will utterly vanish; rather, it is a state of affairs which will generate new shared characteristics, and new links to the nation . . . *The local situation and local uniqueness are not a condition of weakness for the nation* as long as they are under the dome of unity; on the contrary, it is a desirable situation and a genuine source of strength for the nation, whereas *amalgamation which*

abrogates this uniqueness may be a pathological situation which will harm Arab unity.[13]

This point is borne out in the Ninth Regional Congress resolutions, which specify Iraq's unification plan, foreseeing 'a single international entity' but a federative state wherein 'every country will retain its local institutions'. This would preserve the ideological framework favoring unity, but the unified, federal state would be 'balanced and flexible' because after all 'it will express an objective and responsible assessment of the conditions and obstacles which obstruct the process of unity'.[14]

Interviewed in late 1982, the president unexpectedly veered away from a question on the border with Kuwait to pour out his heart:

> Iraqis are now of the opinion that Arab unity can only take place after a clear demarcation of borders between all countries. We further believe that Arab unity must not take place through the elimination of the local and national characteristics of any Arab country. If the people in the Popular Democratic Republic of [South] Yemen and President 'Ali Nasir Muhammad wish to establish unity with Iraq today on the basis of dissolving the Iraqi and Yemeni personalities, I, Saddam Husayn, will personally object to such unity. I will say: Let the two personalities coexist with one another. The question of linking unity to the removal of boundaries is no longer acceptable to present Arab mentality. It could have been acceptable ten or twenty years ago. We have to take into consideration the change which the Arab mind and psyche have undergone. We must see the world as it is. Any Arab would have wished to see the Arab nation as one state with Kuwait as its leader, for example. But these are sheer dreams. The Arab reality is that the Arabs are now twenty two states, and we have to behave accordingly. Therefore, unity must not be imposed, but must be achieved through common fraternal opinion. Unity must give strength to its individual partners, not cancel their national identity.[15]

Finally, in interviews in 1988–89, Saddam Husayn implied that the traditional notion of 'constitutional union' (whether federal or amalgamative) of the Arab states may never come about, and that the pattern of relations which already existed between those Arab countries that cooperated with each other harmoniously may be the final form. The Arabs, he asserted, have already achieved more than 'Abd al-Nasir ever did. 'The outcome of the interaction among the Arab leaders [already] represents the [one] leader awaited by the Arabs,' he concluded.[16] The old notion of unity, he explained in another interview, is gradually giving way to a new one, namely, to improved inter-Arab relations. The existing relations between Iraq, Saudi Arabia, North Yemen, Jordan and Kuwait, he argued, are stronger than those forged between Egypt and Syria within the framework of the UAR (1958–61);[17] namely, between the only two countries in modern Arab history that had actually achieved effective amalgamative unification. The glaring contradiction between Saddam Husayn's idyllic description of Arab harmony that is already in existence, and his own quest for Arab leadership, or his country's acrimonious relations with Kuwait[18] notwithstanding, the theoretical framework is unmistakable: at the end of the 1980s in all but name, Iraq of the Ba'th has relinquished the ideal of Arab unity, replacing it with that of cooperation between fully independent and, apparently, eternal Arab states.

12 Iraq's Opposition Groups and the Iraqi Entity

How typical is the Ba'thist legitimization of the local Iraqi identity of political circles in Iraq other than the ruling party? In the absence of political democracy a field study of public attitudes is impossible. The only alternative, thus, is to study the attitudes of the organized political opposition through their published sources. When the Ba'th came to power the most important such circles were the Iraqi Communist party, the Kurdish Nationalist groupings and the religious Shi'i underground. Between the late 1960s and the late 1980s all three lost much of their clout due to a mixture of severe repression and intimidation, combined with some positive incentives, meant to deprive the leaderships the support of mass following.

The result of these policies was that towards the end of the 1980s the Kurdish and Shi'i opposition foci were, militarily speaking, unable to pose a meaningful threat to the regime and politically speaking all three groups were rendered more marginal than ever before in the history of republican Iraq. However, as no alternative opposition foci have emerged, studying the views of these three groupings may still provide the reader with the views of the most important political groupings outside the Ba'th. And because the three aforementioned groups compete with the Ba'th regime over the hearts and minds of their respective audiences, the views they express, if not actually representing the true feelings of the Iraqi public (or of those of the more limited circles within it towards which the messages are aimed), at least they represent what the various opposition groups believe to be right or, alternately, what are popular with their respective audiences.

Since its inception the ICP and the other Arab Communist parties have always harbored certain reservations in regards to pan-Arabism, and have laid the main ideological stress on the local identities. Thus, in the early and mid-1930s, while expressing general support for the pan-Arab ideal, they were careful all the same to avoid clear-cut support for integrative unity and preferred the federal form. This was the case, for example, with the Congress of the Arab Communist Parties, which convened in 1935; it rejected the slogan of 'unity' [al-wahda], and recommended, instead, 'federations' [*al-ittihad*]. This they did in line with the Comintern's demand that any unification be 'voluntary', 'federal', and that it would safeguard the complete independence of the existing nation-states within the Arab federation,[1] namely, a conception much closer to that of the Arab League than to that of the Ba'th of later years. In the late 1930s the most important Communist leader of the Arab world, the Syrian Kurd, Khalid Bakdash, went even so far as to point out that the Arabs are not one nation. Thus, because of the five attributes of nationhood, as they were defined by Stalin, the Arabs can demonstrate only one: a common language.[2] In 1949 the Soviet union itself, caught in the atmosphere of the cold war, denounced pan-Arabism as 'reactionary', alongside with Zionism, Kemalism and Ghandism.[3] In the second half of the 1950s Arab Communists reverted again to supporting pan-Arabism[4] but when the Egyptian-Syrian unification was announced in 1958 – namely when the theoretical principle was translated into practice – the USSR remained extremely reserved and pretty soon clashed head-on with 'Abd al-Nasir's regime.

The Iraqi Communists, for their part, objected to the Egyptian-Syrian unification, and supported 'Abd al-Karim Qasim's separatist regime and, to counter the slogan of '*Wahda fawriyya shamila*' ['immediate total unity'], raised by the Ba'th and the Nasirites of Iraq, they offered the conception of *al-ittihad* [federation].[5] No doubt, the ICP's objection to Iraq's unification with the UAR stemmed, in part, from practical considerations: the example of Syrian and Egyptian Communists being persecuted and imprisoned under 'Abd al-Nasir could hardly appeal to them. But then there is some evidence that their objection to amalgamative pan-Arabism stemmed also from considerations embedded in Marxist doctrine. One such indication may be found in the famous confrontation between Presidents Gamal 'Abd al-Nasir and 'Abd al-Salam 'Arif on the one hand, and Nikita Khrushchev on the other, during the latter's visit to Egypt in 1964 to inaugurate the Aswan Dam. When the Iraqi President emphasized in his speech Arab nationalism and unity, Khrushchev took the floor to rebut Arif for his 'disregard of deep class division in Arab society'. In his memoirs, Khrushchev defined 'Arab socialism' ('Arif's, but also 'Abd al-Nasir's brand of socialism, fused with pan-Arabism) as an undeveloped phase of Arab political thought, and expressed the hope that it would end up with a ripe form of class consciousness.[6]

As for the ICP, in their official slogan '*watan hurr wa sha'b sa'id*' ['A free homeland and a happy people'] they carefully skirted mention of Arabism altogether, leaving it to the reader to decide whether 'watan' refers to Iraq or to the Arab homeland as a whole. (That 'Sha'b' refers to the local entity is sufficiently clear however, the term usually used for the Arab nation being *umma*.) Indeed, in many of its publications the ICP refers to the Arabs as *'al-Shu'ub al-'arabiyya* [the Arab peoples], rather than 'the Arab-nation'. In times of inter-party tension this practice drew much fire from the Ba'th who claimed that this was evidence of lack of true belief on the part of the ICP in the unity of the Arab nation.[7]

While the ICP was ambivalent, and sometimes clearly hostile towards the notion of Arab unity, however, underneath the umbrella of proletariat internationalism it expressed unreserved allegiance to the concept of an Iraqi people and an Iraqi nation state.

This attachment to the local Iraqi basis of identification may explain why Communist and Communist-inclined intellectuals were and are so prominent among the artists, poets and playwrights who incorporated Mesopotamian themes in their works. This may also explain the great popularity of the Communist press in the Kurdish areas and why, while there were no Kurds (as different from thoroughly-Arabized Kurds) in the Ba'th leadership since its inception, the representation of Kurds at the leadership of the ICP was always high, with a quantum leap at the end of the 1940s and beginning of the 1950s,[8] namely: at the period when the USSR and the Arab Communist parties showed strong reservations towards pan-Arab nationalism. It would seem, then, that the ICP preceded the Ba'th in its belief that, while there is special affinity between the Arab peoples, and that this affinity should be expressed in some political form, this form should not go so far as fully-fledged integration.

As for the other facet of Iraqi nationalism, i.e., internal unity, both in their practice (having a large number of Kurds and Shi'ites among their membership) and in theory the ICP always upheld this unity; even though they traditionally supported the notion of a Kurdish autonomy, they always objected to any secessionist calls.[9]

The religious Shi'i opposition, too, in a way reminiscent of the ICP's commitment to international proletariat solidarity, profess their allegiance to a higher, supra-Iraqi framework, namely, to the establishment of a pan-Muslim political entity. Yet they too are not in a haste to dissolve or fragment the Iraqi nation and its state. Thus, while during World War I and later, during the anti-British revolt of 1920, some Shi'i clergy called for the establishment in Southern Iraq of a Shi'i state that would be based on the *shari'a*,[10] no such calls appeared in the press of the various Shi'i underground movements between 1979 and 1989. On the contrary, even though one comes often across implicitly anti-Sunni texts in this press, the official line of all the movements is ecumenical; they all call upon all the Iraqi Muslims to unite against the Ba'th and promise equality between the various Islamic 'schools' [*madhahib*], as well as between the speakers of Arabic, Kurdish, Persian and Turkish dialects within the future Islamic Iraqi polity.[11] In theory, then, the Shi'i opposition has no reservations towards Arab-Kurdish and Sunni-Shi'i equality and unity within the framework of the Iraqi nation-state. As long as they are in opposition, however, there is no way of studying their practice.

On the no less complex issue of the future of the Iraqi nation and state after the victory of the Islamic revolution there, occasional calls for pan-Islamic unity not withstanding, the main thrust of the written sources unmistakably support the notion that the Iraqi people and its state are not going to dissolve in the crucible of an Iranian-Iraqi union or of a pan-Muslim colossus, at least in the foreseeable future.[12]

This notion is enhanced by the practice of the umbrella organization of the Iraqi Shi'i opposition movements (the Supreme Council of the Islamic Revolution in Iraq [SCIRI]) since it was established in Tehran at the beginning of the Gulf war: not only that it does not encourage the great body of Iraqi exiles in Iran to disappear within the Iranian community, it actively encourages them to preserve their Iraqi identity and to work towards the liberation of their own homeland. It endeavors to create and develop a whole plethora of communal Iraqi institutions, including a distinctly Iraqi military force at the front (the Badr Army), Iraqi mosques, cultural and charity institutions, and it is even engaged in the promotion of a distinctly Iraqi religious Shi'i practice, transplanted from Najaf and Karbala into Komm, namely, the Husayni Processions [*al-mawakib al-husayniyya*], marking the fortieth day to Imam al-Husayn's death at the hands of the Umayad army in Karbala in AD 680.[13] Finally, as pointed out above, unlike the Muslim Brothers in Egypt, who do not hesitate to attack any reference to Egypt's pre-Islamic cultures, the Shi'i opposition chose not to assail the regime over its search of 'Mesopotamian' roots for the Iraqi people. This is not to say that this search is acceptable to them; indeed, it may be safely assumed that, if and when they come to power, they would put an abrupt end to this *Jahili* practice. But as long as they have to rely on voluntary support they apparently choose to concentrate on the essentials of toppling the 'atheist' Ba'th regime and enforcing the Islamic law on all walks of life, leaving more marginal issues aside, so as not to alienate potential supporters unnecessarily. By omission, then, the Shi'i opposition seems to admit that they believe that the 'Mesopotamian' trend has more than marginal following. And by clearly stating their allegiance to the notion of an Iraqi nation state in its present boundaries even after the victory of the Islamic revolution in Baghdad they implicitly admit that they believe that this notion, imported from the West and imposed by the hated Christian imperialist powers, has hit deep roots in the hearts and minds of the Iraqi Shi'i community.

As for the Kurdish national movement, at the inception of its single most important political party, the Kurdish Democratic Party (KDP) in 1946, its official platform demanded 'total independence for Kurdistan' within a (loose) Iraqi federation.[14] This slogan was later replaced by the more realistic conception of Kurdish autonomy, but it cropped up whenever the Iraqi government seemed to contemplate seriously unification with other Arab countries.[15] Under the second Ba'th regime, before the beginning of the war, however, a clear-cut demand for secession and complete independence (though still within the framework of some federal system) was voiced only in the writings of one Kurdish political leader.[16]

When it comes to the more important political parties; Jalal Talabani's Popular Union of Kurdistan (PUK) and more importantly, to the KDP, their demands that appeared in writing were limited to 'full autonomy' that included, *inter alia*, the incorporation of Kirkuk (and its resources), as well as Khannaqin and Jabal Sinjar within the borders of the autonomous area, stopping all efforts to 'Arabize' Kurdish areas, giving greater resources for development, greater representation to Kurds at the center (as promised in the March 1970 KDP-Ba'th agreement), abolishing from the interim constitution those clauses that discriminate against Kurds (as, for example, the definition of the Iraqi people as an integral part of the Arab nation, or the rule dictating that members of the Revolutionary Command Council, the highest political body in the land, would be drawn only from among the members of the Regional-Iraqi Leadership of the Ba'th party, where no Kurds could be found), and other such demands, but not separation.[17]

During the war, as Kurdish hopes to see the demise of the regime had, for the first time since 1975, a real chance to materialize, and as their confrontation with that regime became acute, new voices could be heard. Thus, in his interview with *Le Monde*, in April 1987 and with *Iraq al-Ghad*, a mouthpiece of the ICP in Europe in May 1987, Amin Nushirwan, Assistant Secretary General of the PUK, announced that he 'hopes [to see] the severance of Iraq to a number of small states: Shi'i, Sunni and Kurdish'. When asked about it a year later the secretary general himself, Jalal Talabani, replied 'after a moment of hesitation', in a way that left more question marks than before. Under a democratic regime, he explained, the Kurds will settle for 'a federation', the details of which will have to be defined (thus vaguely implying that, in fact, his demand is for independence, not autonomy). However, if Iraq would remain a dictatorship 'we shall [certainly] opt for establishing an independent and democratic Kurdistan'.[18] Until the end of 1989, the KDP never went on record demanding full independence, but there are growing signs that following the regime's atrocities and the severance of all lines of communication, they, too, are seriously contemplating a complete break.[19]

In summation, then, it seems that, when it comes to Iraqi Arabs, the wish to preserve the Iraqi nation-state is fairly general; neither Ba'this, nor Communists nor Shi'i fundamentalists wish to see the Iraqi people dissolve within the melting pot of a pan-Arab or pan-Muslim super state, at least not in the foreseeable future, and none wishes to see it disintegrate. An important segment, and possibly the majority, of the Kurdish national movement sees things very differently, however. The Kurdish bitterness is matched by the sentiments of large segments of the Arab population of Iraq who feel betrayed by the Kurds, who, as they see it, joined the Iranian enemy in Iraq's most difficult moment. This chasm, separating close to 20 percent of the Iraqi people from the rest of the Iraqi body, poses a grave challenge to Iraq's political community in the foreseeable future.

It is instructive that the central government indicated its despair of the Iraqi Kurds (or its lack of readiness for a meaningful compromise with them) through the 'banishment' of the Kurds from the paradise of the Mesopotamian national myth a full decade before it started their physical banishment from their villages in the north.

Conclusion

In March 1933, a few months before his death, King Faysal I sent some of the more senior politicians in his court a confidential memorandum that described very succinctly how he saw the problems confronting the Iraqi political community more than a decade after the establishment of the Iraqi nation-state:

> In Iraq, there are ideas and aspirations that are totally antagonistic. There are innovating youngsters, including the government officials; the zealots; the Sunna; the Shi'a; the Kurds; the non-Muslim minorities; the tribes; the shaykhs, [and] the vast ignorant majority ready to adopt any harmful notion . . . Kurdish, Shi'i and Sunni tribes who only want to shake off every form of [central] government. My heart is full of sadness and pain because, to my mind, there is no Iraqi nation in Iraq as yet. Rather, there are human masses devoid of any patriotic notion, full of traditions and religious nonsense and absurdities and there is nothing that is binding them together. They are quick to do mischief, inclined towards anarchy, ready to rise at any time against any government whatsoever, and we want . . . to mold a nation out of these masses . . . He who understands the difficulty of molding . . . a nation under such circumstances must recognize the effort necessary for such an achievement.[1]

In July 1968, more than 35 years later, when the Ba'th party took over, though the situation had greatly improved, Iraq's political community was still plagued by deep splits.

The ideological approach and the pan-Arab policies of most of the regimes to rule Iraq since 1921 had not made things any easier. Excluding a period of a few months in 1936–37 under the rule of General Bakr Sidqi (a Kurd) and even more importantly, his Prime Minister Hikmat Sulayman (a Turk), and the four-and-a-half years of General 'Abd al-Karim Qasim's rule in Baghdad, all the other regimes in Iraq expounded a mixed message to their audience. On the one hand, they were encouraged to see themselves as Iraqi nationals and to see in the Iraqi state an object of reverence and sacrifice. On the other hand, however, the long-term existence of the same people and state were called into question by the various unity plans that could be construed as aiming at dissolving Iraq within a greater union.

There is no reason to doubt King Faysal's genuine wish to forge a nation out of the diverse (and often antagonistic) elements in Iraqi society. Indeed, on a number of important levels much was done under Faysal I, and the monarchy in general, in the way of forming the institutions of a nation state in which a nation could be nurtured. With British help, Iraq's territorial borders with its two formidable neighbors were defined; a national army was established in January 1921, a few months before Faysal I became King, and in 1934 it started conscription, usually an important contributor to national cohesion; a large bureaucratic and technocratic machine emerged which coped fairly successfully with the various functions of the state, from education to communication; a centrally-operated system of water control was developed; a legal system was worked out which, despite several drawbacks (in particular, the existence of a separate set of tribal laws and courts) was unique to Iraq and functioned reasonably well. Finally, in spite of serious deficiencies in the governmental systems (governments rarely lasted for more than two years), policy matters, when not dictated by the British, were decided in Baghdad, not in the tribal areas, through a complicated, sometimes violent but generally not ineffective process of political give and take between King, government, parliament, army officers, tribal shaykhs and old and new city establishment in Baghdad. In other words, Baghdad was established as the seat of government and the place where policies were decided upon and from where they were carried out.[2] For a state that was patched together from the three disparate Ottoman provinces of Basra, Baghdad and Mosul, and which had suffered since its first days from Shi'i tribal and religious unrest and from Kurdish revolts, this was no small achievement.

However, King Faysal himself and after him the Regent 'Abd al-Ilah and the formidable Nuri al-Sa'id also worked tirelessly to create a Fertile Crescent Union between Iraq, Syria, Jordan, Lebanon and Palestine. These efforts alienated the Kurds and failed to attract mass Shi'i support. Even some Sunni Arabs feared unification with Syria, either because they suspected that King Faysal would move his seat to Damascus and Iraq would revert to the status of a provincial backwater, or because they feared the competition of the better educated Syrian elite.[3] It is true that in the 1930s, there were also important Iraqi court ideologues, like Sami Shawkat, and politicians, like the brothers Yasin and Taha al-Hashimi, who combined Iraqi pride and ambition with pan-Arabism, but then, even in the minds of these politicians the *long-term* existence of the Iraqi nation (or 'people', *Sha'b* as it was referred to, so as not to confuse it with the more prestigious expression of *umma*, 'nation', reserved for the Arab nation as a whole), was far from clear. More importantly, the Hashimite Royal Family, coming from the Hijaz and, as believed by many, ever nostalgic about their lost rule in civilized, Levantine Damascus, were not Iraq-centered pan-Arabs in the real sense. To them Iraq served as a mere springboard to greater exploits, rather than a permanent power base and the long-term center of their activities.[4] Thus, by their pan-Arab activity the Hashimites, in fact, undermined the faith of their subjects in the durability (and to an extent in the legitimacy) of the very Iraqi nation-state they were endeavoring to create.[5]

The assurance that Iraq was there to stay came in a non-equivocal way for the first time from General Qasim, his Free Officers and their communist supporters following the revolution of 1958. Qasim's view was that even though 'The Arabs are one nation', 'cooperation' rather than unity should be the form of inter-Arab relations, and a clearly-defined Iraqi nation state should remain intact. Indeed, Qasim spoke in no vague terms of an 'eternal Iraqi republic'.[6] Two decades later the Ba'th would adopt a very similar approach, but at the time, when they and their Nasirite allies challenged Qasim's rule, their battle cry was, typically: 'immediate total unity', and Qasim's approach was condemned as treason.[7]

Under the first Ba'th regime and under the 'Arif brothers (1963–68), there were a number of attempts at establishing Iraqi-Syrian-Egyptian and Iraqi-Syrian unity. In themselves, some of these attempts could be reconciled with an Iraqi national identity, because they were aimed at federal unity. But then the Ba'th doctrine challenged the legitimacy of all the Arab states as being the arbitrary creations of foreign imperialism. As for 'Abd al-Salam 'Arif, even though his attempt to unite with Egypt in 1964 in a way that guaranteed that the leadership would be placed securely in 'Abd al-Nasir's Cairo did not take off, this attempt in itself demonstrated where his conviction lied. Similarly, Iraq's voluntary acceptance of 'Abd al-Nasir's leadership throughout his and his brother's rule did not add much to Iraq's self-esteem. In such an ideological atmosphere, any talk of unification with other progressive Arab countries rendered the Iraqi national entity transient in the minds of those who took the unification rhetoric seriously. In part due to this approach, the modern national loyalty in Iraq has been slow to crystallize. As observed by Batatu, in the mid-1970s this loyalty was 'still hazy, uncertain in its direction – Iraqism? pan-Arabism? – unacceptable to Kurds [and] poorly assimilative of the Shi'is'.[8]

Under no other regime and movement was the negation of the Iraqi identity stronger than under that of the Ba'th. As soon as the they came to power in July 1968, they followed party tradition and vigorously propagated for the realization of the party's pan-Arab ideals. Leading politicians pledged boundless sacrifices in the service of the Arab nation, if necessary at the expense of vital Iraqi interests; and party ideologues called upon the Iraqi people in their endeavor to fulfil the party's pan-Arab mission to conduct a 'bitter and arduous struggle' against their own Iraqi identity, or 'Iraqidom' [*al-'iraqiyya*].[9] And even though not in all spheres of political activity the new regime pursued these goals with equal zest, it did enough to create the impression of deep pan-Arab commitment, whether on the Palestinian front or in the realm of Arab unity. Party leaders often called for unification with Egypt and Syria, while criticizing the gross shortcomings of the regimes ruling there. In 1972 Saddam Husayn himself conducted a surrealistic journey to Damascus and Cairo in search of Arab unity. Not surprisingly this attempt failed, but it demonstrated the party's ideological – if not practical – committment. Such credo and policies did little to allay Kurdish fears and Shi'i discomfort and to encourage the Iraqi public in general, and party members in particular, to identify with a short-lived Iraqi people and its nation-state. Yet, at precisely the same time the regime also adopted a contradictory ideological and political line. In the spring of 1969 the first Spring Festival was celebrated in Mosul. Parading alongside various pan-Arab symbols were unmistakable symbols of territorial Iraqi nationalism, which suggested the ancient and lasting nature of the Iraqi people. Likewise, very soon after it came to rule over Iraq the new regime embarked upon an expensive and widely publicized campaign of archeological digs, preservation and reconstruction with the main emphasis on pre-Islamic sites like Babylon, Ashur and Ur. Official encouragement of local folklore and of territorially inspired Iraqi pre-Islamic, as well as Islamic literature and plastic art bore fruit a few years later, but this encouragement started no later than 1969–70.

On the more practical level, the RCC introduced new, particularist-Iraqi, even egotistical legislation. The First Interim Constitution (1968) stipulated that non-Iraqis may not own agricultural land. In the July 1970 Second Interim Constitution it was specified that all members of the RCC (and thus also its chairman, who is by definition the president), government ministers and vice presidents must be Iraqi by birth both of whose parents are Iraqi by birth, and in December 1970 the same rule was applied also to members of parliament.[10] In other words, in terms of their attitude towards the future of the Iraqi nation-state, between 1968 and the end of 1970 the Ba'th regime has been moving in two opposite directions. It preached complete self-sacrifice on the altar of the pan-Arab cause, and some of the ideologues of its ruling party promised to achieve the submergence of the Iraqi people in an as yet non-existent pan-Arab entity. At the same time, however, the same regime was also closing the Iraqi economy and society to non-Iraqi Arabs and enhancing the Iraqi identity, and implying that it would last forever. Furthermore, while there was some difference of views (the Syrian Ba'thi expatriate old-timers among the pan-Arab leadership, and some Iraqis like 'Abd al-Khaliq al-Samarra'i and President Bakr himself, were more active in encouraging the notion of Iraq's pan-Arab commitment, while others, like Saddam Husayn, more conspicuously promoted Iraqi identity), the majority of party leadership had to sanction all important political and ideological decisions. In November 1969 the RCC, which till then had consisted of five senior army officers, was enlarged to include all the members of the Iraqi Regional Leadership of the party and the Iraqi members of the pan-Arab Leadership. The new fifteen-strong RCC included people who represented all shades of party opinion from Saddam Husayn to 'Abd al-Khaliq, the ideological diehard. In short, when considered as it really was at the time, as a collective body, the Ba'thi leadership showed signs of split personality.

This may be explained as result of an ideological conflict when old and new concepts were simultaneously present. The unstable, unpopular infant regime was trying to satisfy all the conflicting political dreams of Iraqi pan-Arabs at once. On the one hand, they wished to sustain a (credible) self-image of deep commitment to Arab unity and readiness for boundless sacrifice for the Arab cause (even though it involved on element of Iraqi self-promotion, as the other Arab regimes were all depicted as cowardly and bankrupt). On the other hand, however, through its enactment and cultural policy the regime delivered the reassuring message that Iraq was there to stay and that, whatever the fate of revolutionary schemes of unification, the revolutionaries had nothing to fear; the Ba'th regime would never loosen its grip over its power base, the Iraqi nation-state, and no one, whether Asad or 'Abd al-Nasir, would be allowed to disinherit them in the name of lofty party ideals. For many party members, who had spent years in jail and exile and who were haunted by the fear of losing power again as they did in 1963, such assurances were no less important than all the party ideals put together and the leadership must have been fully aware of it.[11] In addition, the new laws were instrumental in reassuring other circles in Iraqi society, wary of an influx of Syrians or Egyptians into Iraq as a result of political unification, that their interests would not be compromised.[12] It seems that the new line was also the result of Ba'thi recognition of a wider sentiment; after half a century of statehood, the ordinary Iraqi citizen could no longer view his state, as the party would have it, as an ephemeral and, worse still, an illegitimate creature, conceived and born in sin as the result of unnatural relations between foreign imperialism and the local exploiting classes. The emotional need for a homeland to belong to and identify with in the age of nation-states is no aberration; it is the rule and the Arab nation states are no exception. Finally, as mentioned in Chapter 1, there also seems to have been an additional reason, namely the lack of enthusiasm for sharing with others Iraq's natural wealth (or so the party believed), and there was the general decline during the 1970s in the popularity of integrationist, revolutionary pan-Arabism (indeed, for all its efforts the Ba'th regime of Iraq failed to generate even one successful revolution in the Arab world!). At the peak of its pan-Arab zeal, then, the Ba'th regime had already lost faith in the very central integrationist component of its pan-Arab credo, and started looking for new political and ideological avenues.

The new ideology was slow to manifest itself fully, but its main features appeared soon after the takeover of 1968. Its cornerstone was the admission that the Arab peoples, or nations-in-the making, within their present borders, were there to stay and that, should unity between two or more Arab states ever come about, under no circumstances should it undermine the cohesion of the existing nation-states. As soon as this notion was established, it became clear that, in the words of Bernard Lewis, 'A new future required a different past'.[13] Iraqi national existence was given a breathtaking history of five thousand years – extending from the Dawn of the Dynasties, through Akkad, Babylon, Assur, and Chaldea, the Arab conquests, Harun al-Rashid and his Abbasid Golden Age, and all the way to Saddam Husayn. In 1989 another missing link was added. In addition to the restoration of the statue of King Faysal I, the royal cemetery, too, was renovated at the staggering cost of $3.2 million and re-opened to the general public. Evidently, upholding the Iraqi nation-state was inconsistent with a historical ban on its founder. Another part of this latest development was the publication in Iraq of a great number of academic studies dedicated to the monarchy, and even partly exonerating its politicians, including Nuri al-Sa'id.[14]

What were the sources of inspiration for this non-Ba'thi, Iraq-centered pan-Arabism? As we have seen such tendencies had existed in Iraq itself since the 1920s. A study of the school curriculum prepared for the academic year 1922–23 by the same Sati' al-Husri who, on other occasions, preached egalitarian and self-sacrificing pan-Arabism, shows that when it came to European history, the emphasis was on the study of the unification of Italy by Garibaldi and that of Germany by Bismarck. This study was explicitly connected to the issue of 'the unity of the Arab nation and the Arabhood of Iraq'.[15]

A few years later, in the summer of 1932, it became clearer who the Prussia and Bismark of the Arabs were. Upon his return from a journey in the Arab world, designed to further King Faysal I's plans of Arab unity Yasin al-Hashimi and his party argued that Iraq's impending membership of the League of Nations gave it a political leverage that other Arab states did not possess and thus it should be ready and proud to bear the main brunt of liberating the Arabs.[16]

The notions of service to and leadership of the nation are easily interchangeable, as is evident from the meeting at the home of Colonel Salah al-Din al-Sabbagh, in April 1938, where the draft platform of the new, clandestine 'Association of the Guardians of Arabism' was discussed. It stated that Arab unity could be brought about 'only by force', and that Iraq possessed the necessary military force to achieve it. The liberation and unification of the Arabs were supposed to remain an exclusively Iraqi endeavor 'because independent Iraq is the [only country] capable of striving effectively' towards these two goals.[17] And, as we learned, in his lectures to high school children the Director of Education, Dr Sami Shawkat, spoke of nothing less than an 'Arab Empire' that would be ruled from Baghdad.

There are also historical precedents to the synthesis between pan-Arabism and territorial (or 'Mesopotamian') nationalism. It was the radically pan-Arab government of Prime Minister Yasin al-Hashimi and Rashid 'Ali al-Kaylani (Minister of Interior), which enacted the new Law of Antiquities no. 59 of 1936, which imposed severe restrictions on the export of archeological items.[18] In fact, soon after it came to power in March 1935, this government launched the first campaign in Iraqi history of excavations by Iraqi (as different from foreign) archeological teams, and made it extremely difficult for foreign archeologists to export finds, accusing them of robbing Iraq.[19]

Following the failure of the Rashid 'Ali al-Kaylani pro-Nazi revolt In 1941 the British took control over Iraq's education and, at the expense of aggressive pan-Arabism, much more emphasis was put in the curriculum on ancient Mesopotamian history, and more teachers than before were drawn from the leftist, as different from the pan-Arab, intellectual milieu.[20] Thus, while Saddam Husayn (who commenced his primary education in 1946) and his generation received their radical pan-Arab schooling at home and in the highly-politicized schoolyards and streets of Baghdad, Tikrit, Mosul and Samarra, they heard of Sargon the Akkadian, Hammurabi and Nebuchadnezzar in the classroom. The synthesis may have been largely of their own making.

The post-war years saw a growing interest in the history of ancient Mesopotamia in the academic and intellectual community in general. Thus, for example, 1945 saw the founding of the professional archeological journal *Sumer* which expressed pride in Mesopotamia's unique cultural heritage. Characteristic of the journal's approach is an article by the director general of antiquities in which he reviews the history of civilization in Iraq, beginning with the cultures uncovered at Sulaymaniyya and Halabja in the north, and Tel al-'Ubayd and Tel Hasuna in the south and proceeding to the Sumerians. 'The Sumerians and history,' the author affirms proudly '[both] commence in the Mesopotamian valley.' The reader is also led to conclude that present-day Iraqis are linked with the Sumerians and their predecessors by a bond transcending the connection which exists between successive cultures which have occupied the same stretch of territory. The writer thus calls the first pre-historic man who used a sickle around the sixth millennium BC 'the first Iraqi peasant' and cites with approval a foreign anthropologist's statement that, in appearance, the ancient Sumerians bore 'an astounding resemblance to the heads and bodies of Iraq's present-day inhabitants'.[21]

In the early 1950s Iraq's royal family, too, appeared to take a growing interest in the country's antiquities.[22] However, the Hashimites' interest in the Arab world, and in attaching portions of it to their kingdom, did not diminish.[23] Some of these may have been hesitant beginnings of an ideological fusion between territorial Iraqi nationalism and pan-Arabism. If so, however, the rise of 'Abd al-Nasir, that forced the Hashimites into defensive positions and the eventual destruction of the monarchy in 1958, came before this process could bear fruit; Qasim was not a pan-Arab, and the regimes of the Ba'th of 1963 and the 'Arif brothers showed only limited interest in Iraq's ancient pre-Islamic past.

What were the aims behind the introduction of the new territorial credo, and after twenty years, to what extent have the Ba'th regime succeeded in achieving these aims? While the aims in themselves are fairly clear, without a field study the achievements cannot be gauged to any degree of accuracy. However, it is possible to try and assess the strengths and weaknesses of the new credo, and thus suggest what its chances of establishing roots are.

In focusing attention on the themes of Mesopotamian culture and local folklore the regime had in mind essentially five aims: (a) to provide the Iraqi people with a secular basis for a sense of national identity, thus furthering secularism in Iraq in general; (b) to provide Saddam Husayn, President since 1979, with historical legitimacy by portraying him as the culmination to a continuous succession of great Iraqi rulers from remote antiquity to the present, by emphasizing the role of the 'institution' of inspired leadership in 'sustaining . . . the millennial continuity of the land and people'[24] of Iraq, in bringing out the native ingenuity of the Iraqis and in resurrecting their former glory;[25] (c) to create an historical common denominator that would unite Sunnis and Shi'is, Arabs and Kurds; (d) through the encouragement given to a uniquely Iraqi culture and the revival of Iraq's particular history, to reinforce the Iraqis' sense of uniqueness, hence a degree of separateness from the rest of the Arabs. Internal schisms notwithstanding, a sense of Iraqi identity had emerged under the monarchy.[26] The Ba'th, however, were out to strengthen this identity, to endow it with additional historical and cultural dimensions and give it a higher priority than that given it by previous pan-Arab regimes. The fortification of the Iraqi identity was aimed towards two kinds of audiences. In the first place, it was designed to prevent naïve party members from taking the party's traditional egalitarian and integrationist pan-Arab ideology too seriously, as this could lead to renewed demands that Iraq would give priority to all-Arab interests over its own. Second, it was meant to signal to all those in Iraq who had reservations in regard to integrationist pan-Arabism that the party was, indeed, steering clear from this traditional notion. Finally, (e) the new policy was designed to provide the Iraqi people with a history that would give them great pride as the builders of the first civilization in the history of mankind and their ingenious successors through the ages, and as such the rightful leaders of the Arab nation. This pride was seen as important also in the wider international context. In its own turn, such pride, when generated, was meant to augment the prestige of the party and the man who generated it.

As for the secularizing influence of the Mesopotamian policy, its effect may be very limited. The regime undermined its own secular message when, immediately following Khomeini's rise to power and in order to defeat his charges of Ba'th 'Godlessness', it coated the traditional secular Ba'thi pill with heavy layers of Islamic piety. By the end of the Iran-Iraq war, the religious content of official propaganda was so prominent that it overshadowed any influence which the Mesopotamian component, for all its symbolic importance, might have had. Now, almost two years after the war's end, this trend has remained unchanged. One post-war expression of this Islamic fashion was the announcement by the pan-Arab and Regional-Iraqi Leaderships of the party that, before his death, the co-founder of the Ba'th Party and its chief ideologue, Michel 'Aflaq, had 'embraced Islam as his religion.'[27] If 'Aflaq, a secular Christian, who spent most of his life preaching the confinement of religion to church and mosque, had to become a Muslim in old age, then the ideological concessions to religion in Baghdad in the late 1980s cannot be offset by re-building the temple of Ishtar in Babylon or even by the opening of a beer garden in Nineveh.

The hope that Mesopotamian history could serve as a legitimizing mechanism for the young President seems even less warranted. The Shah of Iran had tried to use Cyrus and the Akhaemenians in a similar manner and had failed. This, despite the fact that, unlike pre-Islamic history in Iraq, pre-Islamic history in Iran did not suffer from a negative image, chiefly thanks to the *Shahname*, Firdawsi's 10th–11th century partly-mythological epic account of pre-Islamic Iranian history.[28]

When the Shah tried to link his throne with that of Cyrus (who had not been mentioned in the *Shahname*, but was re-introduced into Iran's ancient history through the Shah's education system),[29] even those secular intellectuals who had accepted the newly-discovered ancient kings as part of Iran's history, found it difficult to identify the Akhaemenians with the Pahlavis. Intellectuals, Bazaaris and students of religion alike, regarded the Shah's attempt, partly designed to attract Western attention, to tie himself to Cyrus, as presumptuous, verging on the ridiculous.[30]

It has to be made very clear that in Saddam Husayn's Iraq the leader is not subject to ridicule. But rather than wide acceptance of his claim to be the culmination of a chain of great Iraqi leaders, the reason for that seems to be a combination of fear and indifference, the latter stemming from the fact that in Iraq, Mesopotamian history is still relatively little appreciated by the vast majority. Indeed, in his attempt to buttress the legitimacy of his regime by connecting it with Nebuchadnezzar and Hammurabi, Saddam Husayn is trying to build on shifting sands. Much more promising, in that respect, is his claim to be a direct descendent of the family of the Prophet, 'Ali and al-Husayn. Whatever the truth in this claim, here, at least, he is trying to build the foundations of his personal legitimacy on solid rock.[31]

As a common historical thread strengthening internal Iraqi national cohesion the Mesopotamian myth may have some appeal for secularly-inclined Sunni and Shi'i Arabs. If it ever found any favor with the Kurds, this was lost when it was declared to belong exclusively to the Arabs in the late 1970s. More importantly, while a historical myth, and any other unifying ideology, may contribute to national cohesion, under no circumstances can it serve as a substitute for real political partnership. And while there are some signs that Shi'i Arabs are gaining an initial foothold (though clearly not equality) in the corridors of power, this is not the case with Kurds. Even in this age of nationalism based largely on language and culture, the Arab language and culture have not been sufficient as yet to bring about the political unification of all Arabic-speakers. However, within the Iraqi nation-state, the Arabic language has been elevated to a level of unprecedented importance. The process of urbanization has resulted in the erosion of traditional social structures and the old loyalties of extended family, tribe and religion. The large cities have become impersonal and unfamiliar. In addition, 'high culture' is generally imposed through universal education. Under such circumstances, language becomes the main medium for defining one's new identity. This is so in all modern, urbanized societies,[32] doubly so in Iraq, where a powerful totalitarian central government has made formidable and largely successful efforts to penetrate every part of society, or rather to 'nationalize' society, and thus open it up to the regime's inspection, indoctrination and regimentation,[33] and where education has greatly expanded and come under tight government control.[34] Outside the Kurdish areas, in the new highly regimented Iraqi urban society (and, in 1987 some 72 percent of Iraq's population lived in towns),[35] a Kurd who can not, or will not, become thoroughly Arabized is at a clear disadvantage in his contacts with both the vast state bureaucracy and the Arabic speaking majority in general. This situation was made worse by the Iraq-Iran war when many Kurds, in their struggle against the regime, supported Iran. This support, and the terrible retribution that followed, created a greater barrier than ever to Kurdish-Arab reconciliation and integration. Since Qasim's rule, the Kurds have been recognized by the Iraqi constitution as a different nationality [*qawmiyya*] from the Arabs, both forming a united Iraqi 'people' [*Sha'b*]. In 1970 they were promised meaningful autonomy and substantial influence at the center. Ideologically speaking, this is the fulfillment of the most ambitious expectations, save complete independence. But until this ideological commitment is realized, additional ideological-cultural assurances that the Kurds are, indeed, equal partners with the Arabs in Iraq can make little difference.

The 'Mesopotamian' policy may prove much more effective in giving legitimate status to the Iraqi people and to the need to give priority to its interests in the eyes of party members and other pan-Arabs in Iraq, as well as in alleviating the fears of those in Iraq who were traditionally wary of unification plans. There is evidence that the Iraqi stage is ready for such a step; both the Ba'th party, the most radical pan-Arab political organization in Iraq, and the equally radical Islamic opposition, no longer preach the dissolution of the Iraqi people, or nation and its state. This does not mean that the Arab identity of the Iraqis is on the wane. Unless one happens to be Kurdish, to be an Iraqi means also, and perhaps principally, to be an Arab. But while according to traditional Ba'th doctrine, the citizens of Iraq should see themselves as Iraqi Arabs or, in fact, as temporarily Iraqis and eternally Arabs, in the late 1980s the citizens of Iraq are encouraged to see themselves as Arab Iraqis. At the same time, however, there are no signs that Iraq is contemplating isolationism. Indeed, the regime still pays ample tribute to the Arab character of the Iraqi people and to the pan-Arab ideals.[36] This, in itself, is evidence of the great staying power of these ideals among the public, even if their realization is nowhere in sight.

There is, however, a radical change in the way in which the Ba'th regime has been relating to Iraq's Arab connection since the early 1980s, when compared to its approach between 1968 and 1971. While in its early days in power it kept a large force hundreds of kilometers away from its national borders and claimed, with some justification, that it was committed completely to a non-Iraqi pan-Arab cause, since the beginning of the Gulf War Iraq has demanded Arab support for its struggle on its own borders. This demand was justified by the claim (with which at least Syria, Libya, South Yemen, and for a while, the PLO, could not agree), that, in fact, Iraq was defending the whole Arab world against a 'foreign enemy': Iran. This approach, that identifies Iraq's interests with those of the Arab world found its latest expression when Foreign Minister Tariq 'Aziz, in a letter to the Arab League's Secretary General, accused Kuwait of 'hatching plots against the Arab nation' when it asked for help against Iraqi military threats.[37]

In addition to accentuating Iraqi uniqueness, the Mesopotamian dimension has also been used to convince the Iraqi public of Iraq's excellence and seniority among the nations of the world at large. As has been the case with other developing nations, the unpalatable fact that Iraq has to borrow science and technology from the West has been sweetened by the reassuring notion that it was Iraq, from remote antiquity through the Golden Age of the Abbasids, which provided the world with science and technology and that today modern Iraqis are only retrieving what was originally theirs.

The concept of national historical excellence (and the implicit or explicit promise that it could be revived) has a great potential attraction not only in Iraq. This theme in itself is innocuous, even useful. There is no nationalism without history, and every nation needs to be proud of at least some parts of its past, or what it chooses to see as its past. The Ba'th regime, however, has been driving their educational campaign one step further into the danger zones of personality cult, hegemonism and chauvinism. In Ba'thi Iraq pride in national pedigree is intimately connected with an omnipotent, omnipresent and omniscient leader; it serves to justify a claim to seniority among the Arabs; ancient imperial history serves as inspiration for contemporary conquests far byond the borders of the Iraqi nation-state and as justification for Arab hegemony, all in the name of a lofty national cause, as in the case of the regime's promises to follow Nebuchadnezzar's example in Palestine; Kurds are being excluded from the national foundation myth and the last five thousand years of the region's history are presented as an unending ordeal of Iranian anti-Iraqi aggression and racism. If the Ba'th regime continues to play up these and similar motifs and educate its citizens in this spirit even after the Gulf War, then Iraq will run the risk of coming full circle. Rather than realizing the potential of the new ideology to increase political stability by creating a stable balance between the Iraqi and the pan-Arab identities, the regime would be cultivating imperial aspirations, with the corollary that this time, instead of sacrificing all that they have for the sake of the permanent Arab revolution, the leadership would demand of its citizens to be ready for crippling sacrifices for the glory of the Iraqi nation state and its leader.

When a regime with complete control of the media and the educational system embarks upon a consistent long-term cultural-educational policy, its chances of success should not be underestimated. 'Success', in this respect may be seen as the awareness of Iraq's ancient pre-Islamic past as part of the contemporary Iraqi identity. The fact that, despite their complete rejection of the Ba'th regime, the Communists look upon the preservation of Iraqi folklore and the resurrection of Mesopotamian cultures favorably (though not for the same reasons as the Ba'th; the Communists have never spoken in terms of Iraq's glory and superiority), implies a fairly wide acceptance in secular intellectual circles of some aspects of this new national myth. The fact that even the radical Shi'i Islamic opposition does not come out openly against it may imply that the glory that was Mesopotamia is noted even by traditionalists.

How about the wider Arab arena? Is Ba'thi Iraq unique in its endeavor to foster a sense of local-patriotic uniqueness through the creation of an intimate relationship between the people and the ancient history of its particular territory? While a well-substantiated answer to this question requires a more thorough study, a survey of a sample of four countries (Syria, Jordan, Tunisia and Saudi Arabia) suggests that Iraq is not alone. Although less conspicuously, the ruling regimes of the first three, too, have a passion for archeology; they display local pre-Islamic and pre-Arab sites and artifacts on their coins, money notes and stamps; they celebrate festivals in Roman sites and some of them acknowledge in various degrees of clarity the significance of the historical sites to their national identities, and they all encourage the development of local folklore.[38] These policies are not universal: they certainly do not exist in Saudi Arabia and possibly in a few other states, apparently for a combination of religious and dynastic reasons and the relative scantiness of exciting archeological sites in these states. Yet these policies do exist in a number of important Arab states, and they seem to be on the increase. The regimes in these Arab states tend more and more to be legitimizing parts of these countries' local culture that were neglected in the name of pan-Arab uniformity, and some even create local culture artificially. They are not trying to shed their countries' Arabhood, but they are allowing them to become more multi-faceted, with different facets of their personality appearing and receding in different circumstances. While not attempting to predict the shape of things to come, it will be fair to say that at present, local identity at least in these countries is being promoted by the ruling regimes partly through culture, partly through the re-interpretation of history.[39]

On the wider Arab arena, at the end of the 1980s, however, unitarian schemes and sentiments are not completely out of vogue. The unification of the two Yemens on 22 May 1990 has been one such scheme. Much more revolutionary unitarian notions have been expressed in some of the poorer Arab countries, following the collapse of oil prices during the second half of the 1980s and the economic depression that followed. In these countries, notably in Jordan, social protest on the popular level has often been expressed in terms of Islamic Pan-Arabism, and with good reason: it would only be natural for those who criticise the oil-rich Arab states, and demand the re-distribution of "Arab wealth", to speak in pan-Arab terms. This does not mean that the old credo is totally out of vogue. Indeed, the Arab world is a vast one, with different conditions prevailing in its different parts, and thus, while it is legitimate to look for general trends, one should also allow for some variety. Certainly, other, less ambitious and more pragmatic forms of pan-Arabism are possible, if the secular forces in the Arab world manage to contain the present revivalist Islamic upsurge. In a less authoritarian political atmosphere, where Arab regimes were able to rely in a more relaxed way on wide public support, and where the nation-states were accepted as a legitimate, even desirable reality, Arab governments and leaders would have to make less effort to satisfy the pan-Arab expectations of their more radical elements. They would not feel the same compulsive urge to perform the impossible, or the near-impossible, to usher in the messianic age of integrative Arab unity or to realize the aspirations of pan-Arab leadership, aspirations by their very nature mutually exclusive if nurtured (as they are) by more than one Arab state. In such an atmosphere, states and regimes would feel confident within their own borders, secure from encroachment in the name of pan-Arab ideals often indistinguishable from dreams of hegemony. Arab states that had cooperated closely for a whole decade would no longer need to sign agreements of non-intervention in each others' affairs, as Iraq, Saudi Arabia, Egypt and Jordan did in 1989.[40] Fruitful and extensive economic and political cooperation would then be possible, even probable.

Thanks to the common language and culture the affinity between the

Arab nation states is greater than that between most of their European equivalents. Since the states of the Arab East came into being after World War I, however, and especially since the 1950s, when a new brand of radically nationalistic regimes claiming to represent revolutionary socialism came to power in the Arab world at large, this affinity has been used chiefly to undermine the legitimacy of rival regimes, and has thus become an agent of instability and of deepened mistrust. Under different circumstances, this affinity might serve as a foundation for close cooperation. Indeed, it is not unthinkable that Arab states, having achieved full sovereignty and unreserved recognition by their own populations of the legitimacy of their existence, might come full circle and show readiness for some economic and, eventually even political integration; the Gulf Cooperation Council and the Arab Magreb Union may be the first signs of such cooperation. If the intermediate period, however, is too long, there is a very real danger that the separate economies would develop along individual, rather than complementary lines. This would create a formidable obstacle to economic integration, which only an exceptionally strong and committed collective Arab leadership could realistically hope to overcome.

Notes

Preface

1. Clifford Geertz, 'Ideology as a Cultural System', *The Interpretation of Culture* (New York, 1973), p. 193.
2. *Webster's Dictionary*, as quoted in ibid.

Chapter 1:   The Historical Setting

1. Unless otherwise stated, the discussion of Iraq under the monarchy is based mainly on the following sources: Hanna Batatu, *The Old Social Classes and the Revolutionary Movements of Iraq* (Princeton, 1978), pp. 13–106; Phebe Marr, *The Modern History of Iraq* (Boulder, Colorado, and London, 1985), pp. 29–151; Peter Sluglett, *Britain in Iraq, 1914–1932* (London, 1976), *passim*; Marion Farouk-Sluglett and Peter Sluglett, *Iraq Since 1958, From Revolution to Dictatorship* (London and New York, 1987), pp. 1–45.
2. For details see Etan Kohlberg, 'The Evolution of the Shi'a', *The Jerusalem Quarterly*, no. 27, Spring 1983, pp. 109–23.
3. See, for example, Marr, *The Modern History of Iraq*, pp. 5–7.
4. Ernest Main, *Iraq From Mandate To Independence* (London, 1935), p. 165.
5. Marr, pp. 40–1.
6. According to a British source, in the early 1930s some 17 percent of Iraq's population were Kurds (Ernest Main, *Iraq from Mandate to Independence*, pp. 18, 133). According to Batatu's estimation, based on the census of 1947, their share in the population was then 19 percent (p. 40). A Soviet source mentioned in 1970 25 percent (*New Times*, 24 March 1970, as quoted in Ofra Bengio, *The Kurdish Revolution in Iraq* [Tel Aviv, 1989, in Hebrew], p. 217). A Kurdish source claimed that their share in the population in 1975 was 28 percent (Ismet Sheriff Vanly, 'Kurdistan in Iraq', in Gerard Chaliand [ed.], *People Without a country* [London, 1980], p. 157). The two last figures seem too high, the highest figure given by contemporary Western scholars being 20 percent (see Marion Farouk-Sluglett and Peter Sluglett, *Iraq Since 1958, From Revolution to Dictatorship* [London and New York, 1987], p. 23; Marr, p. 5). As for Shi'i Arabs, in 1920 the British estimate was that they comprised 52.4 percent of the population (see Richard Coke, *The Heart of the Middle East* [London, 1926], p. 196). If their population increased at the same rate as that of the other groups, then in the mid-1950s, after the Jews left Iraq, their share should accordingly

144

have been some 54 percent. According to Batatu's estimate (p. 40), in 1947 their share was 51.4 percent. Excluding the Jews, their share was 52.7 percent. According to Batatu's estimate, Sunni Arabs comprised, in 1947, 19.7 percent of the total. Excluding the Jews their share would come up to 20.2 percent. See also Marr, p. 8.

7. Batatu, p. 40; Marr, pp. 9–11.

8. See, for example, Sati' al-Husri, King Faysal's Director of Eduction, accusing young Shi'i school teachers and would-be teachers of loyalty to Iran and Shi'i bias in his *Mudhakkirati fi al-'iraq 1921–1941* (Beirut, 1967), pp. 324–5, 585–90.

9. Batatu, p. 26.

10. Marr, p. 281.

11. Elie Kedourie, 'The Iraqi Shi'is and their Fate', in Martin Kramer, *Shi'ism, Resistance, and Revolution* (Boulder, Colorado, and London, 1987), pp. 152.

12. For statistics see Marr, pp. 143–6; Batatu, pp. 48, 96.

13. See, for example, the speeches made by Faysal after his arrival in Iraq in 1921, Philip Willard Ireland, *Iraq, A Study in Political Development* (London, 1937), pp. 465–9.

14. See, for example Yehoshua Porath, 'Nuri al-Said's Arab unity programme', *Middle Eastern Studies*, vol. 20, no. 4, October 1984, pp. 76–98; Reeva Simon, 'The Hashemite "Conspiracy": Hashemite Unity Attempts 1921–1958', *IJMES*, vol. 5, 1974, pp. 314–27; Khaldun, Sati al-Husri, 'King Faysal I and Arab Unity 1930–1933', *Journal of Contemporary History*, vol. 10 no. 2, April 1975, pp. 331ff

.15 Other reasons were the hope that an Arab union would provide Iraq with strategic depth in its conflict with Iran and Turkey; and the need for ports on the Mediterranean, which union with Palestine, Syria, and Lebanon could secure. See Yehoshua Porath, ibid.

16. Reeva Simon, *Iraq Between the Two World Wars: The Creation and Implementation of a National Ideology* (New York, Columbia Univ. Press, 1986), pp. 75–126.

17. Kedourie, 'The Iraqi Shi'is and their Fate', pp. 153–4; Kedourie, 'The Break Between Muslims and Jews', in Mark R. Cohen and Abraham L. Udovitch, *Jews Among Arabs: Contacts and Boundaries* (Princeton, 1989), p. 26. And see Kedourie, 'The Iraqi Shi'is and their Fate', pp. 145–7, for the mixed position of the *mujtahids* immediately following World War One. In 1941 a few *mujtahids* supported the anti-British pan-Arab revolt of Rashid 'Ali al-Kaylani but their support could stem from their anti-British sentiment and not necessarily from whole-hearted support for pan-Arabism, and, anyway, it came only *after* the revolt won the day (eventually to be crushed by the British). Also, the revolt's leadership was entirely Sunni-Arab. See Hasan al-'Alawi, *Al-Shi'a wal dawla al-qawmiyya fi al-'iraq* (Paris, 1989), pp. 181–6.

18. Marion Farouk-Sluglett and Peter Sluglett, pp. 76–7. For Qasim's cultural-ideological campaign to foster local Iraqi nationalism at the

expense of pan-Arabism, see Chapter 2.

19. Batatu, *The Old Social classes*, p. 832.

20. Samir al-Khalil, *Republic of Fear, The Politics of Modern Iraq* (London, 1989), pp. 214–15. See also Ernest Main, 'Iraq: a Note', *Journal of the Royal Central Asiatic Society*, vol. 20, July 1933, p. 434.

21. For the Shi'a and the Communists see Batatu, pp. 422–24, 649–50, 663, 699–700, 704, 952–3, 983–5, 998, 1046, 1061, 1190–2; tables A-27ff. Batatu refrains from drawing binding conclusions, but his factual account of the places where the pro-Qasim forces chose to make their last stand against the Ba'th in February 1963 is very telling. From interviews with people who grew up under the Monarchy in Baghdad, Basra and 'Amara (conducted in London, January–March 1990) it emerges likewise that, to the extent that they could speak their minds and that they felt that it had any chance at all of success, educated Shi'is in those places were unenthusiastic about the ruling elite's pan-Arab policy. They saw it as a device aimed to legitimize Sunni-Arab rule, and their concern was that within a larger, Sunni-Arab state they would, indeed, be relegated to the status of an insignificant minority.

22. King Faysal I also based some of his legitimacy on his *sharifi* descent. This seems to have been a political asset before he became King. See for example, the letters from the would-be Chief *Mujtahid*, Muhammad Taqi al-Shirazi, and from other Shi'i leaders, to the Sharif of Mecca and his son Faysal in 1919–20, Muhammad 'Ali Kamal al-Din, *Thawrat al-'ishrin fi dhikriha al-Khamsin* (Baghdad, 1971), pp. 78–9, 81, 135, 181–3, 211–12, 328, 333–4, 338. Elie Kedourie on a similar approach by groups of activist Shi'i notables in Baghdad, Kazimiyya and Karbala, 'The Iraqi Shi'is', ibid., p. 146; Amal Vinogradov, 'The 1920 Revolt in Iraq Reconsidered: The Role of Tribes in National Politics', *IJMES*, vol. 2, April 1972, p. 135. When he became King, however, his pedigree notwithstanding, his support for the British and for Sunni-Arab rule turned the *mujtahid* against him. Kedourie, pp. 149–51.

23. Marr, pp. 40–42, 51, 146; Farouk-Sluglett and Sluglett, pp. 23–30.

24. Marr, pp. 281–2.

25. Hasan al-'Alawi, *Al-Shi'a wal-dawla al-qawmiyya fil-'iraq*, pp. 197–8.

26. Marr, p. 282.

27. Marr, pp. 283–4. While the nationalizations in themselves were a part of 'Arif's wider policy of preparing the grounds for Iraqi-Egyptian unification, rather than pre-meditated anti-Shi'i acts, it is possible that the predominance of the Shi'a in certain sectors of private enterprise (like finances and foreign and large internal trade) and their poor representation at the policy-making level made it easier for 'Arif and his Sunni-Arab ruling elite to nationalize these sectors. Without an effective lobby in the corridors of power, the Shi'i entrepreneurs were defenseless against 'Arif's nationalizations. Some Shi'is, however, feel very differently. According to Hasan al-'Alawi (pp. 213–16), the

whole nationalizations policy under 'Abd al-Salam 'Arif was geared to exclude the Shi'a from leading roles in the economy, under the false guise of 'Arab socialism'.

28. See, for example, their demands of Faysal I to reserve half of the places in his cabinet and in the government administration to Shi'is, Peter Sluglett, *Britain in Iraq, 1914–1932* (London, 1976), p. 306; and in the mid-1930s, Hasan al-'Alawi, p. 183. And some Shi'i support for the Rashid 'Ali revolt see ibid., pp. 181–6.

29. See Hanna Batatu, 'Iraq's Underground Shi'a Movements . . . ', *Middle East Journal*, no. 4, vol. 35, Autumn 1981, pp. 578–94.

30. For example: Hasan al-'Alawi, pp. 200–8; Muhsin al-Hakim calling the Muslims of Iraq to support the new activist Ulama Group (*jama'at al-'ulama*) of Najaf, *Liwa al-Ikhwa al-Islamiyya* (Baghdad), 22 January 1959; *al-Dawa Chronicle* (London), no. 4, August 1980, pp. 3, 6; *al-Massar* (London), 28 October 1987; *al-Nashra* (Cyprus), no. 5, December 1983, pp. 23–5; *Jeune Afrique*, 25 January 1984, p. 50; Mahdi al-Hakim to *Impact International*, 25 April – 8 May 1980, p. 5; *Tariq al-Thawra* (Tehran), no. 29, February–April 1983, pp. 14–15; an interview with Grand Ayat Allah Muhsin al-Hakim, *al-Hayat*, 19 January 1961; *al-Hayat*, 24 November 1966; 18 November 1967.

31. For additional details on the genesis of the Ba'th party in Syria, see: Kamel S. Abu Jaber, *The Arab Ba'th Socialist Party: History, Ideology and Organization* (New York, 1966); John F. Devlin, *The Ba'th Party, A History from it Origins to 1966* (Stanford, Calif.: Stanford Univ., 1979); Patrick Seale, *The Struggle for Syria: A Study of Post-War Arab Politics 1945–58* (London, 1965) (henceforth: Seale, *The Struggle for Syria*). As for Iraq, unless otherwise stated, the following summary is based on Majid Khadduri, *Republican Iraq* (London, 1969), (henceforth: Khadduri, 1969) pp. 10, 189ff.; Devlin, pp. 106–12, 231ff.; Hanna Batatu, *The Old Social Classes and the Revolutionary Movements of Iraq*, (henceforth: Batatu, 1978); pp. 722ff.; The Arab Ba'th Socialist Party, the Pan-Arab Leadership, *The Reasons for the Disintegration of Party Rule in Iraq* [in 1963] (submitted to the Eighth Pan-Arab Congress in Damascus, April 1965; translated into Hebrew and annotated by Ofra Bengio, Tel-Aviv Univ., 1981) (henceforth: ABSP, *Reasons*). There are minor differences between the various sources. For the party line on religion, see, for example, Michel 'Aflaq, *Fi sabil al-ba'th* (For the Sake, or On The Road of Resurrection) (Beirut, 1974) (henceforth: 'Aflaq, *Fi sabil*), pp. 122–34, 168–78, 201–17; Saddam Husayn, *Fi al-din wal-turath* (On Religion and Heritage), (Baghdad, 1977) (Henceforth: Husayn, *Fi al-din*).

32. See, for example, 'Abd alla 'Abd al-Da'im, *Al-Jil al-'arabi al-jadid* (Beirut, 1961), throughout the book.

33. Devlin, p. 109.

34. Khadduri, 1969, p. 19; Devlin, pp. 109, 114; Batatu, 1978, pp. 789–91, 810, 1004.

35. Uriel Dann, *Iraq Under Qassem* (Jerusalem, 1969) (henceforth: Dann, 1969) pp. 40, 42, 71.

36. See 'Aflaq's hind-sight severe denouncement of this anti-Communist campaign, blaming it conveniently on Sa'di's faction, Jubran Shamiyya (ed.), *Silsilat Sijill al-Ara* (Beirut), January–February 1966, pp. 90–1.

37. For his version of these years, that is fairly accurate in many details, despite its attempt to glorify Husayn, see his semi-official biography, Amir Iskandar, *Saddam Husayn, the Fighter, the Thinker, the Man* (Paris, 1980), pp. 94ff.

38. Majid Khadduri, *Socialist Iraq* (Washington, D.C., 1978), pp. 18–19.

39. *Thawrat 17 tammuz, al-tajriba wal-afaq*, the resolutions of the Eighth Regional Congress (Baghdad, January 1974), pp. 167–72.

40. *Thawrat 17 Tammuz*, pp. 179–80.

41. Bengio, pp. 31–2. Kurdish rule, however, did not extend to the large cities and the main roads.

42. This disappearance is explained as the result of two processes: many Shi'is left the party when 'Ali al-Sa'di was ousted from it in the wake of the November 1963 debacle, and for reasons not related directly to their sectarian affiliation, those who stayed, received a far harsher treatment by the 'Arif police in jail than their Sunni counterparts. Some of them died, and for others clandestine party activity became to risky. For details see Batatu, pp. 1077ff.

43. Amazia Baram, 'The Ruling Political Elite in Ba'thi Iraq 1968–1986, the Changing Features of a Collective Profile', *International Journal of Middle East Studies*, vol. 21, no. 4, November 1989, pp. 447–93.

44. For Shi'i activists charges that the Ba'th are 'atheists' for example, *Tariq al-Thawra*, no. 25, ibid., p. 10; *al-Dawa Chronicle*, no. 4, August 1980, p. 1; no. 17, September 1981, p. 7; no. 22, February 1982, pp. 1, 6. For Ba'th accusations see below.

45. *Al-Muharrir*, 19 December; *al-Anwar*, 20 December 1966; Amir Iskandar, pp. 114ff.

46. See Amazia Baram, 'Ideology and Power Politics in Syrian-Iraqi Relations 1968–1984' in Moshe Ma'oz and Avner Yaniv (eds), *Syria Under Assad: Domestic Constraints and Regional Risks* (London, 1986), pp. 125–39.

47. Ofra Bengio, *The Kurdish Revolution in Iraq* (Tel-Aviv, 1989), p. 27; and interviews.

48. See Amazia Baram, 'Saddam Husayn: A Political Profile', *The Jerusalem Quarterly*, no. 17, Fall 1980, pp. 115–44.

49. See Fouad Ajami's analysis, 'The End of Pan-Arabism', Tawfic E. Farah (ed.) *Pan-Arabism and Nationalism* (Boulder, Colorado and London, 1987), pp. 96–114.

50. Compare, for example, The National Bureau of Culture, *Political Report The Tenth National Congress* (Baghdad, March 1970), pp. 18–38, 74–8, 80–1, 85–7; Ahmad Hasan al-Bakr, *Masirat al-thawra fi khutab wa tasrihat al-ra'is* (Baghdad, 1971), pp. 231–2;

Saddam Husayn, *al-Jumhuriyya*, 13 May 1969; with *Thawrat 17 tammuz al-tajriba wal afaq* (The Resolutions of the Eighth Regional Congress, Baghdad, January 1974), pp. 124–31, 167–70; also 121, 222, 224, 162–6; Michel 'Aflaq, *Baghdad Observer*, 10 October 1977; Typically the most central reason given to the Iraqi public by the Ba'th party for the failure of unity talks with Ba'thi Syria in 1978–79 was that the Syrian regime in fact coveted Iraq's oil riches but was not willing to pay for it the political price that Iraq demanded, namely, Iraqi hegemony within the future union (*Al-Taqrir al-markazi lil-mu'tamar al-Qutri al-tasi', haziran 1982*, The Central Report of the Ninth Regional Congress of June 1982 [Baghdad, January 1983], pp. 323–5.

Chapter 2:   The Ba'th in Power: The Political and Ideological Setting

1.   For example, *al-Hayat*, 22, 26, 27, 28 June; 1, 11, 12 July; 2, 4, 20 August 1969; *al-Nahar*, 5 July, 31 August, 26 September 1969; *Nida al-Watan*, 26 June, 21 July 1969; *al-Jarida*, 15 June, 16, 28, 30 August, 18 September 1969; *al-'Amal* (Beirut), 8 August 1969; *al-Thawra*, (hence: *Th*); al-Jumhuriyya (hence: *Jum*), 8 May, 12–13 August, 29 September 1969; 8–25 February, 24 March 1977; Edith and E. F. Penrose, *Iraq, International Relations and National Development* (London and Boulder, 1978), pp. 373–4; *Saddam husayn warith al-shah (Munazzamat al-'Amal al-Islami*, Tehran, 1981); *Tariq al-Thawra* (Tehran) no. 25, Rajab, 1402; *al-Dawa Chronicle* (London), no. 4, August 1980; no. 10, February 1981; no. 22, February 1982; no. 30, October 1982; no. 37, May 1983; no. 38, June 1983; no. 39, July 1983; no. 40, August 1983; *Imam* (The Iranian Embassy in London), April–May 1982; *al-Jihad* (Tehran), 6 September 1982; *Impact International*, 25 April–8 May 1980. *Alif Ba*, 16 April 1980, p. 15. 'A. Najaf, *al-Shahed al-shahid* (Tehran, *Jama'at al-'ulama al-mujahidin*, 1981), pp. 12, 27, 45; *Amnesty International News Release* (London), 10 March, 12 June, 1980; Amnesty International, *Report and Recommendations . . . to the Government of the Republic of Iraq*, 22–28 January 1983, pp. 21,39; *Sawt al-Iraq*, September 1983; *al-Nahar* (Beirut, 25 June 1983); Iraq's FM Tariq 'Aziz confirming executions, *Reuter*, from Kuwait, 20 July 1983; *al-Shira'* (Beirut), 1 August 1986. There are no reliable figures as to the total number of Shi'i deportees. According to Iranian sources, it rose in 1989 to close to five hundred thousands (including forty thousand Kurds). See *Tehran Times*, 28 February 1989, p. 1.

2.   A. Baram, 'The Ruling Political Elite in Ba'thi Iraq', ibid.

3.   For example, Marr, pp. 240–3, 261–4, 268–70, 272; Edith and E. F.Penrose, *Iraq, International Relations and National Development* (London and Boulder, 1978), pp. 452–60; Marion Farouk-Sluglett

and Peter Sluglett, pp. 137–40; Amazia Baram, *Iraq of the Ba'th 1968–1989: An Anatomy of Political Change* (forthcoming, due in 1991).

4. See Saddam Husayn, *Fi al-din wal-turath*, ibid.

5. Saddam Husayn, *al-Thawra wal-nazra al-jadida* (Baghdad, 1981), pp. 79–80. See also, ibid., pp. 101–4. And see in the resolutions of the Eighth Regional Iraqi Party Congress of January 1974, *Thawrat 17 tammuz al-tajriba wal-afaq* (Baghdad, 1974), pp. 162–4; and Saddam Husayn to the Popular Front, *Jum*, 26 April 1974; President Bakr on Revolution Day, *Jum*, 18 July 1974. And Saddam Husayn, *'Hawla iqamat al-ishtirakiyya fi qutr 'arabi wahid' (On the Establishment of Socialism in One Arab Country)*, *Afaq 'Arabiyya*, June 1978, pp. 2–9.

6. Bengio, pp. 36–7.

7. For reports on the use of poison gas and the flight of refugees to Iran and Turkey, see, for example, *NYT*, 22 June 1988; *The Independent*, 28 December 1988; *The Times*, 19 October 1988; *WP*, 8 September 1988; 14 March 1989. For Iraqi official admissions of mass-transfers of Kurds from Qal'at Diza (13,500 families) and nearby villages (1780 families) see the communique of the Iraqi Embassy in London, *INA*, 26 June, *FBIS-Daily Report*, 27 June 1989, p. 12; the figure of 250,000 was mentioned to the author by American officials in Washington, D.C. The Iraqi authorities claim that they compensated each family from Qal'at Diza with $30,000 (or around ID 10,000) per family and that families were given the choice where they wanted to go in Kurdistan (the Iraqi Embassy in London, ibid.). These claims could not be confirmed. See also *al-Iraq* (Baghdad), as quoted in *FBIS-Daily Report*, 19 June 1989, p. 20; Tariq 'Aziz to *al-Qabas*, 31 October 1988, in *FBIS-Daily Report*, 21 November 1988, p. 27.

8. For details, see Marr, pp. 220–5, 244–6, 291ff; Farouk-Sluglett and Sluglett, pp. 132–4, 178–81, 187–90, 200–5; Majid Khadduri, *Socialist Iraq* (Washington, D.C., 1978), pp. 148–64, 166–7, 173–4; Naomi Sakr, 'Economic Relations Between Iraq and Other Arab Gulf States', in Tim Niblock (ed.), *Iraq, the Contemporary State* (London, 1982), pp. 150–67; my articles, 'Qawmiyya and Wataniyya in Ba'thi Iraq, A Search of a New Balance', *MES*, vol. 19, no. 2, April, 1983, pp. 188–200; 'The June 1980 elections to The National Assembly in Iraq', *Orient*, vol. 22, no. 3, September 1981, pp. 391–412; 'Ideology and Power Politics', in Ma'oz and Yaniv, ibid.; 'Saddam Husayn: A Political Profile', *The Jerusalem Quarterly*, no. 17, Fall 1980, pp. 115–44. For an attempt to re-evaluate the political, economic and social policies of the Ba'th regime in an historical perspective, see A. Baram, *Iraq of the Ba'th, 1968–1989: An Anatomy of Political Change* (forthcoming, due in 1991).

9. See my early works, 'Mesopotamian Identity in Ba'thi Iraq', *Middle Eastern Studies*, vol. 19, no. 4, October 1983, pp. 426–55; 'Culture in

the Service of *Wataniyya'*, *Asian and African Studies*, vol. 17, no. 1–3, November 1983, pp. 265–313.

10. For Sa'ada's position see, for example, *Dustur al-hizb al-suri al-qawmi al-ijtima'i* (n.p. 1958) pp. 7–8; and for the views of the proponents of Egyptian Nationalism, see Israel Gershuni and James P. Jankowski, *Egypt, Islam, and the Arabs, the Search for Egyptian Nationhood 1900–1930* (Oxford and New York, Oxford University Press, 1986), pp. 40–54, 77ff. For Sati' al-Husri's views see for example his *al-'Uruba awwalan* (Beirut, 1958), pp. 113–15, 125–6; *Difa' 'an al-'uruba* (Beirut, 1957) pp. 52, 63, 70–9; *Ma hiya al-qawmiyya* (Beirut, 1959) pp. 251–2; *Hawla al-qawmiyya al-'arabiyya* (Beirut, 1961) pp. 94–103, 105. For a somewhat different approach during his early days in Iraq in charge of school curricula, see his *Mudhakkirati fi al-'iraq 1921–1941*, vol. 1 (Beirut, 1967), p. 216 on the 1922/3 curriculum.

11. 'Aflaq, *Fi sabil al-ba'th* (Beirut, 1974), pp. 181–3.

12. Ibid., pp. 219–220. And his position on Pharaonicism and on Antun Sa'ada's party, ibid., pp. 168–70.

13. See, for example, ibid., pp. 122–34.

14. al-Bazzaz, *Hadhihi qawmiyatuna* (Cairo, 1964), pp. 244–5. See also, ibid., pp. 62, 66, 95–6, 137–8, 234–5, 241, 401–3. Also in his book, *Min wahi al-'uruba* (Cairo, 1963), pp. 38–9, 55.

15. An explanation of the law states that the symbol of the sun 'represents the Arab sun[!]' and suggests: (a) freedom i.e. the revolution of 14 July, 1958; (b) it is 'the symbol of justice that was widespread in ancient Mesopotamia among the ancient inhabitants of Iraq before the Christian era'; (c) the symbol suggests 'Iraq's ancient name Araki or 'Land of the Sun'. The star is also characterized as an 'Arab star' (see Supplement B, Emblem of the 'Iraqi Republic, Law 57 of 1959; *WI*, no. 151 of 5 April 1959, pp. 1–2). The eight-pointed star is far more widespread in ancient Mesopotamian art then in its Arab Islamic counterpart. Indeed, clauses B and C show the regime to be aware thereof, and eager to bring it to the attention of the public. See a further hint in this direction in the law establishing the national flag, no. 102 of 1959; *WI*, no. 189 of 27 June 1959. The Iraqi state symbol was abolished by the 'Arif regime, the reason given being that the old symbol did not match 'the spirit of the revolution and the goal of unification'. See Law 86 of 1965, *WI*, no. 1125, of 8 June 1965, p. 3. 'The Arab Eagle' replaced it. Ibid. See also the modification of the national flag, whereby the new ensign 'expresses the noble Arab aims that the blessed [Ba'th] revolution [of February 1963] came to practice', Law 28 of 1963, *WI*, no. 812 of 8 June 1963. The 'Arab' eagle was fashioned after 'Abd al-Nasir's Egypt's national emblem.

16. *Sumer*, Baghdad, vol. 15, 1959, pp. 59ff. The Akkadian term 'dumuzi' means 'the good son'; this description was also applied to Qasim.

Chapter 3: Folklore and Mesopotamian Culture

1. There were folklore related activities during 'Arif's rule but they were quite limited. Thus *Firqat al-Rashid lil-Funun al-Sha'biyya* included dancers, singers, and musicians employed however on a partial salary (*Th*, 12 July 1968; *Jum*, 7, 8, 14, February 1967). Regarding painting exhibitions related to folklore, see also *Jum*, 21 March 1967; 25 April 1967. Collection of folk songs, *Jum*, 6 February 1967; letters from readers and reporters demanding more intensive research in this field, *Jum*, 6, 7, 8, 17, 21, February 1967, 14 March 1967).

2. Law 37 of 1969, *WI*, no. 1704, 12 March 1969, pp. 3–5. And see the law, replacing an administrative decree, which puts emphasis on fostering folklore, Law 146 of 1975, *WG*, no. 31, 4 August 1976, p. 2. Development of Arab-Islamic Heritage and Folklore, Resolution no. 21, 1972, *WG*, no. 10, 6 March 1974, pp. 6–7. A Folklore Directorship was established with wide powers to run a 'Folklore Center'. See more on this below.

3. *Th*, 11 May 1975.

4. *Jum*, 17 January 1969.

5. *Jum*, 20 May 1969; 19 January, 6 April, 22 August, 7, 10 September 1970. *al-Turath al-Sha'bi (TuSh)*, no. 7, vol. 11, p. 63.

6. *TuSh*, no. 4 vol. 1 (Dec. 1969), p. 164. Law 18 of 1971 'Folklore Center', the official newspaper (*WG*), no. 25, 23 June 1971, p. 11. For additional institutions see, *Afaq 'Arabiyya (AA)*, September 1977, pp. 94–5, *Th*, 12 April 1979.

7. *Jum*, 7 May 1969.

8. *Th*, 12 April 1979; *Culture and Art in Iraq* (Baghdad, 1978), pp.157–162; *TuSh*, no. 7, vol. 11, 1980, pp. 60–2, 64–5. More on encouragement to traditional crafts see, *Jum*, 3 April 1969; 30 March 1970; *Th*, 17 May 1972; 20 May, 3 August 1979; RCC Resolution 18 of 1971, *TuSh*, no. 7–8, 1971, pp. 178–180; and ibid., vol. 1, no. 4, Dec. 1969, p. 164; vol. 2 no. 1, September 1970, p. 179; no. 4, Dec. 1970, p. 182.

9. Law 120 of 1974, First Amendment of Law of Antiquities no. 59, of 1936, *WG*, no. 4, 22 January 1975, pp. 9–12.

10. See, for example, *Jum*, 22 January 1979; 26 July 1979; *Th*, 18 May 1972, p. 24; 7 February, 3 March, 13, 16, 20, 23, May; 2 June, 8 July, 30 September, 3 October 1975; 4 February, 17 April, 1977; 9 July, 5 October 1979; *TuSh*, no. 7–8, vol. 2, March–April 1971, p. 180. *Th*, 18 May 1972; *Jum*, 7 October 1982; *Th*, 24 February 1969; *Tariq al Sha'ab*, 17 January 1978; *TuSh*, no. 7, year eleven, July 1980, pp. 65–6. Regarding Soviet guidance and influence in the development of folklore troupes see *al-Thaqafa al-jadida*, February 1972, pp. 163–8. See also below in the discussion of the Communist position regarding the promotion of folklore.

11. *TuSh*, no. 1, vol. 1, September 1969, p. 126; no. 9 second year,

March–April 1971, p. 172; *Culture and Arts in Iraq* (Baghdad, 1978), p. 144.

12. *al-Muthaqqaf al-'Arabi*, September 1970, pp. 157–8.
13. *al-Muthaqqaf al-'Arabi*, ibid.
14. *Jum*, 28 October 1972, p. 3.
15. *Jum*, 25 April 1980, p. 1. And See also ibid., 22, 23, April.
16. *Th*, 10 July 1981, p. 6. For another, similar, festival replete with political themes see, *Th*, 21 October 1981, p. 4. And see a similar festival in the mixed Sunni-Shi'i area of Dyala, which was attended by Sa'd Qasim Hammudi, a Shi'i member of the Regional Leadership, *Jum*, 29 July 1981.
17. *The Central Report of the 9th Regional Congress, June 1982* (Baghdad, January 1983), p. 230. For more on folk songs and their development see, *Tariq al-Sha'b*, 23 June, 14 July, 18 August 1976.
18. See, for example, *Th*, 25 May 1969; 19 March 1975; *The Middle East*, February 1979, pp. 122–3; *TuSh*, no. 4, vol. 1, Dec. 1969, p. 164; no 1, vol. 2, September 1970, p. 179. The demand to write in the colloquial language had at least one important precedent: the famous poet, Ma'aruf al-Rusafi, in several instances, demanded that classical Arabic be put aside in favor of the more practical spoken tongue. *al-Aqlam*, August 1968, pp. 3–12. See also regarding the playwright 'Adil Kazim, *al-Thaqafa al-Jadida*, April 1972, p. 159.
19. See, for example, *Th*, 12 August 1977; 5, 27, July 1979; 1 October 1979; and especially 13 February 1980. Also, *Funun*, 10 Dec. 1979, p. 56; *Afaq 'Arabiyya*, January 1980, p. 129.
20. For example, *Jum*, 23 January 1988. And see the plan for the 12 dunam 'Baghdad Clock' and center, *Jum*, 22 January 1988.
21. *Jum*, 17 January 1969.
22. *Jum*, 18 October 1982. The moving force behind the reconstruction of old private houses seems to be Engineer Ihsan Fathi. In 1986 he was made head of the new architecture department at al-Mustansiriyya University. See his book with Jabra Ibrahim Jabra, *Baghdad bayna al-ams wal yawm* (Baghdad, 1987), pp. 135, 192. And John Warren and Ihsan Fathi, *Traditional Houses in Baghdad* (Sussex, 1982). Fathi used to preach for preservation of old buildings before the Ba'th takeover but only under the Ba'th he managed to get official support (an interview with a foreign diplomat).
23. *Baghdad Observer*, 26 February 1989.
24. Milton Viorst, *The New Yorker*, 19 October 1987, p. 86.
25. Regulation no. 57 of 1970, 'Iraqi Fashion House', *WG*, no. 20, 19 May 1971, p. 7.
26. *Culture and Art in Iraq* (Baghdad, 1978), p. 165. See also photographs of a few costumes: *Jum*, 5 July 1977. See also *Th*, 19 May 1972; *al-Khalij al-'Arabi*, no. 7, 1977, p. 101; *TuSh*, no. 7–8, vol. 2, March–April 1971, p. 180; no. 7, vol. 11, 1980, pp. 63–4.
27. 'Abd al-Noor Aboud, *Iraq Today*, 16–31 Dec. 1977.

28.	Before the outbreak of the Gulf War the Iraqis thought it wise to improve ties with the USA (the Soviets imposed a partial embargo on arms to Iraq for more than a year of the war). Baghdad's first diplomatic move was to send the Fashion House to hold a show in Washington, as a subtle reminder to the Americans of the West's indebtedness to Iraq for the contributions to world civilization by the Sumerians, Akkadians and Babylonians. This exhibition was reported in *The Washington Post*, 17 August 1980.

29.	*Th*, 19 October, 31 July, 2, 4, August 1979. See also, for example, *Th*, 19 May 1972; 16 May 1975; 13, 25, February 1980; *Jum*, 23 February 1971; 12 April 1974; *Baghdad Observer*, 18 January 1980. The performance also included Kurdish costumes. See *Jum*, 19 February 1972.

30.	*Jum*, Weekly Supplement, 3 February 1979, p. 1, 10, 11.

31.	*Jum*, 14 October 1982, p. 8.

32.	Saddam Husayn, *al-Thawra wal-nazra al-jadida* (Baghdad, 1981), p. 81–2.

33.	*Mithaq al-'amal al-watani wal-qawmi* (Baghdad, 15 Nov. 1971), pp. 49–50. See also Sami Ahmad al-Mawsili, *al-Aqlam*, no. 8, vol. 8, Dec. 1972, pp. 2–6.

34.	See also, for example, the stress on Folklore Center delegations to the south to learn from the locals and purchase folk products, as well as to collect proverbs, folk stories, songs, poems and dances, *Jum*, 30 October 1972, p. 3.

35.	*Th*, 9 July 1979, p. 8. See also the Mosul Festivals designed to express 'patriotic-Iraqi unity', through various folklore performances, *Jum*, 11, 13, 15 April 1970; 10 April 1973; 23 March 1974; 11, 16 April 1975; *Th*, 11 April 1975. A most interesting solution to this problem appeared in the mid-1980s, when the party newspaper's daily cartoons commenced portraying 'an Iraqi man' as a mixture: he wears a Kurdish head covering and Arab dress. See, for example, *Th*, 16 November 1984. And see Saddam Husayn wearing a Kurdish head covering and a safari suit in many posters.

36.	Communique, *TuSh*, no. 1, vol. 1, p. 3. See also, for example, similar stress but accompanied by a warning against cultural isolationism, Salman al-Tikriti, *TuSh*, no. 10, vol. 1, June 1970, pp. 4–5; and no. 1, vol. 1, p. 10 ;*Th*, 12 May 1969.

37.	Muhammad Khalifa, *Th*, 24, 25, 26, February 1969. And see Mahmud 'Abta, *TuSh*, no. 1, vol. 1, pp. 4–5; Fadil Akram, in a Prologue in the book by Hillu Mansur, *Suwar mulawwana, dirasa fi al-shi'r al-sha'bi* (Baghdad, 1970), p. 4.

38.	Lutfi Khuri, *TuSh*, no. 9, vol. 1, May 1970, pp. 3–6; and ibid., no.7, vol. 11, 1980, pp. 59–60. And at the All-Arab Folklore Congress in Baghdad, *Jum*, 2–5 March 1977. Also: *TuSh*, no. 9, vol. 1, May 1970, pp. 3–6; no. 7, vol. 11, 1980, pp. 59–66. And folklore as preserving 'the pan-Arab personality' of the Palestinian people, see *Jum*, 4 March 1977; *Th*, 6 March 1977

39. Dr 'Abd al-Hamid Yunis, *al-Aqlam*, no. 3, vol. 8, 1972, pp. 19–20. See also, assertion of 'certain differences' between Arab countries, although they have more in common, *Th*, 6 March 1977, cultural editor's column.

40. The Iraqi Sami Mahdi, *Th*, 31 March 1977. And see reports in the Iraqi Press on the Baghdad Conference for Folklore, 16–19 April 1986.

41. See also report on 'flood of letters' received by the editors supporting the use of the spoken Iraqi language in poems and songs, and calling for national broadcasts to be opened up to popular poets who write in dialects, *Jum*, 8 September 1970.

42. See, for example, Dr Khalid al-Jadir on the National Folklore Troupe, *Th*, 23 May 1975; and 16 May 1975; *Afaq 'Arabiyya*, on the movie 'Art of Samarra', February 1980, p. 126; *Th*, on folkloric ceramics, 14 December 1968, p. 25; *Th*, 11 June 1969; Dr Salman 'Isa, Director of Antiquities , *Jum*, 1 April 1970; *Jum*, 19 January 1970, p. 16; and see more below.

43. *Jum*, 23 February 1971, p. 12; and see also, ibid., 24 February 1971, p. 5.

44. *TuSh*, no. 7, vol. 11, 1980, pp. 63–4.

45. See, *Th*, 24 February 1969; *TuSh*, no. 1, vol. 1, September 1969, p. 3, 5–10.

46. Najjah Hadi al-Kubba, response to attack, *TuSh,* no. 8, vol. 5, 1974, p. 149. See also Sami Mahdi, *Th*, 24 March 1977, p. 6.

47. *TuSh*, no. 1, vol. 1, pp. 9–10.

48. By Taha Baqir, see *Sumer*, no. 1, vol. 6, 1950, pp. 42–80. For a new translation see Dr Sami Sa'id al-Ahmad, *TuSh*, no. 6, 7, 8, 11, 12, 1977; 2, 3, 5, 6, 8, 9, 1978; 5, 6, 7, 10, 1979. This according to Ja'far al-Kawwaz, *Faharis al-turath al-Sha'bi, 1969–1979* (Baghdad, 1980).

49. Salman al-Tikriti, *TuSh*, no. 2, vol. 1, October 1969, pp. 28–30; no. 8, vol. 1, April 1970, p. 23ff.

50. Majid 'Abdallah al-Shams, ibid., no. 11, vol. 1, July 1970, pp. 36–54.

51. Taha Baqir, ibid., no. 4, vol 2, December 1970, pp. 137–43.

52. Salman al-Tikriti, ibid., no. 10, vol. 1, June 1970, pp. 3–4.

53. 'Abd al-Jabbar Mahmud al-Samarra'i, ibid., no. 3, vol. 1 November 1969, p. 6. See also Taha Baqir, ibid., no. 1, vol. 2, September 1970, pp. 9–15; Salman al-Tikriti, ibid., no. 5, vol. 1, January 1970, pp. 11–18; cover page, no. 2, vol. 3, October 1971; George Habib, 'Aramaic Expressions in [our] Colloquial Language', ibid., no. 11, vol. 3, pp. 35–40.

54. On the connection between Sumerian songs and those of Southern 'Iraq today, see, for example, Dr Fawzi Rashid, *Afaq 'Arabiyya*, November 1977, pp. 81–3; S. Brock, on the Dispute Poem as a link between Sumerian and modern Syriac literature, *Bayn al-Nahrayn*, no. 28, vol. 7, 1979, p. 426; 'Abd al-Rahman, on the continuity of children's names, ibid., no. 17, vol. 5, pp. 7–12. On a Soviet study claiming that present day Iraqis are descendants of the Sumerians, the Akkadians etc.,

and anthropologically distinct from the Syrians, *Jum*, 4 April 1970; see also, *Th*, 23 February, 3, 25 March 1975.

55.   Khalil Hamudi (archeologist), *Afaq 'Arabiyya*, September 1977, pp. 94–5.
56.   *Jum*, 5 February 1973, p. 4.
57.   *Th*, 14 July 1976, last page. The reviewer praised the dance but pointed out that, while the dance related to Hammurabi [beginning of 2nd millennium BC], the decorations were from the period of Nebuchadnezer the Second [middle of 1st millennium BC] and the combination thus being an anachronism.

Chapter 4:   A Passion for Archeology

1.   There is no information on the year 1966–1967. *Sumer*, vol. 21, 1965, p. 144; vol. 22, 1966, p. 129; vol. 23, 1967, p. 215; vol. 24, 1968, p. 127–8; vol. 25, 1969, p. 166; vol. 26, 1970, pp. 255–6; vol. 29, 1973, p. 125.
2.   See, Consumer Price Index Number in Baghdad and Its Suburbs, The Central Bank of 'Iraq, *Bulletin* no. 3, July–September 1974, Table 26, pp. 40–1. The years 1969–73 were especially difficult, with lower oil revenues due to a dispute with the IPC oil company and its nationalization in June 1972. Given this, the substantial raise in the allotment to the Directorate of Antiquities was striking. Before the oil boom of 1973–74, inflation in Iraq was low, and the authorities did not make efforts to disguise it. The official information in those years seems to have been fairly accurate.
3.   Dr 'Isa Salman, *Jum*, 19 February 1969.
4.   Introduction, *Sumer*, vol. 25, 1969, pp. a–j.
5.   *Jum*, 23 July 1970; also ibid., 1 April 1970, p. 10.
6.   *Jum*, 1 April 1970.
7.   Fa'iz Muhsin, *Jum*, 4 February 1970.
8.   *Sumer*, vol. 30, 1974, p. 353.
9.   *Sumer*, vol. 33, 1977, p. 7; vol. 34, 1978, p. 5–7; *Bayn al-Nahrayn*, no. 29, vol. 8, 1980, p. 106; *Jum*, 14 April 1978; *Th*, 1 June 1980. For other dams see, *Jum*, 29 December 1987.
10.   Law 80 of 1979, 'State Organization for Antiquities and Heritage', *The Weekly Gazette*, no. 7, 13 February 1980, pp. 4–6.
11.   Mu'ayyad Sa'id, *ibid.*, vol. 35, 1979, the English part, pp. 12–13. See also the Arabic part, pp. 9, 19.
12.   E. Cody, *Washington Post News Service*, in *The Jerusalem Post*, 16 November 1979. More about generous government funds for additional reconstruction, see *Sumer*, vol. 35, 1979, p. 23.
13.   Yearly Reports on Archeological Digs and Reconstruction can be found in the editor's introductions to *Sumer*, and in the last part of each volume which includes the reports of the activities of the directorate.

14. Mu'ayyad Sa'id, ibid.; and also *Sumer*, vol. 30, 1974, p. 354. And vol. 35, 1979, the English part, p. 12–13. The law prohibits exports of antiquities unless undertaken by the directorate for the purpose of research. Penalties for illegal exports were set at seven years in prison and a heavy fine. (See Law 120 of 1974, *WG*, no. 4, 22 January 1975, pp. 9–12).

15. *Th*, 6 August 1980. See also *al-Qadisiyya* (Baghdad), 25 October 1987. Iraq threatened to call off archeological cooperation with whosoever refused to restore archeological finds to their source. See, *Sumer*, vol. 33, 1977, in English, pp. 6–7; *Th*, 15 May 1972, p. 6; *New York Times*, 2 January 1980.

16. *Jum*, 14 October 1982, p. 3. On the results of these efforts see, *Th*, 6 August 1980; *Herald Tribune*, in *HaAretz*, reported the Louvre's willingness to give the Hammurabi Stele to Iraq on 'long-term loan' (9 April 1980). France, Britain and the University of Chicago agreed to return sundry items (*Reuters, UPI*, Baghdad, 6 August 1980).

17. *Sumer*, vol. 24, 1968, pp. a–j; *Jum*, 1 April 1970, p. 10.

18. Based on reports on the visits of the public to museums, and a comparison between the period of the 'Arifs and the Ba'th period. See, *Sumer*, 1965, p. 141; 1968, p. 123; and comparison with 1969, p. 155; 1970, p. 243–5; 1972, p. 93; 1973, p. 122; 1970, English part, p. 244; 1972, English part p. 97; *Jum*, 14, 16, January 1969; 1 April 1970, p. 10; *Th*, 20 April 1972; 20 January 1975, p. 8.

19. *Sumer*, vol. 26, 1970, English part, p. 244.

20. *Baghdad Observer*, 8 September 1983, 'Museums'. Apparently the Ramadi museum houses antiquities from Tel-Aswad (29 kilometers north-west of Ramadi), a site whose history began at the dawn of the Sumerian dynasties and extended through the 3rd dynasty of Ur. Near Irbil there is a pre-historical site (the 4th and 5th millennium BC).

21. *Jum*, 2, 31, January 1969. See also the visit of Saddam Husayn and General 'Ammash in Babylon in order to encourage the reconstruction, *Jum*, 11 April 1970; 2 February 1971; a Hungarian diplomatic delegation in Babylon, *Jum*, 20 January 1971; report on a peak number of visitors in Babylon, *Jum*, 29 January 1970.

22. *al-Ta'akhi*, 12 April 1975; See also, for example, German delegation in Babylon, ibid.; and Numayri in Babylon, *ibid.*, 10 April 1975; Indira Ghandi in Nineveh, *Th*, 20 January 1975; Secretary General of the Bulgarian Communist Party 'Excited by the Mesopotamian Civilization', *Jum*, 12 April 1974; delegations from around the world in honor of the Ba'th anniversary, in Babylon, *Th*, 9 April 1975; Arab delegations at Assyrian sites, *Th*, 19 May 1975; the Soviets in Babylon, *Tariq al-Sha'b*, 16 August 1977; Saddam Husayn drags the Bulgarian President to Babylon, *Th*, 31 May 1980, the cover page.

23. *Sumer*, vol. 25, 1969, English part, p. 156; vol. 26, 1970, p. 244; *Jum*, 14 April 1978; *Th*, 18 January, 5 July, 16 November 1979.

24. *Jum*, 1 August 1970, p. 5.

25. Jamil Rufa'il surveying exhibitions in Iraq's museums in honor of Revolution Day, *Th*, 1 August 1975; See also, *Sumer*, vol. 25, English part, p. 158–9; Dr 'Isa Salman, Director of Antiquities, *Jum*, 23 July 1970; Fa'iz Muhsin, *Jum*, 4 February 1970; *Th*, 30 January 1972; *Th*, 7 July 1977; *Jum*, 14 April 1978; *Th*, 16 August 1980; 5 July 1979. And more.

26. *Th*, 15 December 1979, p. 16; *Sumer*, vol. 30, 1974, p. 3, 5, 7; *Th*, 21 April 1975, p. 6; 2 March, 7 May, 1979; *Afaq 'Arabiyya*, April 1980, p. 156.

27. *Culture and Art in Iraq* (Baghdad, 1978), pp. 49, 91–3.

28. *Jum*, 1 April 1970, p. 10; *Th*, 20 April, 1972; 5, 21 March 1975, p. 8; 11, 26 July 1979, p. 8; *France Pays Arabes*, August 1981, p. 20; See also the annual report in *Sumer*, in the various volumes, on reconstruction of sites, and especially on the five-year plan to reconstruct the city of Ashur, vol. 35, 1979, pp. 21–3, and also, ibid., pp. 271–400. And 'The Facelift of Assur', see *The Baghdad Observer*, 2 August 1988. In Nineveh the walls were partially reconstructed, one of the gates was reconstructed and a beer-garden was built for the tourists. According to tourists' reports until late 1988 not much was done in Ashur.

29. Preservation of Aqaraquf, al-Hatra, Ur, Samarra and Babylon was launched in 1960 by the Qasim regime. However, according to reports in *Sumer*, work was discontinued at most of the sites in the mid-1960s. See *Sumer*, no. 1–2, eighteenth year, 1962, p. 5–14; no. 1–2, twentieth year, 1964, introductory pages; and 22nd year, 1966, introduction; and also year twenty-three, 1967, ibid.

30. 'Isa Salman, *Sumer* vol. 26, 1970, pp. e–g, and see also *Jum*, 2 February 1971, p. 4.

31. *Sumer*, vol. 34, 1978, pp. 8–9; vol. 35, 1979, pp. 9, 16–20, 30–93, 249–294; and Resolutions of the International Symposium on Babylon, Assur, and Himrin, ibid., pp. 601–2. Joseph Craft, *The New York Times*, 2 January 1980; *Jum*, 25 February 1980; *Th*, 13, 15, April, 31 May 1980. *The New Yorker*, 20 October 1980, pp. 151–3.

32. *Sawt al-Talaba*, July 1981, pp. 27–9. According to an Iraqi archeologist (London, summer 1982), the work was very complicated and difficult and demanded a high degree of expertise, therefore the sums of money alloted were not in themselves an indication of the total effort invested in Babylon. In fact, the 'State Organization of Antiquities' was unable to use up the budget it had been allocated (see also *Sawt al-Talaba*, ibid., p. 29). Since 1987–88 priorities changed, and instead of careful reconstruction the president instructed his archeologists to build Babylon without delay. And see below.

33. Dr 'Isa Salman, to Vice President 'Ammash, *Th*, 3 February 1971, p. 5.

34. Visit of the Deputy Prime Minister to Babylon, *Th*, 24 February 1981, p. 6. Eventually the first phase alone cost $80m. See *AP* from Baghdad, 19 January 1988.

35.   Interview with the projects director by the *Washington Post News Service*, as quoted in *The Jerusalem Post*, 16 November 1979. And see also Dr Mahdi, *Sumer*, vol. 35, 1979, p. 19.

36.   *Th*, 24 February 1983, and see report of the Director General of the General Institution for Antiquities and Heritage, Mu'ayyad Sa'id, regarding substantial expenditures on excavations and reconstruction [of Islamic sites] in Samarra, as directed by Saddam Husayn 'to accentuate Iraq's antiquities and send its civilizational roots into the depths of history' and how the excavations proved 'the glory that was Mesopotamia', *Jum*, 14 October 1981.

37.   *AP*, from Baghdad, 19 January 1988; *Financial Times*, 15 October 1987; *Th*, 25 January 1987; 23 January, 1989; and see Saddam's instructions to allocate ID 60m to the province of Babylon for preparations to the 1988 Babylon Festival, *Th*, 31 August, 1988.

38.   *Babylon City Guide 1988* (The Ministry of Culture and Information, The Department of Antiquities and Heritage, Baghdad, 1988).

39.   Dr Zaku, *al-Fikr al-Jadid*, 14 May 1977; see also below, the section on art.

40.   *Th, 26* July 1979.

41.   See, for example, Muhammad Nasir Khalil's definition whereby Ishtar was 'a whore and a warrior', *Sumer*, 1979, p. 61. In fact Ishtar was no 'whore' as she received no payment for sexual intercourse. She was, indeed a goddess of fertility and had a lively sexual appetite. The ancient Babylonian rite of Ishtar, though fertility rite, did not involve mass-prostitution.

42.   See opening ceremony, *Jum*, 23 September 1981, and a comparison of Saddam Husayn with Nebuchadnezzar emphasizing the superior achievements of the former over the latter, commercial advertisement, *Observer*, London, 20 July 1980.

43.   *Jum*, 23 September 1981, p. 6.

44.   Ibid.

45.   See, for example, Sati' al-Husri's story on the great Iraqi-Arab poet of the 1st half of the 20th century, Muhammad Mahdi al-Jawahiri from Najaf, who soon after the establishment of the monarchy in Iraq requested a position as teacher in the Ministry of Education but resisted demand that he would give up his Iranian citizenship and apply for Iraqi citizenship. Ultimately, he gave in to the pressure but published an anti-Iraqi poem in a newspaper to explain that, were it not for his family, he would not have chosen Iraq, preferring Iran, 'its air . . . and sky'. See Sati' al-Husri, *Mudhakkirati fi al-'iraq* (Beirut, 1967), vol. 1, pp. 588–90. And see also, ibid., pp. 323–7; 419–21; 585–8, 591–9.

46.   See, *Th, Jum*, 21 September 1987, the President's visit to Babylon to inspect preparations for the Festival and see the Iraqi press throughout the following month. Also, *Th*, 21 October, p. 7, and last page; *The Baghdad Observer*, 5 March 1987.

47.   *Jum*, 23 September 1988. And see, *Th, Jum*, 24 September through 3

October 1988. And interviews with foreign diplomats who had attended the Festival, London, Nov. 1988, Sept. 1989–March 1990.

48. *Time Magazine*, 21 May 1990, p. 23.
49. *The Central Report of the Ninth Regional Congress, June 1982*, pp. 149–150, 234.
50. *Majallat Kuliyyat all-Adab*, no. 23, (1978), pp. 12–13; 'Iraqi Culture Center, London, *Iraqi Art of the 50s* (1979), p. 15; *Ur* (Iraqi Culture Center, London), Special Issue, 1981, pp. 82–3.

Chapter 5:   Mosul's Spring Festivals: Mesopotamian Rites

1. *Jum*, 11 April 1969.
2. *Jum*, 21 April 1969.
3. Jum, 11 April 1970. The General Secretary of the Ministry of Tourism on the contribution of the festival to the glory of Iraq in the past and present and to the unity of the various communities in Mosul, ibid., 16 April 1970.
4. *Jum*, 11 April 1970. See also, ibid., April 13, 15.
5. *Jum*, 21 April 1971, p. 10. See also, ibid., 12, 15, 16, April 1971. The Festival in the next two years, see *Jum*, 11 April 1972; *Th*, 10 April 1973.
6. *Th*, 11 April 1975, p. 4. For more details and photos see ibid., 16 April 1975.
7. See the attempt to establish an interconnection between the Arabs of southern Iraq, the Arabs of its north and the Kurds, through the unearthing of the historical roots of the National Kurdish Festival, Nevruz, at the end of the third millennium BC in a Sumerian city in Southern Iraq, where the Spring Festival celebrated the betrothal of the Goddess Inana to the God Dumuzi (Tammuz). Reportedly this festival was still celebrated in Abbasid Iraq, though in a different form. *Jum*, Weekly Supplement, 23 March 1974, pp. 8–9.
8. *Th*, 13 April 1976; 10, 17, April 1977. In 1978 the Festival was combined with the First Iraqi Festival for University Youth in Mosul. *Jum*, 15 April 1978, pp. 8–9; and see also, *Th*, 13 April 1978; *Baghdad Observer*, 14 April 1979.
9. *Jum*, 16 April 1980, cover page. (On the content of the festival, see also, ibid., 17 July, pp. 1, 8. In 1981 the Festival was proclaimed as an all-Iraqi holiday, The First National Spring Festival (*Th*, 17 April 1981)
10. *al-'Iraq*, 15 April 1984. See also *al-Tali'a al-Adabiyya*, March 1984, p. 123, on the Mosul Festival being the 'ressurection' of the 'great heritage' of Babylon's spring festivals.
11. *Jum*, 8 April 1988, p. 4.
12. *Th*, 16 November 1979.
13. Ibid.

14. *Th*, 29 April 1984; *al-'Iraq*, 15 May 1984. For the seventh annual festival see ibid., 26 April 1986, p. 5.
15. *al-Aqlam*, no. 1, January 1984, p. 6; *al-'Iraq*, 6 January 1987. See also the guided tour given to poets and novelists attending the Abu Tamam Festival in Babylon, Ashur, Nimrud and other ancient Iraqi sites, *al-Aqlam*, 11, 1972, p. 105–6.
16. In 1984 the First Festival of Ta'mim and in 1987 the First Festival of Nineveh were designed to launch a series of provincial festivals. See, *Th*, 21 October 1987; *al-Qadisiyya*, 7 March 1987. Both were held under the president's auspices, and both involved archeology, folklore and sports.
17. See this approach also in Sati' al-Husri, *Mudhakkirati fi al-iraq*, vol. 1, 1921–1927, (Beirut, 1967), p. 215, which distinguishes between the history of the Iraqi homeland and that of the Arab nation. And see more below.
18. See, for example, *Th*, 13 April 1976; 11 April 1975.
19. See, for example, *Jum*, 11 April 1969; 11 April 1970; 21 April 1971; 23 March 1973; *Th*, 11 April 1975; 10 April 1977.
20. *al-Ta'akhi*, 12 April 1975.
21. Saddam Husayn, at a June 1975 convention of teachers convoked to reform the teaching curricula of history, *al-Thawra wa al-nazra al-jadida* (Baghdad, 1981), p. 80–1.
22. Sa'ad Jawad, *'Iraq and the Kurdish Question 1958–1970* (Ithaka Press, London, 1981), p. 247ff.
23. Though an officer, Shihab, who inaugurated the celebrations in 1969, was close to Saddam Husayn. Taha Yasin Ramadan who was very faithful to Saddam Husayn inaugurated the festival in 1970 and in 1973 (*Jum*, 11 April 1970; *Th*, 10 April 1973). The 1972 festival was launched by Sa'dun Ghaydan (he continued to serve in Husayn's government and also in the RCC until June 1982) (*Jum*, 11 April 1972). In 1975 it was the Kurdish Vice President, Taha Muhyi al-Din Ma'ruf (*Th*, 11 April 1975), who Saddam appointed as a member of the RCC (the first Kurd) in June 1982, and who continued to serve as Vice President. In 1976–1977 and in 1979, it was 'Izzat al-Duri, an intimate of Husayn who served since 1979 as Deputy Chairman of the RCC (*Th*, 13 April 1976; 17 April 1977; *Baghdad Observer*, 14 April 1979). Information for the other years is lacking.

Chapter 6: Mesopotamian Symbols in Official Iraq

1. *Reuter*, 6 April 1970, *Sijill al-ara*, April-June 1970, p. 298.
2. See: *Encyclopedia of Islam* 2nd ed. (*EI*, II), vol. 1, pp. 1034–5.
3. al-Muthanna was also the name of a national pan-Arab club with fascist leanings in Iraq in the 1930s. H. Batatu, *The Old Social Classes and the Revolutionary Movements of Iraq* (Princeton, 1978), pp. 297–9.

4. There is bitter controversy among Iraqi historians in regard to al-Mukhtar's movement. In the second half of the 1970s, a SOAS graduate, Dr Faruq 'Umar Fawzi, defended the central government, especially the Abbasid, but also the Umayyad one, and attacked historians who saw al-Mukhtar's movement and its like as early liberation movements. See *al-Mawrid*, no. 2, vol. 8, summer 1979, p. 30; *Afaq 'Arabiyya*, September 1977, pp. 76–83.
5. *Jum*, 17 April 1970.
6. Dr Samira Kazim al-Shamma', *Manatiq al-sina'a fi al-'iraq* (Baghdad, 1980), pp. 329–37. Pre-Islamic Arab names appear also at the *nahiya* level; al-Khawarnaq, all-Hira, al-Munadhara.
7. The president was apparently referring to the Garden of Eden, thought to have been located in southern Iraq; to the flood in the story of Gilgamesh, and to Udpishtim, the Sumerian 'Noah'. And compare to 'Abd al-Wahhab al-Bayyati's poem about the unrequited love of Ashurbanipal: 'Ashurbanipal loved me / A city he built for his love for me surrounded by walls / He dragged the sun into [the city], chained / And fire, and slaves . . . and the river of Paradise.' *Diwan*, vol. 3 (Beirut, 1975?), p. 135.
8. Saddam Husayn, *Th*, 4 February 1983.
9. *Th*, 1 July 1980, p. 6; And see also on Iraq's contribution to the UN: a replica of Hammurabi's ancient stele. *Iraq Today*, 15–31 October 1977, p. 3.
10. Map of Baghdad, The General Institute for Tourism, 1977, scale 1:50,000. These names are new and were given after 1970–71. Compare to a tourist map of 1970 on a scale of 1:30,000, published by *The General Survey Directorate Press*.
11. Compare to a Sumerian girl's face in A. Moortgat, *The Art of Ancient Mesopotamia* (London, New York, 1969), plate 26.
12. *WG*, no. 36, 8 September 1976, p. 6. And compare to the mythological bearded bull, in *Ur*, published by the Iraqi Cultural Center in London, no. 3, 1981, p. 68.
13. *al-'Iraq*, vol. 2, no. 165, 1 August 1982. Due to the war, the congress did not convene in Baghdad.
14. Yvert and Tellier, *catalogue de Timbres Poste* (Paris, Amiens, 1985), pp. 67ff.
15. *Baghdad Observer*, 24 March 1986; 27 October 1987; *Jum*, 11 March 1969; 2 February 1973; *Middle East News Agency (MENA)* (Cairo), 25 July 1973; *Th*, 11 June 1983; *Wall Street Journal*, 6 April 1981; *Th*, 20 March 1990.
16. Law 29 of 1927. See: *Iraq Government Gazette*, no. 15, 9 April 1927, p. 117. And the use of hallmarks borrowed from Babylon, Ashur and Sumer by private commercial establishments under the monarchy, see for example, *Iraq Government Gazette*, no. 3, 1949, p. 6; no. 11, 12 March 1950, p. 7; no. 22, 28 May 1950, p. 5.
17. *Th*, 6 January 1978.

18. Law 1 of 1968, *WG*, no. 16, 1968; Resolution no. 1, 1968, ibid. The Law and the Resolution came out in 28 January 1968.
19. *Th*, 6 January 1978. The Mesopotamian star also appears in four other decorations. (*Th*, ibid.).
20. See,*Jum*, 14 October 1982; 30 October 1981; 29 July 1981; *Th*, 25 September 1981; 26 July 1981; 14 December 1981.
21. *Jum*, 9 September 1984.
22. Th, 22 September 1983, p. 9.
23. See, for example, *Th*, 23 December 1986.
24. *Th*, 6 March, 11 April 1987.
25. For example, *Th*, 5 March 1988; *Ruz al-Yusuf* (Cairo), 1 May 1989, *FBIS-Daily Report*, 19 July 1989, p. 24; *Jum* 29 December 1989.
26. Law 57 of 1980, the fourth amendment to the Law of Personal Status, *WI*, no. 2766, 31 March 1980, p. 528. The most interesting clause in this amendment stipulates that a woman shall not be considered 'rebellious' if she disobeyed her husband when the latter did not see to it that their home would be within a reasonable distance from her place of employment, so that she can 'reconcile her obligations at home with those at work'. See clause 2B. This clause is clearly outside the *Shari'a*. And for the claim that most laws under Saddam Husayn were inspired by Hammurabi's laws, see *Th*, 13 July 1987. The claim is not substantiated.
27. Article 66, *WI* 1625 of 21 September 1968.
28. Article 56, *al-Dustur al-mu'aqqat wa ta'dilatuhu* (Baghdad, 1976), p. 29.
29. Article 18 of the 1968 Constitution, p. 3, cf. *al-Dustur al-Mu'aqqat*, ibid., Article 18, p. 9.
30. Law 228 of 1970, The National Council, *WI* 1950, 28 December 1970, p. 1. In Law 55 of 1980, The National Assembly, *WI* 2764, 17 March 1980, pp. 486–96, this limitation, is somewhat moderated with the stipulation that a member's mother may be a citizen of any Arab country.
31. Law 47 of 1986, the First Amendment to Law 812 of 1984, regarding the Physicians' Association Council. *WI* 3098, 19 May 1986, p. 218.
32. Law 68 of 1985, *WI* 3059, 19 August 1985, p. 594, amending Law 43 of 1963, *WI* 818, 19 June 1963, p. 1.

Chapter 7: Art with Local and Mesopotamian Components

1. *Iraqi Art of the Fifties* (London, The Iraqi Culture Center, 1979); *Ur*, Special Issue on Contemporary Arab Art, London, The Iraqi Culture Center, 1981, pp. 78, 82–3.
2. Fadil Muhammad al-Bayati, *The Momument in Memory of the Glorious Revolution of July 14* (Baghdad, 1961?), p. 1–3, 17.
3. Famous artists of the middle generation are Shakir Hasan al-Sa'id;

Hashim al-Samarji; Ibrahim Rashid; Mahud Ahmad; Tariq Mazlum; Suhayl al-Hindawi and Sa'd al-Ka'bi. The younger generation includes artists like: Dara Hama Sa'id, 'Ali Salim, 'Abd al-Sahib al-Rikabi and many others. There is also a growing number of ceramic artists like Siham al-Sa'udi and Nuha al-Radi, within whose works it is easy to identify strong Mesopotamian influences. For more details see, for example, *Afaq 'Arabiyya*, June, 1984; November-December, 1980; *Jum*, 26 July 1982; *Alif Ba*, 2 April 1980; *Baghdad International Festival of Art* (Baghdad, 1986); *Th*, 5 February 1978; *Tariq al-Sha'b*, 27 April 1978.

4. 'Exhibitions', *Afaq 'Arabiyya*, June 1978, pages not numbered. Also the Scientific Supervisor of the General Institution of Antiquities, Abu Suf, *Jum*, 14 April 1978.
5. *Th*, 10 October 1983.
6. *Jum*, 9 June 1980, picture and explanation.
7. Sa'adoon Fadhil, *M. Ghani, Exhibition of Bronze Maquettes* (Europe, Baghdad, 1979); *Afaq 'Arabiyya*, June, 1978.
8. *Jum*, 5 April 1980. This is, very probably, an Italian influence; cf. Boromini's figure looking disdainfully at Berninis' Fountain, Piaza Navona, Rome. Rahhal was educated in Rome.
9. *Th*, 2 September 1976 and interviews with tourists.
10. *al-Fikr al-jadid*, 21 May 1977, pp. 4–6.
11. *Jum*, 6 March 1971, p. 12.
12. *Th*, 24 September 1979.
13. *Culture and Arts in Iraq* (Ministry of Culture and Arts, Baghdad, 1978), p. 168.
14. *Sawt al-Talaba*, July 1981, p. 41. And compare to the Sumerian Princess figure in *Ur*, no. 3, 1983, p. 34. And compare to picture of a beautiful Iraqi model with large eyes and perfectly arched eyebrows in a costume from The Iraqi Fashion House, which is a very faithful replica of the splendid dress and tiara of the Sumerian Princess: *Culture and Arts in Iraq*, p. 165.
15. *Afaq 'Arabiyya*, no. 7, March 1976, p. 96. Figures thought to represent Gilgamesh and Enkidu on a green jasper cylinder seal from the era of the Dawn of the Dynasties (2,500 BC), in a publication by the Iraqi Culture Center in London in honor of the Gilgamesh exhibition, ibid.: *The Epic of Gilgamesh* (London, January–March, 1982).
16. See also Ghani, in *The Influence of Calligraphy on Contemporary Arab Art* (London, Iraqi Culture Center, 1980), plate 35, and the medal given to outstanding workers (the Work Medal), *WI* 2988, 9 April 1984, p. 278.
17. Cf. Anton Moortgat, *The Art of Ancient Mesopotamia* (London and New York, 1969), figure 61.
18. Cf. A. Moortgat, plate 26.
19. For example, Hamed Madhi, *Naif Art in Iraq* (Baghdad, 1982). The more important among them are Muhammad al-Safi (b. 1922), Kazim

Khalil sa'id (b. 1922), Hamid Madi (b. 1927); Sa'diya Mun'im Furat (b. 1947).

20. See *Th*, 12 July 1976.
21. *The Baghdad Observer*, 3 December 1989. In an earlier explanation, relayed to the present author in 1983, the two halves were to symbolize a broken heart. This secular approach went out of vogue at the end of the war. The names of all the martyrs of the 1920–1941 anti-British revolts, of those who died in the uprisings of 1952 and 1956, and of the fallen soldiers up to the end of the October 1973 war, are engraved in plaques in a museum underneath the plateau. Apparently, the names of the soldiers who died in the Gulf War (over 100,000 in all) were not included as of yet (ibid.).
22. See for example, *Th*, 29 February 1984; 18 November 1984; *al-'Iraq*, 17 July 1987; *Alif Ba*, 8 January 1986; *Th*, 28 April 1985.
23. Saddam Husayn claims to be a descendent of Imam 'Ali. See, for example, a speech by Deputy Chairman of the RCC 'Izzat Ibrahim in Najaf, in celebration of 'Ali's birthday, *Th*, 15 March 1987. For the drawing see, ibid., 28 April 1985.
24. *Th*, 18 November 1984; also for example, *Th*, 16 February 1986; 6, 8, March 1986; 20 December 1987; 14, 21, 28, February 1988.
25. For example, *Th*, 8 February 1988; 27 April 1988.
26. *Th*, 11 June 1990.

Chapter 8: Mesopotamian Inspiration in Theatre and Poetry

1. Al-Shawaf (1924–   ) wrote no less than ten verse dramas. See *The Baghdad Observer*, 9 March 1987; Nur al-Din Faris, *al-Thaqafa al-Jadida*, February 1978, pp. 121–4. Babylonian-inspired plays appeared very early in modern Iraqi history, but they were aimed at very limited audiences. 'Nebuchadnezzar', by the Chaldean priest Khuri Hirmiz, was written and produced in 1888–89, in the clerical school of Mosul; see *al-Mawrid* 2/4 (December 1973), p. 83; *Present Day Iraqi Culture*, pp. 4–8. 'The Ruins of Babylon' was written in Mosul in 1913 probably for the same audience. These plays seem to be the origin of a view prevalent among Iraqi intellectuals, that the Jews collaborated with the Persians in their onslaught against Chaldean Babylon in the 6th century BC and helped bringing it down. For Iraqi politicians' use of this theme, see below.
2. *Th*, 5 January 1969, p. 18.
3. Yasin al-Nasir, *al-Fikr al-Jadid*, 15 January 1977; *al-Aqlam* 6/1 (October 1969), p. 97; *Th*, 23 April; 16 May, 1 June 1972.
4. Yasin al-Nasir, *al-Fikr al-Jadid*, 15 January 1977; *al-Aqlam* 6/1 (October 1969), p. 97.
5. For example, *Thawrat 17 tammuz al-Tajriba wal-afaq* (Baghdad, 1974), pp. 162–73; Saddam Husayn, *Afaq 'Arabiyya*, June 1978, pp. 2–9.

6. Yasin al-Nasir, *al-Fikr al-Jadid*, 15 January 1977.
7. Sami 'Abd al-Hamid, *Tariq al-Sha'b*, 6 April 1978; *al-Fikr al-Jadid*, 31 December 1976, p. 4; 14 May 1977; 6 May 1978; *Tariq al-Sha'b*, 12 May 1977; *Afaq 'Arabiyya*, July 1979, p. 130–1.
8. *Th*, 23 April 1975, p. 8.
9. *Al-Tali'a al-Adabiyya*, March 1977, p. 25; *al-Fikr al-Jadid*, 8 April 1978, pp. 4–5; *al-Idha'a wal-Tilifiziun*, May 8, 1977, pp. 36–8.
10. *Al-Fikr al-Jadid*, 6 May 1978, p. 9.
11. *al-Tali'a al-Adabiyya*, November, 1984, pp. 130–1. Also ibid., March 1984, pp. 122–3.
12. al-Sayyab, *Diwan* (Beirut, 1971), pp. 437–9.
13. *Diwan*, pp. 482–5. Cerberus of course, borrowed from Greek mythology, but the rest of the poem's symbols are Mesopotamian.
14. *Diwan*, pp. 471–3.
15. '*Tammuz Jaykur*', ibid., pp. 410–11.
16. *Diwan*, p. 486. See also '*Tammuz wal-madina*', pp. 414ff; for other poems, see, for example, pp. 271, 487–91, 627.
17. *Diwan*, pp. 324–5.
18. 'Abd al-Wahhab al-Bayyati, *Tajribati al-Shi'riyya* (Beirut, 1968), p. 22–3, 70–1, 74–6, 80–2.
19. Al-Bayyati, in *Shi'r*, 10/37 (Winter 1968), pp. 70–1; *Tajribati*, p. 39; *Diwan* (Beirut, 1974?), vol. 3, pp. 70–1, 161.
20. Al-Bayyati, 'The Return from Babylon,' *Diwan* (Beirut 1972), vol. 2, pp. 103–5.
21. Ghali Shukri interviewing al-Bayyati, *Dirasat 'Arabiyya*, September 1971, pp. 84–5; *Tajribati*, pp. 41–2, 61–3.
22. *Diwan*, vol. 2, pp. 128–130.
23. Ibid, pp. 203–5.
24. Tarrad al-Kubaysi, *Maqalat fi al-asatir fi . . . Shi'r al-Bayyati* (Damascus, 1974), pp. 56–7.
25. *Diwan*, vol. 2, p. 252.
26. '*Qasa'id Hubb . . .* ', in *Diwan*, vol. 3, pp. 135–46.
27. For example, Naji 'Alush's introduction to al-Sayyab's *Diwan*, p. DDD; Shmuel Moreh, *Modern Arabic Poetry 1800–1970* (Leiden, 1976), pp. 246–7; *al-Aqlam*, 6/12 (January 1971), p. 6.
28. *Jum*, March 16, 1969.
29. *Tajribati al-Shi'riyya*, pp. 60–1. And see also p. 45.
30. For example, 'A Stranger on the Gulf', written when he was an exile in Kuwait, *Diwan*, pp. 317–22. And poems written in London, ibid., pp. 269–88.
31. *Al-Aqlam* 8/9 (1973), 100–2; *Jum*, 25, 26, December 1970; 2 January, 13 April 1973; Desmond Stuart, *Poet of Iraq, Abdul Wahhab al-Bayyati* (London, 1976), 1–5.
32. *al-Qadisiyya*, 22 January 1987.
33. Hajim al-Salihi, *Th*, 29 April 1986.
34. *Th*, 30 April 1986. See also 'Abd al-Razzaq 'Abd al-Wahid, *Th*, 29

February 1984; Muhyi al-Din Isma'il, *Th*, 30 April 1985; and for an attempt to imitate al-Bayyati see Ghazay Dar' al-Ta'i, *al-Tali'a al-Adabiyya*, August 1985, p. 56.

35. Dr Nafi' 'Aqrawi, *Th*, 27 April 1988.
36. *al-Tali'a al-Adabiyya*, March 1984, pp. 3–29; June 1984, p. 97; *al-Qadisiyya*, 28 November 1987, p. 10; *Jum*, 4 April 1988.
37. *Th*, 25 April 1984.
38. al-Bayyati, *Bustan 'A'isha* (Cairo, 1989), pp. 8, 13.
39. *Th*, 12 July 1981. In the early years, Shafiq 'Abd al-Jabbar al-Kamali was a minister, and a member of the pan-Arab leadership and RCC; he was dismissed from his positions under pressure from Saddam Husayn. He was subsequently active in the cultural sphere until the early 1980s, when he disappeared, reportedly imprisoned. Kamali was a poet and painter in his own right.

Chapter 9: The Changing Features of the Past: Re-writing History

1. *al-Thawra al-'Arabiyya*, no. 6–7, vol. IV (1973), p. 187.
2. Jamal Baban, *Afaq 'Arabiyya*, March 1980, p. 98; *Th*, Weekly Supplement, 15 December 1979, p. 16. See also *Jum*, Weekly Supplement, 16 March 1969, p. 1; Jum, 14 March 1969, p. 3; 30 March 1970, p. 11; Dr Isa Salman, ibid., 16 January 1969, p. 5; 23 July 1970; *Th*, 31 May 1972; 14 July 1978; 10 December 1979; Dr al-Khatib, *Th*, 29 April 1980; on the treatment of Mesopotamian history in the new concise Iraqi Encyclopedia, *Th*, 23 November 1980; Dr Fawzi Rashid, *Afaq 'Arabiyya*, July 1979, pp. 92–9; Dr Ahmad, *Baghdad Observer*, 6 August 1979.
3. Prof. R. Landa as quoted by *Jum*, 4 April 1970; and see Hamid Sa'id, *Th*, 26 December 1981. And see below.
4. See for example Dr Bahnam Abu Suf, *Bayn al-nahrayn (BN)*, no. 1, vol. I (1973), pp. 8–9; no. 5, vol. II (1974), p. 5; Muhammad Husayn Jawdi, *Ta'rikh al-fann al-'iraqi al-qadim*, pp. 31, 36–7, 238–9; Dr Kazim al-Janabi, *Jum*, 4 February 1970; 23 July 1968; Fa'iz Muhsin, *Jum*, 4 February 1970; Engineer Shamil Kubba, *Jum*, Weekly Supplement, 16 February 1974, pp. 1, 8, 9; the editor, *BN*, no. 1, vol. I (1973), pp. 3–5; Father Antonio Nakud, ibid., no. 2, vol. I, pp. 241–2; the art column of *Th*, 9 July 1979, last page.
5. Jamil Rufa'il, '*Tammuz shahr al-sa'd . . .* ', *Th*, 17 July 1979. See also, *Afaq 'Arabiyya*, vol. I, no. 2 (October 1975), pp. 86–90.
6. *BN*, no. 1, vol. I (1973), pp. 3–5, 7 respectively. There can be no doubt that, in using the terms 'our' and 'we', the editor refers to Iraqis, not Arabs, and all Iraqis, not just Chaldeans. See also the editorials, ibid., no. 5, vol. II (1974), pp. 3–4; No. 9–10, vol. III (1975), pp. 3–4; no. 17, vol. V (1977), pp. 3–6; letters to the editor from Chaldean priests, no. 2, vol. I (1973), pp. 112–31, 241–2.

7.   'Abd al-Latif Sharara, *'Dawr al-'iraq fi bina' al-mustaqbal al-'arabi'*, *al-Aqlam*, no. 9, vol. VI (August 1970), pp. 27–9.

8.   See for example, *Jum*, 19 January 1970, p. 16; 5 January 1971, p. 12; Weekly Supplement, 16 February 1974, pp. 1, 8, 9; Dr Khalid al-Jadir, *Th*, 23 May 1975; *Th*, 11 July 1979, p. 8; Jamil Rufa'il, ibid., 11 October 1979; on 5,000 years of Iraqi music, ibid., p. 11; an historian from Mosul University on the mysterious ways of 'transmission of heritage from one nation to another', *Adab al-Rafidayn*, no. 9 (1978), pp. 99–113; *Th*, 16, 20, 23, May 1975; *Th*, Weekly Supplement, 2 August 1979; Khalid Khalil Hammudi, *Afaq 'Arabiyya*, September 1977, p. 94; Dr Shawqi Khalifa, *al-Khalij al-'Arabi*, no. 7 (1977), p. 101; Dr Fawzi Rashid (Director of the Iraqi Museum) on the Sumerian nature of southern-Iraqi songs, *Afaq 'Arabiyya*, November 1977, pp. 81–3; Dr 'Abd al-Hadi al-Fu'adi on the connection between Sumerian and Akkadian proverbs and their modern Iraqi counterparts, *Sumer*, vol. XXIX (1973), pp. 83–106; vol. XXX (1974), pp. 27–46; Dr Salih Ahmad al-'Ali (Chairman of the Iraqi Academy of Science), *al-Mawrid*, vol. VIII, no. 2 (summer, 1979), pp. 19–25.

9.   Salman Tikriti, *al-Mawrid*, vol. II (1973), no. 1, pp. 95–104; Amir Iskandar, *Afaq 'Arabiyya*, no. 2, vol. I (October 1975), p. 66. Dr Bakiza Rafiq Hilmi, *Majallat al-majma' al-'ilmi al-'iraqi* (henceforth *MMII*), vol. XXV (1974), pp. 172–204; vol. XXVI (1975), pp. 184–99; for an earlier attempt see Prof. Naji Ma'ruf of Baghdad University, *Asalat al-hadara al-'arabiyya* (Baghdad, 1969), p. 12. And compare to his book under Qasim where Semites and Arabs are not identical, *al-Madkhal fi ta'rikh al-hadara al-'arabiyya* (Baghdad, 1960), pp. 5, 9.

10.   The Governor of the Mosul Province speaking at the Festival, *Th*, April 11, 1975, p. 4. See also *Jum*, April 21, 1975, p. 10; April 11, 1970; Weekly Supplement, March 23, 1974, pp. 8–9; *Th*, April 13, 1976; April 10, 17, 1977. For the same dichotomy between the ancients, 'Iraqis and Egyptians', and 'the Arab Muslims', see Dr Faysal al-Samir, *al-Muthaqqaf al-'Arabi*, (*MA*), no. 1, vol. V (September 1973), p. 56.

11.   *al-Turath al-'Ilmi al-'Arabi*, no. 1, vol. I (1977), pp. 4–9. Articles and books with the same approach are numerous. See for example, Dr Muhammad Mustafa Radwan, *al-Mirbad* (issued by the Faculty of Humanities, Basra University), no. 1, vol. I (1968), pp. 23–34; Dr Muhammad Amara, *Afaq 'Arabiyya*, March 1976, pp. 2–3.

12.   Zuhayr Ahmad al-Qaysi, *BN*, no. 16, vol. IV (1976), pp. 311–15. Dr Hans Guterbock, *BN*, no. 1, vol. I (1973), pp. 103–6; Dr Mundhir al-Bakr, *al-Khalij al-'Arabi*, no. 2 vol. II (1975), pp. 32–5; Rida Jawad al-Hashimi, identifying Arabs with Chaldeans but not with Assyrians or Akkadians, *Afaq 'Arabiyya*, December 1980, pp. 168–71.

13.   Hatim Muhammad al-Sakr, *Afaq 'Arabiyya*, August 1978, p. 144.

14.   Saddam Husayn, *'Hawla kitabat al-ta'rikh'*, *Afaq 'Arabiyya*, May 1978, pp. 11, 13. See also, *al-Mawrid*, no. 2, vol VII (summer 1979),

pp. 7–18; Dr Ahmad Susa, *Hadarat al-'arab wa marahil tatawwuriha 'ibra al-'usur* (Baghdad, 1979) (henceforth: Susa, *Hadarat*), p. 5.

15. See, for example, Philip Hitti, *History of the Arabs* (London, 1937), pp. 3, 8. This account was very popular in Iraqi school text books since the early days of the Monarchy. See, for example, Darwish al-Miqdadi (a Palestinian student of Hitti in the AUB), *Ta'rikh al-umma al-'Arabiyya* (Baghdad, 1931), pp. 13–15. And school curriculae, *Wizarat al-ma'arif, Minhaj al-dirasa al-mutawasita* (Baghdad, 1931, 1940), pp. (respectively) 16–18 and 28–30. In the later version the Semitic waves are actually called 'Arab'. For an earlier Arab source see 'Izzat Darwaza, *Mukhtasir ta'rikh al-'arab wal-islam* (Cairo, 1924), 17–18. And see Iraq's Director of Education Sami Shawkat's *Hadhihi ahdafuna* (Baghdad, 1939), p.32.

16. Baqir, *Afaq 'Arabiyya*, March 1977, p. 75. See also his article, *Afaq 'Arabiyya*, March 1978, pp. 76–83. 'Ali al-Shawk more prudently calls the Semitic tongues 'the languages of the Arab peninsula'. (*Afaq 'Arabiyya*, July 1979, pp. 102–3). See also Ihsan Ja'far, *Afaq 'Arabiyya*, December 1979, pp. 56–9; Dr 'Adil Jasim al-Bayyati, a teacher in the Faculty of Humanities at Baghdad University, *Afaq 'Arabiyya*, January 1979, pp. 50–2; Dr Fadil 'Abd al-Wahid, *Afaq 'Arabiyya*, November-December 1980, pp. 257; Ahmad Susa, *The Arabs and Jews in History* (Switzerland, 1980?), pp. 20–3; *Hadarat* p. 11. Susa bases himself (correctly) on J. B. Philby, *The Background of Islam* (Alexandria, 1947), pp. 10–11; Sabatino Moscati, *Ancient Semitic Civilizations* (London, 1957), p. 35ff. He could, in fact, supplement his sources with *The Encyclopedia Britannica* (London, 1973), vol. 20, p. 208, which, with due academic restraint, suggests that the most likely places to be considered as the origin of the speakers of the proto-semitic language are the Arabian Peninsula and Mesopotamia.

17. See, for example, the supplement to the resolutions of the 11th pan-Arab Congress, *Th*, 9 April 1979; 'Aflaq, *Fi sabil al-ba'th* (Beirut, 1974), pp. 111–21, 180.

18. Ahmad Susa, *Hadarat*, pp. 18, 77–85, see also pp. 94, 99–100.

19. Munif al-Razzaz, *Afaq 'Arabiyya*, March 1978, pp. 4–5.

20. Baqir, *Afaq 'Arabiyya*, March 1977, p. 75. See also, Dr Ilyas Farah, *Afaq 'Arabiyya*, August 1977, p. 6; Farah, *Afaq 'Arabiyya*, January 1979, pp. 2–4; *Afaq 'Arabiyya*, March 1980, pp. 5–8; *Th*, 18 June 1979; 10 February 1980; Munif al-Razzaz, *'al-judhur al-ta'rikhiyya lil-qawmiyya al-'arabiyya'*, *Afaq 'Arabiyya*, March 1978, pp. 2–5; Faruq Khurshid, *'al-Adab al-sha'bi wal-wahda al-'arabiyya'*, *Afaq 'Arabiyya*, June 1977, pp. 108–11.

21. Baqir, *Afaq 'Arabiyya*, March 1977, pp. 73–5; see also Susa, *Hadarat*, pp. 131–3.

22. See, for example, Munif al-Razzaz, *Afaq 'Arabiyya*, March 1978, pp. 2–5; Salah al-Mukhtar, *Th*, 11 July 1979; Ihsan Ja'far, *Afaq 'Arabiyya*, December 1979, pp. 56–9; Susa, *Hadarat*, pp. 102–4.

23. Razzaz, *Afaq 'Arabiyya*, March 1978, pp. 2–5. See the same approach in *'Mas' alat al-aqalliyyat al-qawmiyya* . . . ', supplement to the resolutions of the 11th pan-Arab Congress, *Th*, 9 April 1979; and Salah Muktar, *Th*, 11 July 1979.
24. Susa, *Hadarat*, pp. 29–30, 102–3.
25. Susa, ibid., pp. 10, 30, 34, 107–108. Philby did not commit himself. See J. B. Philby, *The Background of Islam* (Alexandria, 1947), p. 9. See similar views in Susa, *The Arabs and Jews* . . . , pp. 42–6; Dr Bakiza Rafiq Hilmi, *MMII*, vol. XXV (1974), pp. 172–204; vol. XXVI (1975), pp. 184–199; Salah al-Mukhtar, *Th*, 11 July 1979; Ilyas Farah quoting a French authority, *Afaq 'Arabiyya*, January 1979, pp. 3–4; and quoting Susa, *Afaq 'Arabiyya*, March 1980, pp. 5–7. According to *The Encyclopedia Britannica* (ibid.), it is possible that the epigraphic South Arabian language is phonologically closest to the ancient proto-Semitic language (if, indeed, the latter ever existed). This is still a far cry from what Susa claims to have been written by Philby.
26. Chaim M. Rabin, 'Semitic Languages', *Encyclopedia Judaica* (Jerusalem, 1972), vol. XIV, p. 1154; George Roux, *Ancient Iraq* (London, 1964), pp. 125–7.
27. Susa, *Hadarat*, pp. 15–16, 64–7; see also Baqir, *Afaq 'Arabiyya*, March 1977, pp. 73, 75.
28. See the speech of the Minister of Culture where he presented the reconstruction of Babylon as a contribution to the 'heritage of our Arab nation' (*Sumer*, 1979, p. 9). See also, for example, Khalid Kishtainy, 'The Geographical and Historical Legacy . . . ', (Exeter, July 1981), p. 3; a letter to the president from the 1st Festival of Iraqi Cinema (*Afaq 'Arabiyya*, September 1979, pp. 130–5); report on a new film, *Th*, Weekly Supplement, 25 October 1979; Dr Khalid al-Jadir, (a professor of the history of art in Baghdad University), on 'Arab Construction', meaning the Babylonian winged bull and the Dome of the Rock alike, *Th*, 16, 31 October 1979; Sumerian Ur as part of 'Arab civilization', *Th*, 16 November 1979; see also, *Th*, 13, 15, April 1980, last page.
29. Ramadan, *Uktubr* (Cairo), 6 March 1988.
30. Susa, *Hadarat*, pp. 30–1, 177–8. For more expressions of pride in the pre-eminence of Mesopotamia, see Kishtainy, 'The Geographical . . . ', ibid., p. 3; Dr 'Adil al-Bayyati, *Afaq 'Arabiyya*, January 1979, pp. 50–71; on the special role of Sumer [!] and Babylon as part of the general Arab contribution to modern European civilization, Pierre Rossi *'Annahu al-ta'rikh al-haqiqi lil-'arab', Afaq 'Arabiyya*, June 1979, pp. 102–5. For more see below.
31. Susa, *Hadarat*, pp. 30–1. See also, Baqir, *Afaq 'Arabiyya.*, March 1977, pp. 40–51; March 1978, pp. 76–83; Dr Salih Ahmad 'Ali concentrated almost exclusively on the contribution of ancient Iraq (*al-Mawrid*, vol. VIII, Summer 1979, no. 2, pp. 19–25). A history teacher in Mosul University, *Adab al-Rafidayn*, no. 9, (1978), pp. 99–113.
32. RCC Communique, *Jum*, 2 October 1978. The Babylonian theme was

missing altogether from the communique issued by the pan-Arab leadership (ibid., 3 October 1978). See also Nuri Najam, *Th*, 18 April 1979; '*Yawmiyyat al-thawra*', ''*Iraq nuqtat ish'a'*, *Th*, 21 May 1980; Rida Jawad al-Hashimi, *Afaq 'Arabiyya*, November-December 1980, pp. 170–1.

33. Bakr, *Masirat al-thawra, 1968–70* (Baghdad, 1971), pp. 60–5; also 5–6, 11, 57–9.

34. Saddam Husayn in an impromptu speech to the masses in Southern 'Iraq, *Th*, 20 March 1979.

35. Saddam Husayn, special supplement, *Wa'i al-'Ummal*, 17 February 1979.

36. Saddam Husayn, *Th*, 20 March 1979. See also his speeches *Wa'i al-'Ummal*, 7 July 1979; *Th*, 1 July 1980; '*Iraq al-sha'b, tariq al-rifah wal-taqaddum* (Baghdad, December 1978), p. 11; Na'im Haddad, *Th*, 1 July 1980; Ghanim Jasim, *Baghdad Observer*, 16 May 1981; *Th*, 13 April 1980; Salah al-Mukhtar, *Th*, 11 July 1979. For an attempt to justify Nebuchadnezzar's exile of the Jews as liberation from 'their own wickedness', see Salah al-Mukhtar, '*al-sabi al-babili sabi am tahrir*', *Th*, 22 June 1979. For the accusation that the Jewish exiles in Babylon served as a fifth column, which aided Cyrus in taking the city, see Dr Fawzi Rashid, Director of the Iraqi Museum during the late 1970s, *Afaq 'Arabiyya*, November–December 1980, p. 231. For more on Iraqis, Persians and Jews see below.

37. On several occasions Saddam Husayn warned that Iraq faced a real danger of disintegration into 'three mini-states: a mini-state for the Sunna, a mini-state for the Shi'a and a mini-state for the Kurds'. See *Th*, 9 February 1980; *Afaq 'Arabiyya*, November–December 1980, p. 7; *Th*, 21 June 1980. And denouncing Iran for her effort to foment 'sectarian grudges', *INA*, 19 August 1980; the Iraqi military attache in London, *al-Dustur*, 9 March 1981; Foreign Minister Sa'dun Hammadi, *al-Dustur*, 23 March 1981; Hani Wahib, *Th*, 17 December 1980.

38. Saddam Husayn, to army officers, *Th*, 21 June 1980.

39. *Wa'i al-'Ummal*, special supplement, 17 February 1979.

40. In *qada* al-Balad, *Th*, 26 October 1979. See also '*Iraq al-sha'b* . . . , p. 11; other speeches: in Maisan in a public rally, and in Dhi Qar to soldiers, *Th*, 20 March 1979; in air force headquarters, *Th*, 23 April 1979; to Iraqi youth, *Wa'i al-'Ummal*, 7 July 1979. Other speeches, *al-'Iraq*, 16 April 1980; *Th*, 21 June 1980; *Th*, 1 July 1980; to party cadres, *Th*, 13 July 1980; to parliament on the Iraqi-Iranian war, *Th*, 5 November 1980; on '*Id al-adha, Afaq 'Arabiyya*, November–December 1980, p. 23; an interview, *Th*, 20 January 1981; *al-Hawadith*, 17 April 1981.

41. Brig, General 'Abd al-Razzaq Yusuf, *Jum*, 17 December 1989; *Jum*, 7 June 1990; *al-Qadisiyya*, 29 November 1989; *Th*, 22 December 1989; and Iraqi leadership also *al-Qadisiyya*, 2 December 1989. See also Ghanim Jasim, *Baghdad Observer*, 16 May 1981; 'Abd al-Latif

Sharara, *al-Aqlam*, no. 9, vol. VI (August, 1970), pp. 27–30. Editorial, *Th*, 20 June 1980; 'Abd al-Ghani 'Abd al-Ghaffur, *Th*, 15 December 1980; Hani Wahib, *Th*, 31 January 1981. p. 8; 'Yawmiyyat al-thawra', *Th*, 21 May 1980; Hamid Sa'id, ibid., 26 December 1981; Theodor Jibkov in Babylon, *Th*, 31 May 1980, p. 1; Hani Wahib, ibid., p. 4; Pierre Rossi, *Afaq 'Arabiyya*, June 1979, pp. 102–5; a poem, *Th*, Weekly Supplement, 2 February 1980. On Salah al-Din and other leaders, presented as Iraqis – some of them inaccurately, like 'Ammad al-Din Zanki – and their contribution to Arab unity and victory over the Crusaders, see Dr Rashid al-Jamili, *Th*, Weekly Supplements, 5, 12, July 1979; see also, 'al- *'Iraq nuqtat ish'a'*, *Th*, 21 May 1980, back page. Nuri Najam, *Th*, 18 April 1979.

42. *Sumer*, vol. XXV (1969), pp. a–j.
43. For example: Dr Fadil 'Abd al-Wahid, *Afaq 'Arabiyya*, November–December 1980, pp. 257–9; Dr Fawzi Rashid, ibid., pp. 228–231; Dr Sami Said Ahmad, 'A Sumerian Poem on Persian Aggression', *Baghdad Observer*, 28 April 1981; Hadi al-Jubburi, *Th*, 10 December 1980; Ghanim Jasim on "Persian hostility to Iraq when the Babylonian Civilization Flourished', *Baghdad Observer*, 28 April 1981; Hani Wahib, *Th*, 17 December 1980; Shakir Sabir al-Dabit, *Ta'rikh al-munaza'at bayna al-'iraq wa iran* (Baghdad, The Ministry of Culture, 1984), gives the fullest list of Iran's hostile acts against the Arabs until the era of Salah al-Din. And see poems by the well-known poets 'Ali al-Hilli, Muhammad Jamil Shilsh and Shafiq al-Kamali, *Afaq 'Arabiyya*, November–December, 1980, pp. 144–85.
44. 'Aziz, *Iraqi News Agency, (INA)*, November 1, *FBIS-Daily Report*, 2 November 1988, p. 28.
45. For example, Information Minister Latif Nusayyif Jasim, *The Baghdad Observer*, 7 September 1987.
46. *Jum*, 26 July 1981.
47. Sa'd al-Bazzaz, *Gulf War, The Israeli Connection* (translation from the Arabic Namir Abbas Mudhaffar) (Baghdad, 1989), pp. 17, 19, 23, 28, 33. In reality the Iraqi Jewish community in Israel has no set political views in regard to contemporary Iraq. Some of the more prominent Israeli politicians of Iraqi descent were in fact very active in trying to find an Israeli-Iraqi modus vivendi.
48. 'Aziz to *The Voice of Lebanon*, 4 December 1987, *FBIS*, 7 December 1987.
49. See, for example, Saddam Husayn to Kuwaiti reporters, *KUNA*, 15 February 1989, *FBIS-Daily Report*, ibid. p. 36.

Chapter 10: The Mesopotamian Myth, Pan-Arabism and Islam

1. For example 'Aflaq in the 11th pan-Arab Congress, *Baghdad Observer*, 10 October 1977; and on the 32nd anniversary of the party, *Th*, 7 April 1979; and 'Aflaq in *Jum*, Weekly Supplement, 27 April 1980.
2. *Faysal ibn Husayn fi Khutabihi wa aqwalihi* (Baghdad, 1945), p. 263.
3. Ibid, p. 252. See also 236, 243–4, 247–8, 258, 263–4.
4. Ibid, p. 241.
5. Sami Shawkat, *Hadhihi ahdafuna* (Baghdad, 1939), p. 3.
6. 'An Arab Empire', ibid., p. 33.
7. 'Iraq's Future . . . ', ibid., p. 81.
8. Khaldun Sati' al-Husri (introduction and annotation), *Mudhakkirat Taha al-Hushimi* (Beirut, 1967), pp. 254–9. And presenting Bismarck as model for imitation in school curriculae, see Sati' al-Husri, *Mudhakkirati fi al-'iraq 1921–1927* (Beirut, 1967), vol. I, p. 215–16. And see in the Conclusion.
9. Fadil al-Jamali, *al-'Iraq bayna ams wal-yawm* (Baghdad, 1954), pp. 4–7, 28–9.
10. An indication of the attitude of fundamentalist Islamic circles may be provided in *al-Mukhtar al-Islami* (Cairo), no. 25, vol. III, 17 June 1981). This magazine regarded the claim to 'Assyrian and Chaldean civilizational affiliation' as proof of 'Ba'th sterility', 'atheism' and its 'total bankruptcy' (pp. 71, 73).
11. al-Tabari, *Ta'rikh al-rusul wal-muluk* (Leiden: Brill, 1964), vol. II, p. 657.
12. al-Tabari, ibid., pp. 658, 662, 665; Ibn Qutayba, *Kitab 'uyun al-akhbar* (Cairo, 1928), vol. II, first edition, p. 201; Ibn al-Faqih, *Mukhtasir kitab al-buldan* (Leiden: Brill, 1885), pp. 98, 261; Mujir al-Din al-Hanbali, *Kitab al-uns al-jalil* (n.p., n.d.), vol. I, pp. 133–6.
13. Ibn Wadih al-Ya'qubi, *Tarikh* (Leiden: Brill, 1969), vol. I, pp. 69–71.
14. Khalid Kishtainy, 'The Geographical and Historical Legacy . . . , p. 4.
15. Donald Kirk from Baghdad, *The New Republic*, 22 February 1988, p. 10. And interviews with Iraqis, London, October 1989–March 1990.
16. For example party officials of the upper-medium echelon, *al-Qadisiyya*, 6 June 1987, p. 7. And see interviews with citizens visiting the ruins of Babylon during the Music Festival there, in the Iraqi press, 2 September 1987, ff. And interviews with foreign diplomats, who discussed this issue with Iraqi officials.

Chapter 11: A New Vision of Arab Unity: From Integration to Confederation

1. Almost every Ba'thi document mentions Arab unity, being the party's highest ideal. However, almost as a rule Ba'th ideologues in Iraq since 1968 (and to a large extent also in earlier years) refrained from discussing the specific form of the future united state. A glaring example is a book that was meant to sum up the approach to unity of the ''Aflaqite' branch and which draws upon the most important writings of the most important Ba'th old-timers, people like 'Aflaq, 'Aysami, Razzaz, Baytar and others, as well as on major party documents in that respect. *al-Wahda fi turath al-Ba'th wa fi baramij al-ahzab al-'arabiyya* (first edition, Beirut, 1975). The book compares Ba'th thought in regard to unity to that of other Arab parties but remains completely silent over the final form of unity.

2. *'Muqaddima, ba'd al-muntalaqat al-nazariyya'*, Nidal hizb al-ba'th . . . *'ibra mu'tamaratihi al-qawmiyya 1947–1964* (Beirut, 1972, 2nd edn), vol. 1, p. 174.

3. 'Aflaq, *Fi sabil al-ba'th* (Beirut, 1974), p. 219.

4. See Avraham Ben-Tzur, 'The Neo-Ba'th Party of Syria', *Journal of Contemporary History*, vol. 3, 1968, p. 161–81.

5. See, for example, a quotation from the *'Muntalaqat'* as an illustration to an account of Saddam Husayn's initiative to unite Iraq, Syria and Egypt in 1972, *Th*, 17 April 1972, p. 3; and another quotation from the same source to the effect that the state apparatus is charged with responsibility for the class interests of the 'popular masses', *Th*, 21 September 1976; and on the meaning of freedom and democracy, *Th*, 18 April 1975; and on the connection between unity and socialism, *Th*, 5 May 1975; and on the link between the political *avant guarde* and the masses, *Th*, 8 May 1975.

6. *Al-Thawra al-'Arabiyya*, 1969, p. 575.

7. *'Ba'd al-muntalaqat,'* ibid., pp. 186–8.

8. *Ba'd al-muntalaqat*, ibid., p. 186. Author's underlining.

9. Sa'dun Hammadi, *Ara hawla qadaya al-thawra al-'arabiyya* (Beirut, December 1968), pp. 228–9.

10. See 'Aflaq as in Ilyas Farah, *Tatawwur al-idyulujiyya al-'arabiyya al-thawriyya* (Beirut, 1973), pp. 105, 109; Farah, ibid., pp. 46–9, 204; 'Aflaq, *al-Ba'th wal-wahda* (Beirut, 1973), pp. 16–29; President Bakr, *Masirat al-thawra fi khutab wa tasrihat al-ra'is* (Baghdad, 1971), p. 233. And see an article by Sabah Salman who was close to Saddam Husayn on Arab unity that would 'eliminate the local (or: regional) entities and mentality', *Th*, 17 April 1972.

11. *INA*, 19 March 1971 in Jubran Shamiyya, *Silsilat Sijill al-Ara* (Beirut), January–March 1971, p. 199.

12. Saddam Husayn interviewed in *Alif Ba*, as in *Iraq Today*, 1–15 March

1979. And in Arabic in *Wa'i al-'Ummal*, 17 February 1979. See also Dr Ghanim Muhammad Salih of the Dept. of Political Science, Baghdad University, *Th*, 12 April 1979.

13. '*Jawla fi fikr Saddam Husayn*', *Afaq 'Arabiyya*, July, 1981, p. 32. Author's underlining.

14. *The Central Report of the Ninth Regional Congress, June 1982* (Baghdad, January 1983), p. 301.

15. An interview given by Saddam Husayn to editors of Kuwaiti newspapers in Fas (Morocco) on 8 September 1982. It was broadcast two days later in Baghdad in Arabic. See *FIBS-Daily Report*, 14 September 1982, p. E4. And see Taha al-Qaysi, Iraq's Ambassador to Bahrain: 'the issue of Arab unity is no longer one of removing borders or regimes but of obtaining unity of objectives', *Gulf News Agency*, 3 December, *FBIS-Daily Report*, 8 December 1988, p. 21. And Saddam Husayn's speech on Army Day, January 6, *FBIS-Daily Report*, 6. January 1989, p. 30. It seems that even in a hypothetical integrationist Arab unity Saddam could not envisage an Arab reality without a leading country (Kuwait, in this case).

16. Saddam Husayn to a Jordanian Committee, *INA*, February 6, *FBIS-Daily Report*, 8 February 1989. And see the veteran ideologue Sa'dun Hammadi, to Milton Viorst, *The New Yorker*, 19 October 1987, p. 96.

17. Saddam Husayn to *al-Tadamun* (Beirut–Paris), 4 February 1988.

18. On 19–21 July 1990 Iraq accused Kuwait of robbing it of oil, and threatened to settle their border dispute by military means.

Chapter 12: Iraq's Opposition Groups and the Iraqi Entity

1. Hanna Batatu, *The Old Social Classes*, pp. 407, 818–20, 1153–5.

2. Mustafa Ghalib, *al-Hizb al-shuyu'i al-suri* (N.P., 1964), pp. 92–4; Ilyas Murqus, *Ta'rikh al-ahzab al-shuyu'iyya fi al-watan al-'arabi* (Beirut, 1964), pp. 149–50.

3. Batatu, *The Old Social Classes* pp. 820–1.

4. Ilyas Murqus, ibid., pp. 237–66.

5. See Uriel Dann, *Iraq Under Qassem* (Jerusalem, 1969), p. 69ff; Batatu, ibid., pp. 818–32.

6. George Lenczowski, *Soviet Advances in the Middle East* (Washington, D.C., 1972), p. 138. Also p. 80.

7. For example, 'Aziz al-Sayyid Jasim, *Masa'il marhaliyya fi al-nidal al-'arabi* (Beirut, 1973), pp. 428–32; The Resolution of the Sixth pan-Arab Congress, October 1963, in *Nidal hizb al-ba'th al-'arabi al-ishtiraki 'ibra mu'tamanatihi al-qawmiyya 1947–1964* (Beirut, 1971), p. 182.

8. Between 1949 and 1955 all the Secretaries General and 31.1 percent of the members of the Central Committee of the ICP were Kurds. See

Batatu, *The Old Social Classes*, pp. 520, 572, 608, 699, 718, 821, 964, 1046, 1102, 1216–23.

9. See, for example, a passionate call to the Kurdish parties of Iraq to join the Arabs in their fight against the Ba'th regime, 'keeping away from national isolationism and the spread of negative feelings against the Arabs', with the aim of establishing 'real autonomy' in Kurdestan, *Tariq al-Sha'b* 12, 51st Year, July 1986, p. 6, and no. 7, ibid., February 1986, p. 1; and no. 6, ibid., January 1986, pp. 1, 10; and no. 1, ibid., August 1985, p. 1.

10. Eli Kedourie, 'Reflexions sur L'histoire du royaume d'Iraq 1921–1958', *Orient*, no. 11, 1959, p. 55–79, as quoted in Amal Vinogradov, 'The 1920 Revolt in Iraq Reconsidered: The Role of Tribes in National Politics,' *IJMES*, vol. 2, April 1972, pp. 123–139.

11. For Shi'i-Sunni ecumenism, see for example, *Liwa al-Sadr* (Tehran), 9 February 1983, p. 13; the Head of the Supreme Council of the Islamic Revolution in Iraq, Ibid, 22 October 1989; *Tariq al-Thawra* (Tehran), 13 Jamadi I, 1401, pp. 11–12; The legacy of the spiritual leader of the Shi'i opposition, Muhammad Baqir al-Sadr, *al-Dawa Chronicle (DCH)* (London), 3 July 1980, p. 2; for Kurdish-Arab-Persian equality see, for example, *Liwa al-Sadr* (Tehran), 9 February 1983, p. 13; relating to all deportees from Iraq: Kurds, Iranians and Arabs as 'Iraqis', *DCH*, 1 May 1980, p. 2; 8 December 1980, p. 5; 10 February 1981, p. 4.

12. For example, *al-Jihad* (Tehran), organ of *al-Da'wa*, 52, pp. 3–4; *Saddam Husayn Warith al-shah* (Tehran, 1981), p. 7; *DCH* 40, p. 8; The head of SCIRI to *Imam*, 1, vol. 3, January 1983, p. 31.

13. Since the late 1950s the fortieth day to al-Husayn's death (20 Safar) has been commemorated in Iraq by a three-day mass procession from Najaf to Karbala. In 1977 the processions were forbidden by the Ba'th. This caused major disturbances that rocked the regime. Iraqi Shi'ites take pride in that event and see in it the first Islamic revolution, preceding the one in Tehran in 1979. This event became a symbol of Iraqi, no less than Shi'i sacrifice and self-assertion. See, for example, *DCH* 22, February 1982, p. 4; *Liwa al-Sadr*, 25 September 1989, pp. 8–10. And see the emblem of the military units under SCIRI a Koran and a hand holding a rifle on the background of the map of Iraq which is placed at the center of the globe (*Liwa al-Sadr*, 22 October 1989, p. 11). And 'the true duty' of this Badr Army being 'the liberation of Iraq', *Liwa al-Sadr*, 15 October 1989, p. 5. For a detailed analysis of the political credo of the religious Shi'i opposition, see A. Baram, *National Integration and Exclusiveness in Political Thought and Practice in Iraq Under the Ba'th 1968–1982*, Ph.D. thesis, The Hebrew University, Jerusalem, 1986.

14. David Andrews (ed.), The *Lost Peoples of the Middle East* (Salisbury, 1982), p. 134, as quoted by Ofra Bengio, *The Kurdish Revolution in Iraq* (Tel-Aviv, 1989), p. 19.

15. Bengio, pp. 19–20

16. Jamal Nabaz, leader of the small Kurdish Socialist Party, *Hawla*

al-mushkila al-Kurdiyya (Europe, 1969), pp. 13, 22, 59. Also pp. 8–10, 15. To Nabaz 'the Kurdish problem . . . is that of a nation with its own particular homeland but without its own political entity'. The Arab and the Kurds, to his mind 'have no common aims', certainly not 'the legend of common struggle against imperialism', nor do they have a 'common destiny' or 'common interests'.

17. Interviews with Kurdish activists in Europe, summer and fall 1982; for documents see, for example, *al-Kadir* 14–15, Fourth year, July–August 1972, pp. 2–5, 12; no. 18, fifth year, August 1973, pp. 16–23, 27–9, 30–41; no. 24, sixth year, September 1974, pp. 3–8, 14–17, 23–33; and see The International Relations Committee, KDP, *The Historical Place of the Kurdish National Liberation Movement* (Europe, September 1977), calls for the downfall of the 'Tikriti clique' and the establishment of a truly democratic government that would find a 'democratic solution' to the Kurdish problem. See also Bengio, pp. 60–71. According to Edmund Ghareeb, *The Kurdish Question in Iraq* (Syracuse, Syracuse University Press, 1981), p. 162, in early 1974 (when the confrontation with the regime was re-opened) there was talk in Kurdish circles of independence. Yet, the KDP documents remained within the demand for autonomy.

18. *Le Monde*, 16 April 1987, in *FBIS-Daily Report*, 30 April 1987, p. E2; *al-Ghad* (Europe), 29 March 1988, p. 2. And implying Kurdish national independence outside the Iraqi nation state but as a member of an Islamic family of nations in an interview to *Kayhan*, 3 December 1987, p. 20.

19. See interview with Hushiyar Zaybari, member of the KDP Central Committee, confirming his party's allegiance to Iraq's territorial integrity, *Iraq al-Ghad*, 15 March 1988, p. 3. That this position is being reconsidered emerges from a number of interviews conducted by the author in London in October, November and December 1989.

Conclusion

1. 'Abd al-Razzaq al-Hasani, *Ta'rikh al-wizarat al-'iraqiyya* (Saida, 1953), part III, pp. 286–93.

2. For a succinct discussion of the achievements of the state under the monarchy, see Roger Owen, 'Putting the State Back In. Some Thoughts on Batatu's Account of Class and Class Politics in Iraq Before 1958'. Paper prepared for a conference on *The Iraqi Revolution of 1958: The Old Social Classes Revisited*, University of Texas at Austin, 10–11 March 1989. And see Marr, pp. 29–151; Batatu, *The Old Social Classes*, particularly pp. 26–35.

3. E. B. Main, 'Iraq: a Note', *Journal of the Royal Central Asiatic Society*, vol. 20, July 1933, p. 343. The Colonial Office in London, too, felt that in case of unification Faysal would probably transfer his crown

completely from Iraq to Syria, as Damascus is 'an infinitely pleasanter town than Baghdad' and for other reasons. See Khaldun Sati' al-Husry, 'King Faysal I and Arab Unity 1930–33', *Journal of Contemporary History* Vol.10, No.2, April 1975, pp. 330–1. See also pp. 323–4. And see Yehoshua Porath, 'Nuri al-Sa'id's Arab Unity Programme' *MES* vol. 20, no. 4, October 1984, p. 78.

4. See f.n. 3. And for 'Abd al-Ilah's designs on Syria in the late 1940s and early to mid-1950s see Reeva S. Simon, 'The Hashemite "Conspiracy": Hashemite Unity Attempts, 1921–1958', *IJMES*, Vol.1 (1974), p. 318.

5. See, for example, Sati' al-Husri, Faysal's Director of Education, stressing the ephemeral and implying the illegitimate nature of the Iraqi state when he reprimanded Iraqi teachers for objecting to the privileges given to non-Iraqi Arab teachers, *Mudhakkirati fi al-'iraq*, Part One, 1921–27 (Beirut, 1967), pp. 261–2.

6. Uriel Dann, *Iraq Under Qassem*, p. 67.

7. Uriel Dann, ibid., p. 69ff.

8. Batatu, *The Old Social Classes*, p. 36.

9. For example, 'Aziz al-Sayyid Jasim, *al-Muthaqqaf al-'Arabi*, July 1970, pp. 8–9; and *Th*, 10 June 1969; Ilyas Farah, *al-Tarbiya wal-siyasa* (Beirut, 1975), p. 35, a speech in Mosul in June 1972; Ahmad Hasan al-Bakr, *Masirat al-thawra fi khutab wa tasrihat al-ra'is* (Baghdad, 1971), pp. 58–9; also 63, 95, 134–5, 203–8, 242; 'Abd al-khaliq al-Samarra'i, *Jum*, 29 August 1970.

10. See Chapter 6, footnotes 26–30. The first elections to parliament were actually conducted only a decade later, in 1980. In subsequent years this principle was applied to many other official offices.

11. See, for example, an interview with Saddam Husayn, *Iraq Today*, March 1–15, 1979; *Wa'i al-'Ummal*, February 17, 1979.

12. See, for example, fierce objection to the influx of Egyptian workers into Iraq before and during the Gulf War for fear that it is designed 'to change the social [read: religio-communal] balance in Iraqi society', *Al-Dawa Chronicle* (monthly of the [Shi'i] Islamic Da'wa Party, London), No.5, September 1980, p. 3; No.15, July 1981, p. 4. This objection is in glaring contrast to the Da'wa's official call for all-Islamic, Sunni-Shi'i cooperation.

13. Bernard Lewis, *History Remembered, Recovered, Invented* (Princeton, 1975), p. 11.

14. Reports in the Iraqi press reproduced in *FBIS-Daily Report*, 21 June 1989; *The Independent* (London), 30 August 1989; *The Independent Magazine* 14 October 1989. For academic studies see, for example, Su'ad Ra'uf Shir Muhammad, *Nuri al-Sa'id wa dawruhu fi al-siyasa al-'iraqiyya 1932–1945* (Baghdad, 1988); 'Abd al-Razzaq Ahmad al-Nasiri, *Nuri al-Sa'id . . . hatta 'am 1932* (Baghdad, 1988).

15. Sati' al-Husri, *Mudhakkirati fi al-'iraq*, ibid., p. 216.

16. Khaldun Sati' al-Husri, 'King Faysal I and Arab Unity 1930–33',

Journal of Contemporary History, vol. 10, no. 2, April, 1975, p. 327; based on *al-Ikha al-Watani*, 14 July 1932.

17. Khaldun Sati' al-Husri (ed.), *Mudhakkirat Taha al-Hashimi* (Beirut, 1967), pp. 254–9.
18. *Sumer*, second year (1946), no. 1, p. 78.
19. For Leonard Wooley's complaints and account of a decline in archeological digs see Brian M. Fagan, *Return to Babylon* (Boston, 1979), pp. 250, 276, 279; and see also pp. 248–9. And *Sumer*, no. 1, sixth year, 1950, p. 225.
20. Reeva S. Simon, 'The teaching of History in Iraq Before the Rashid Ali Coup of 1941', *MES*, Vol.22, No.1 (January 1986),p. 49
21. Dr Naji al-Asil, *Sumer*, no. 2, first year, 1945, pp. 3–7. See also the letter by the well-known poet Ma'ruf al-Rusafi to the newspaper editor, ibid., p. 155; and the expert at the National Museum, Akram Shukri,ibid., no. 1, first year, pp. 131–4; and the constant resort to the terms 'the ancient inhabitants of 'Iraq' 'ancient 'Iraqi culture' etc, see Taha Baqir, Director of the Iraqi Museum, ibid., no. 1, third year, January 1947, pp. 12–14; and no. 1, fourth year, January 1948, pp. 86–8; and the assertion of the editorial board that they believe in the 'strong ties between the ancient and the new', ibid., no. 1, 6th year 1950, p. 114; and see also Dr al-Asil, no. 1, ninth year, p. 173, and fifth year, 1–11; seventh year, pp. 20, 103–4.
22. Thus, for example, the National Museum honored Faysal's accession to the throne with an exhibition on 'Iraq's Long History which is still mostly unknown', which was inaugurated by the young Faysal II in person (*Sumer*, no. 2, ninth year, 1953, p. 265). See his visit to the museum, ibid., no. 2, second year, pp. 265–9. And see the official booklet issued in honor of his coronation, Iraq Today (Baghdad, 1953), pp. 26–32. Faysal II was the first Hashimite ruler to have been born in Iraq.
23. See for example Reeva Simon, 'The Hashemite "Conspiracy": Hashemite Unity Attempts, 1921–1958', *IJMES*, vol. 5 (1974), pp. 318–21.
24. Compare Bernard Lewis, *History*, pp. 101–2.
25. The most typical works with this idea in mind are two panegyrical books written by the little-known author Zuhayr Sadiq Rida al-Khalidi and published in Baghdad in 1988–89, *Saddam Husayn wa rijal al-hadara fi al-iraq*, with an introduction by First Deputy PM Ramadan, and *Mundhu nushu' al-hadara hatta saddam husay*. In these books, that received wide publicity in Iraq, Husayn is depicted as the culmination of a chain of historical giants, from Hammurabi, through Ashurbanipal to Nebuchadnezzar the Chaldean. For typical academic panegyrics in the same vein see, for example, the Assyriologist from Baghdad university Dr Fadil 'Abd al-Wahid, comparing his president favorably with a mythological hero like Gilgamesh and a historical military leader like Sargon the Akkadian, and the well-known and very able Medieval historian Faruq 'Umar Fawzi equating him with al- Mansur, the founder

of Baghdad and the 'founding khaifa' of the Abbasid empire, and other Abbasid *khulafa'*, *al-Thawra*, April 29, 1984.

26. An interview with Sylvia G. Haim-Kedourie, Oxford, February 21, 1990. When it suited their political aims the educated elite of the large cities were very quick to adapt and adopt the new concept of Iraqi nationalism. Thus, for example, since 1919 political activists in Baghdad and Mosul presented the British authorities with demands of Iraqi independence, based on the right for self-determination as it had been defined by President Woodrow Wilson in the wake of World War I. In the same way, in 1921 some notables, like Sayyid Talib of Basra and 'Abd al-Rahman al-Kaylany, Baghdad's *naqib al-ashraf*, propagated in the name of Iraqi identity and interests against the imposition of a Hashimite prince from the Hijaz as King of Iraq. See, for example, Ireland, *Iraq*, pp. 305, 320–1.

27. *Baghdad Radio*, 24 June 1989, in *FBIS-Daily Report*, 26 June 1984, p. 10.

28. The *Shahname* was a mixture of myth and real history, leaving out altogether such major figures like Cyrus, Cambyses and Xerxes (Bernard Lewis, *History*, pp. 5, 40; Roy Mottahedeh, *The Mantle of the Prophet* [London, 1986], p. 311). Yet, even the fictitious kings and heroes it introduced, like the noble hero Rustam and the ingenious, inventor-king and tyrant Jamshid, were regarded as true historical figures, and became the subject of great popular interest and admiration. Thus, even though many aspects of this history were described in less than enthusiastic terms, in its entirety Iranian pre-Islamic history gained in Iran an essentially positive connotation. For example, medieval Muslim kings in Iran used to visit sites like Persepolis (commonly believed to have been built by Jamshid), and leave there inscriptions testifying to their respect for their pre-Islamic predecessors (Mottahedeh, pp. 313–14).

29. Mottahedeh, p. 312; Bernard Lewis, ibid.

30. See Mottahedeh, pp. 312–14. And interviews with Iranian intellectuals who preferred to remain anonymous, Washington, D.C., February through August 1989; Oxford, September 1989 through March 1990.

31. *Th*, 15 March 1987; 4 March 1988; Communique of the GC of the Armed Forces, *Th*, 26 August 1987. A book that came out in 1989, dedicated to the study of tribes in Iraq, describes Saddam's tribe from his mother's side, Al Nasir, as emanating from the prophet's family (see Yunis al-Shaykh Ibrahim al-Samarra'i, *al-Qaba'il al-'iraqiyya* (Baghdad, 1989), vol. II, pp. 655–6. An earlier book by the same author does not mention Al Nasir among these tribes which emanated from the prophet. See his *al-Qaba'il wal-buyutat al-hashimiyya fi al-'iraq* (Baghdad, 1988).

32. See Ernest Gellner, *Thought and Change* (London, 1972), pp. 155–64; *Nations and Nationalism* (Oxford, 1988), especially pp. 35–8, 57ff.

33. Khalil's *Republic of Fear* is dedicated, in large part, to this issue. See, in particular, Chapters 1–4.

34. In 1968–69 the number of primary school pupils was just over one million, and there were 286 000 secondary school students and 34 600 university students. In 1987–88 the figures were nearly three million; 985,000; and 153,000 respectively. See Central Statistical Organization, *Annual Abstract of Statistics (AAS), 1970,* p. 502; *1987,* pp. 210–26. In the mid-1970s education became compulsory and since 1978 adults, too, were compelled to learn to read and write. This illiteracy eradication campaign was taken advantage of by the regime to indoctrinate the population.

35. *AAS, 1987, p. 46.*

36. After the cease-fire in the Iraq-Iran war in August 1988 the Ba'th regime embarked with renewed zest on a propaganda campaign designed to prove to the Iraqi and Arab public that Iraq is, indeed, still fully committed to the Arab cause. The latest example thereof is Saddam Husayn's speech to army officers on Faw Day in which he pledged to retaliate against any country that would attack not just Iraq, but also any other Arab country. (See *The Jerusalem Post,* 19 April 1990.) This, however, did not prevent Iraq from threatening a sister Arab state, Kuwait, with use of force over a border and oil production dispute. *Ha-Aretz,* 19–23 April 1990.

37. For the Iraqi letter to the Secretary General of the League see *Ha-Aretz,* 25 July, 1990. For the ubiquitous claim that Iraq is defending all the Arabs in its war against Iran see, for example, Saddam Husayn to *al-Hawadith,* 17 April 1981; *al-Thawra al-'Arabiyya,* 1980, pp. 7, 18–20, 34; Ilyas Farah, *Afaq 'Arabiyya,* November–December 1980, pp. 69–70; Shafiq al- Kamali, a poem, *ibid.,* September 1979, pp. 10–11; Tariq Aziz, *The Iran-Iraq Conflict* (London, 1981).

38. For a detailed account see Amatzia Baram, 'Territorial Nationalism in the Contemporary Middle East: a Progress Report', due in *Middle Eastern Studies,* December 1990.

39. In some cases, like Egypt and Tunisia, this process started a few decades ago. For Egypt during the 1920s and 1930s see Israel Gershoni and James P. Jankowski, *Egypt, Islam and the Arabs: The Search for Egyptian Nationhood, 1900–1930* (New York and Oxford, Oxford University Press, 1986), especially p. 164ff. On the level of political practice, too, local interests are being placed higher than before on the national scale of priorities by the various Arab regimes. In the case of Syria the reference is to the emergence of pan-Syrian notions and later to the alignment with Iran. For other countries and organizations see Fouad Ajami, 'The End of Pan-Arabism' in Tawfic E. Farah (ed.), *Pan Arabism and Arab Nationalism* (Boulder and London, Westview, 1987), pp. 96–114. See there also a report on a poll carried out in Kuwait University and showing that the pan-Arab ideal no longer enjoys wide support. Another poll reported by Hassan Nafaa ('Arab Nationalism: a Response', *ibid.,* p. 145), conducted in ten Arab countries, however, shows opposite results. These polls demonstrate the

grave difficulties of conducting field studies that touch upon sensitive political issues in the contemporary Arab world.

40. For Iraq signing such an agreement with Saudi Arabia after the latter supported it during eight years of war to the tune of at least $40b, see *Baghdad Radio*, 27 March, *FBIS-Daily Report*, 28 March, p. 22. for the ACC Charter see, *INA*, 26 February, *FBIS-Daily Report*, 28 February 1989, p. 29; Saddam Husayn promising 'non-interference', *MEED*, 9 December 1988.

Bibliography

Books and Articles

Abu Jaber, Kamel S., *The Arab Ba'th Socialist Party: History, Ideology and Organization* (Syracuse University Press, 1966).

'Aflaq, Michel, *Fi sabil al-ba'th* (Beirut, 1974).

'Aflaq, Michel, *Nuqtat al-bidaya* (Beirut, 1973).

Ajami, Fouad, 'The End of Pan-Arabism' in Tawfic E. Farah (ed.), *Pan Arabism and Arab Nationalism* (Boulder and London, Westview, 1987).

'Alawi, Hasan al-, *Al-Shi'a wal-dawla al-qawmiyya fil-iraq* (Paris, 1989).

Arab Ba'th Socialist Party, *The Central Report of the 9th Regional Congress, June 1982*, (Baghdad, Jan. 1983).

Arab Ba'th Socialist Party, *al-Minhaj al-thaqafi al-markazi* (Baghdad, 1977).

'Aysami, Shibli al-, *al-Wahda al-'arabiyya min hilal al-tajriba* (Beirut, June 1971).

'Aysami, Shibli al-, *Hizb al-ba'th al-'arabi al-ishtiraki, marhalat al-arba'inat al-ta'sisiyya* (Beirut, 1974).

Aziz, Tariq, *The Iran-Iraq Conflict* (London, 1981).

Bakr, Ahmad Hasan al-, *Masirat al-thawra fi khutab wa tasrihat al-ra'is* (Baghdad, 1971).

Baram, Amazia, *National Integration and Exclusiveness in Political Thought and Practice in Iraq Under the Ba'th 1968–1982*, Ph.D. thesis, Hebrew University, Jerusalem, 1986.

Baram, Amazia, 'Culture in the Service of Wataniyya', *Asian and African Studies (AAS)*, 17/103 (Nov. 1983).

Baram, Amazia, 'Ideology and Power Politics in Syrian-Iraqi Relations', in Moshe Maoz and Avner Yaniv (eds), *Syria Under Assad: Domestic Constraints and Regional Risks* (London, 1986), pp. 125–39.

Baram, Amazia, 'Mesopotamian Identity in Ba'thi Iraq', *Middle Eastern Studies (MES)*, 19/4 (Oct. 1983).

Baram, Amazia, 'The Ruling Political Elite in Ba'thi Iraq 1968–1986, the Changing Features of a Collective Profile', *International Journal of Middle East Studies*, vol. 21, no. 4, November 1989, pp. 447–93.

Baram, Amazia, 'Saddam Husayn: A Political Profile', *The Jerusalem Quarterly*, no. 17, Fall 1980, pp. 115–44.

Batatu, Hanna, *The Old Social Classes and the Revolutionary Movements of Iraq* (Princeton, 1978).

Bayati, Fadil Muhammad al-, *The Monument in Memory of the Glorious Revolution of July 14* (Baghdad, 1961?)

Bayyati, 'Abd al-Wahhab al-, *Bustan 'a'isha* (Cairo, 1989).

Bayyati, 'Abd al-Wahhab al-, *Diwan* (Beirut, 1972, 1974).

Bayyati, 'Abd al-Wahhad al-, *Tajribati al-Shi'riyya* (Beirut, 1968).

Bazzaz, 'Abd al-Rahmand al-, *Hadhihi qawmiyatuna* (Cairo, 1964).

Bazzaz, 'Abd al-Rahmand al-, *Min wahi al-'uruba* (Cairo, 1963).

Bazzaz, Sa'd al-, *Gulf War, The Israeli Connection* (translation from the Arabic Namir Abbas Mudhaffar) (Baghdad, 1989).

Bengio, Ofra, *The Kurdish Revolution in Iraq* (Hebrew) (Tel-Aviv, 1989).

Ben-Jelloun, Tahar, *Azzawi* (Geneva, May 1980).

Ben-Tzur, Avraham, 'The Neo-Ba'th Party of Syria', *Journal of Contemporary History*, vol. 3, 1968, pp. 161–81.

CARDRI (Committee Against Repression and for Democratic Rights in Iraq), *Saddam's Iraq, Revolution or Reaction?* (London, 1986).

Chaliand, Gerard (ed.), *People Without a Country* (London, 1980), p. 157.

Coke, Richard, *The Heart of the Middle East* (London, 1926).

Dabit, Shakir Sabir al-, *Ta'rikh al-munaza'at bayna al- 'iraq wa iran* (Baghdad, The Ministry of Culture, 1984).

Da'im, 'Abd alla 'Abd al-, *Al-Jil al-'arabi al-jadid* (Beirut, 1961).

Dann, Uriel, *Iraq Under Qassem* (Jerusalem, 1969).

Darwaza, 'Izzat, *Mukhtasir ta'rikh al-'arab wal-islam* (Cairo, 1924).

Devlin, John F., *The Ba'th Party, A History from its Origins to 1966* (Stanford California, Stanford University Press, 1979).

Fadhil, Sa'adoon, *M. Ghani, Exhibition of Bronze Maquettes* (London, Baghdad, 1979).

Farah, Ilyas, *al-Tarbiya wal-siyasa* (Beirut, 1975).

Farah, Ilyas, *Tatawwur al-idyulujiyya al-'arabiyya al-thawriyya* (Beirut, 1973).

Faris, Shams al-Din, *al-Manabi' al-ta'rikhiyya lil-fann al-jidari al-'iraqi al-mu'asir* (Baghdad, 1974).

Farouk-Sluglett, Marion and Sluglett, Peter, *Iraq Since 1958, From Revolution to Dictatorship* (London and New York, 1987).

Fathi, Ihsan and Jabra Ibrahim Jabra, *Baghdad bayna al-ams wal yawm* (Baghdad, 1987).

Fathi, Ihsan and John Warren, *Traditional Houses in Baghdad* (Sussex, 1982)

Faysal I, King of Iraq, *Faysal ibn Husayn fi Khitabihi wa aqwalihi* (Baghdad, 1945).

Geertz, Clifford, *The Interpretation of Culture* (New York, 1973).

Gellner, Ernest, *Nations and Nationalism* (Oxford, 1988).

Gellner, Ernest, *Thought and Change* (London, 1972).

Gershoni, Israel, and Jankowski, James P., *Egypt, Islam and the Arabs, The Search for Egyptian Nationhood 1900–1930* (Oxford, New York, Oxford University Press, 1986).

Ghalib, Mustafa, *al-Hizb al-shuyu'i al-suri* (N.P., 1964).

Ghareeb, Edmund, *The Kurdish Question in Iraq* (Syracuse, 1981).

Hammadi, Sa'dun, *Ara' hawla qadaya al-thawra al-'arabiyya* (Beirut, Dec. 1968).

Hanbali, Mujir al-Din al-, *Kitab al-uns al-jalil* (n.p., n.d.), vol. I.

Hasani, 'Abd al-Razzaq al-, *Ta'rikh al-wizarat al-'iraqiyya* (Saida, 1939).

Hitti, Philip, *History of the Arabs* (London, 1937).

Husayn, Saddam, *Fi al-din wal-thurat* (Baghdad, 1977).

Husayn, Saddam, 'Hawla iqamat al-ishtirakiyya fi qutr 'arabi wahid', *Afaq 'Arabiyya*, June 1978.

Husayn, Saddam, *'Iraq al-sha'b, tariq al-rifah wal-taqaddum* (Baghdad, Dec. 1978).

Husayn, Saddam, *al-Thawra wal-nazra al-jadida* (Baghdad, 1981).

Husri, Sati' al-, *al-'Uruba awwalan* (Beirut, 1958).

Husri, Sati' al-, *al-'Uruba bayna du'atiha wa Mu'aridiha* (Beirut, 1957).

Husri, Sati' al-, *Ahadith fi al-tarbiya wal mujtama'* (Beirut, 1962).

Husri, Sati' al-, *Difa' 'an al-'Uruba* (Beirut, 1957).

Husri, Sati' al-, *Ma hiya al-qawmiyya* (Beirut, 1959).

Husri, Sati' al-, *Hawla al-qawmiyya al-'arabiyya* (Beirut, 1961).

Husri, Sati' al-, *Mudhakkirati fi al-'Iraq 1921–1941*, vol. 1 (Beirut, 1967).

Husri, Khaldun Sati' al-, (introduction and annotation), *Mudhakkirat Taha al-Hashimi* (Beirut, 1967).

Husri, Khaldun Sati' al-, 'King Faysal I and Arab Unity 1930–33', *Journal of Contemporary History*, vol. 10, no. 2.

Ibn al-Faqih, al-Hamadhani, *Mukhtasir kitab al-buldan* (Leiden: Brill, 1885).

Ibn Qutayba, Abu Muhammad 'Abd Allah, *Kitab 'uyun al-akhbar* (Cairo, 1928), vol. II.

Iraq, Ministry of Education (wizarat al-ma'arif), *Minhaj al-dirasa al-mutawasita* (Baghdad, 1931, 1940).

Iraqi Culture Center, *Contemporary Arab Art* (London, 1981).

Iraqi Culture Center, *Contemporary Iraqi Ceramics* (London, 1978).

Iraqi Culture Center, *Iraqi Art of the 50s* (London, 1979).

Iraqi Culture Center, *Seven Iraqi Artists* (London, May–June 1979).

Iraqi Culture Center, *The Epic of Gilgamesh* (London, Jan.–March 1982).

Iraqi Culture Center, *The Influence of Calligraphy on Contemporary Arab Art* (London, Feb.-March, 1980).

Ireland, Philip Willard, *Iraq, A Study in Political Development* (London, 1937).

Iskandar, Amir, *Saddam Husayn, the Fighter, the Thinker, the Man* (Paris, 1980).

Jamali, Fadil Muhammad al-, *al-'Iraq bayna ams wal-yawm* (Baghdad, 1954).

Jasim, 'Aziz al-Sayyid, *Masa'il marhaliyya fi al-nidal al-'arabi* (Beirut, 1973).

Jawad, Sa'ad, *Iraq and the Kurdish Question 1958–1970* (Ithaka Press, London, 1981).

Jawdi, Muhammad Husayn, *Ta'rikh al-fann al-'iraqi al-qadim* (Najaf, 1974).

al-Kawwaz, Ja'far, *Faharis al-turath al-Sha'bi, 1969–1979* (Baghdad, 1980).

Khadduri, Majid, *Republican Iraq* (London, 1969).

Khalil, Samir al-, *Republic of Fear, The Politics of Modern Iraq* (London, 1989).

Kohlberg, Etan, 'The Evolution of the Shi'a', *The Jerusalem Quarterly*, no. 27, Spring 1983, pp. 109–23.

Kubaysi, Tarrad al-, *Maqalat fi al-asatir fi . . . Shi'r al-Bayyati* (Damascus, 1974).

The Kurdish Democratic Party (KDP), *the Historical Place of the Kurdish National Liberation Movement* (Europe, Sept. 1977).

Lewis, Bernard, *History Remembered, Recovered, Invented* (Princeton, 1975).

Main, Ernest, *Iraq from Mandate to Independence* (London, 1935), pp. 18, 133.

Main, E. B., 'Iraq: a Note', *Journal of the Royal Central Asiatic Society*, vol. 20.

Madhi, Hamed, *Naive Art from Iraq* (London, 1983).

Mansur, Hillu, *Suwar mulawwana, dirasa fi al-shi'r al-sha'bi* (Baghdad, 1970).

Marr, Phebe, *The Modern History of Iraq* (Boulder, Colorado, 1985).

Maruf, Naji, *Asalat al-hadara al-'arabiyya* (Baghdad, 1969).

Maruf, Naji, *al-Madkhal fi ta'rikh al-hadara al-'arabiyya* (Baghdad, 1960).

Miqdadi, Darwish, *Ta'rikh al-umma al-'arabiyya* (Baghdad, 1931).

Moortgat, Anton., *The Art of Ancient Mesopotamia* (London, New York, 1969).

Moreh, Shmuel, *Modern Arabic Poetry 1800–1970* (Leiden, 1976).

Moscati, Sabatino, *Ancient Semitic Civilizations* (London, 1957).

Mottahedeh, Roy, *The Mantle of the Prophet* (London, 1986).

Muhammad, Su'ad Ra'uf Shir, *Nuri al-Sa'id wa dawruhu fi al-siyasa al-'iraqiyya 1932–1945* (Baghdad, 1988).

Munazzamat al-'Amal al-Islami, *Saddam Husayn Warith al-shah* (Tehran, 1981).

Murqus, Ilyas, *Ta'rikh al-ahzab al-shuyu'iyya fi al-watan al-'arabi* (Beirut, 1964).

Nabaz, Jamal, *Hawla al-mushkila al-Kurdiyya* (Europe, 1969).

Najaf, 'A, *al-Shahed al-shahid* (Tehran, 1981).

Niblock, Tim (ed.), *Iraq, the Contemporary State* (London, 1982).

Owen, Roger, 'Putting the State Back In. Some Thoughts on Batatu's Account of Class and Class Politics in Iraq Before 1958'. Paper prepared for a conference on *The Iraqi Revoution of 1958: The Old Social Classes Revisited*, University of Texas at Austin, March 10–11, 1989.

Penrose, Edith, and E. F. *Iraq: International Relations and National Development* (London, 1978).

Philby, J. B. *The Background of Islam* (Alexandria, 1947).

Republic of Iraq, Ministry of Culture, *Culture and Arts in Iraq* (Baghdad, 1978).

Republic of Iraq, Ministry of Culture and Information, *Present Day Iraqi*

Culture (Baghdad, 1970).

Republic of Iraq, Ministry of Culture, *al-Thawra wal-tanmiya fi al-'iraq* (Baghdad, 1981).

Republic of Iraq, Ministry of Information, *al-Dustur al-mu'aqqat wa ta'dilatuhu* (Baghdad, 1976).

Roux, George, *Ancient Iraq* (London, 1964).

Sakr, Naomi, 'Economic Relations Between Iraq and Other Arab Gulf States', in Tim Niblock (ed.), *Iraq, the Contemporary State* (London, 1982), pp. 150–67.

Samarra'i, Yunis al-Shaykh Ibrahim al-, *al-Qaba'il al-'iraqiyya* (Baghdad, 1989).

Samarra'i, Yunis al-Shaykh Ibrahim al-, *al-Qaba'il wal-buyutat al-hashimiyya fi al-'iraq* (Baghdad, 1988).

Sayyab, Badr Shakir al-, *Diwan* (Beirut, 1971).

Shamma', Dr Samira Kazim al-, *Manatiq al-sina'a fi al-'iraq* (Baghdad, 1980).

Shawkat, Sami, *Hadhihi ahdafuna* (Baghdad, 1939).

Sluglett, Peter, *Britain in Iraq, 1914–1932* (London, 1976).

Stuart, Desmond, *Poet of Iraq, Abdul Wahhab al-Bayyati* (London, 1976).

Susa, Ahmad, *Hadarat al-'arab wa marahil tatawwuriha 'ibra al-'usur* (Baghdad, 1979).

Susa, Ahmad, *al-Rayy wal hadara fi wadi al-rafidayn* (Baghdad, 1968).

Susa, Dr Ahmad, *The Arabs and Jews in History* (Switzerland, 1980?).

Tabari, Abu Ja'far Muhammad ibn Jarir, *Ta'rikh al-rusul wal-muluk* (Leiden: Brill, 1964; Cairo, Dar al-Ma'arif, 1960–66).

'Uluji, 'Abd al-Hamid, and al-Rawi, Nuri, *al-Madkhal ila al-fulklur al-'iraqi* (Baghdad, 1962).

al-Ya'qubi, Ibn Wadih, *Tarikh* (Leiden: Brill, 1969), vol. I.

Yvert and Tellier, *catalogue de Timbres Poste* (Paris, Amiens, 1985).

Newspapers, Journals and Magazines

Adab al-Rafidayn (annual publication by the Faculty of Humanities, Mosul University).

Afaq 'Arabiyya (intellectual monthly magazine, Baghdad).

al-'Amal (daily, Beirut and Tunis).

al-Anwar (daily, Beirut).

al-Aqlam (intellectual monthly magazine, Baghdad).

Alif Ba (weekly, Baghdad).

Baghdad Observer (daily, Baghdad).

Bayn al-Nahrayn (cultural quarterly, issued by the Chaldean church in Mosul).

al-Dawa Chronicle (monthly issued by the Islamic Da'wa Party, London).

Dirasat 'Arabiyya (intellectual monthly, Beirut).

al-Dustur (weekly, London).

al-Fikr al-Jadid (Communist, cultural weekly, Baghdad).

Funun (cultural monthly, Baghdad).

al-Ghad (Communist monthly, Europe).

HaAretz (liberal daily, Israel).

al-Hawadith (independent weekly, Beirut and London).

al-Idha'a wal-Tilifiziun (weekly dedicated to radio and television, Baghdad).

Imam (monthly, the Embassy of the Islamic Republic of Iran in London).

Impact International (fortnightly, News and Media Ltd., London).

The Independent Magazine (weekly, London).

Iraq (fortnightly, Baghdad).

al-'Iraq (daily of the pro-Ba'th Kurdish Democratic Party, Baghdad).

al-'Iraq al-Jadid (cultural monthly magazine under Qasim).

Iraq al-Ghad (a monthly magazine, London).

Iraq Today (a fornightly, Baghdad).

The Jerusalem Post (daily, Israel).

Jeune Afrique (weekly, Paris).

al-Jarida (daily, Beirut).

al-Jihad (weekly issued by the Islamic Da'wa Party, Tehran).

al-Jumhuriyya (Jum) (The Government Daily, Baghdad).

al-Kadir (monthly of the Kurdish Democratic Party, Europe).

al-Khalij al-'Arabi (quarterly issued by the Center for Gulf Studies, Basra University).

L'Iraq Aujourd'hui, (weekly, Baghdad).

Liwa al-Ikhwa al-Islamiyya (irregular, Baghdad).

Liwa al-Sadr (weekly, issued by the Supreme Council of the Islamic Revolution of Iraq, Tehran)).

Majallat Adab al-Mustansiriyya (quarterly of the Faculty of Humanities in that university, Baghdad).

Majallat Kuliyyat al-Adab (an annual publication of Baghdad University).

Majallat al-Majma' al-'ilmi al-'iraqi (an annual publication of the Iraqi Academy of Science).

al-Massar (Islamic, irregular, London).

al-Mawrid (cultural quarterly issued by the Ministry of Information and Culture, Baghdad).

al-Mirbad (a literary quarterly issued by the Faculty of Humanities, Basra University).

al-Mizmar al-Shahri (cultural monthly, Baghdad).

al-Mu'allim al-Jadid (educational quarterly issued by the Ministry of Education, Baghdad).

al-Mu'arrikh al-'Arabi (quarterly issued by the Iraqi Historical Society, Baghdad).

al-Mukhtar al-Islami (monthly of the Muslim Brotherhood, Cairo).

al-Muthaqqaf al-'Arabi (intellectual monthly magazine, Baghdad).

Nida al-Watan (daily, Beirut).

al-Qabas (daily, Kuwait).

al-Qadisiyya (a daily issued by the Ministry of Defense, Baghdad).

Ruz al-Yusuf (cultural magazine, Cairo).

Sawt al-Talaba (monthly, the National Union of Students, Baghdad).
Silsilat Sijill al-Ara (Sijill al-ara) (monthly collection of articles in the Arab press and news agency reports, editor Jubran Shamiya, Beirut).
Sumer (an annual publication of the Department of Antiquities, Baghdad).
al-Ta'akhi (Kurdish daily, Baghdad).
al-Tadamun (an Arabic language magazine, London).
al-Tali'a al-Adabiyya (cultural youth monthly, Baghdad).
Tariq al-Sha'ab (Communist political daily, Baghdad).
Tariq al-Thawra (monthly of the Movement of the [Iraqi] Islamic Masses, Tehran).
Tehran Times.
al-Thaqafa (Communist monthly, Baghdad).
al-Thaqafa al-jadida (Communist monthly, Baghdad).
al-Thawra (Th) (the ruling Ba'th party daily, Baghdad).
al-Thawra al-'Arabiyya (the internal magazine, for the eyes of Ba'th party members only, Baghdad, irregular).
al-Turath al-'Ilmi al-'Arabi (quarterly, issued by the Center for the Revival of Arab Scientific Heritage, Baghdad University).
al-Turath al-Sha'bi (folklore monthly, Baghdad).
Ur (cultural magazine, The Iraqi Culture Center, London).
Wa'i al-'Ummal (worker's union weekly, Baghdad).
al-Waqa'i' al-'Iraqiyya (WI) (in English: The Government).
Weekly Gazette (WG), (the official magazine, Baghdad).

Western Magazines

International Journal of Middle East studies (IJMES) (an academic quarterly, Cambridge University Press).
Middle Eastern Studies (an academic quarterly, LSE, editor: Elie Kedourie).
The New Yorker (cultural magazine, New York).
Orient (academic quarterly, Hamburg, Germany).

News Agencies

Gulf News Agency.
Iraqi News Agency (INA).
Kuwait News Agency (Kuna).
Middle East News Agency (MENA) (Cairo).

Translations of daily broadcasts

British Broadcast Corporation (BBC-SWB) (summary of world broadcastings, the Middle East and Africa, London).
Foreign Broadcast Information Service-Daily Report (FBIS-Daily Report – Middle East and Africa) (Washington, D.C.).

Index